BATTLEGROUND ALASKA

BATTLEGROUND ALASKA

Fighting Federal Power in
America's Last Wilderness

Stephen Haycox

University Press of Kansas

Published by the
University Press of Kansas
(Lawrence, Kansas 66045),
which was organized by the
Kansas Board of Regents
and is operated and funded
by Emporia State University,
Fort Hays State University,
Kansas State University,
Pittsburg State University,
the University of Kansas,
and Wichita State University

Library of Congress Cataloging-in-Publication Data
Names: Haycox, Stephen W.
Title: Battleground Alaska : fighting federal power in America's
    last wilderness / Stephen Haycox.
Description: Lawrence : University Press of Kansas, 2016. |
    Includes bibliographical references and index.
Identifiers: LCCN 2015044255| ISBN 9780700622153 (hardback) |
    ISBN 9780700622733 (ebook)
Subjects: LCSH: States' rights (American politics) | Federal
    government—United States. | Alaska—Politics and
    government. | Public lands—Alaska. | Environmental
    protection—Alaska—History. | Natural resources—Alaska—
    Management—History. | Wildlife management—Alaska—
    History. | Environmental policy—Alaska. | Environmental
    policy—United States. | Alaska—Environmental conditions.
    |Alaska—Economic conditions. | BISAC: HISTORY / United
    States / State & Local / West (AK, CA, CO, HI, ID, MT, NV, UT,
    WY). | NATURE / Environmental Conservation & Protection. |
    POLITICAL SCIENCE / Public Policy / Environmental Policy.
Classification: LCC JK311 .H39 2016 | DDC 333.109798—dc23
LC record available at http://lccn.loc.gov/2015044255

British Library Cataloguing-in-Publication Data is available.

Printed in the United States of America

10 9 8 7 6 5 4 3 2 1

The paper used in this publication is recycled and contains
30 percent postconsumer waste. It is acid free and meets the
minimum requirements of the American National Standard for
Permanence of Paper for Printed Library Materials Z39.48-1992.

for DAGMAR, and in memory of Morgan Sherwood

CONTENTS

On January 25, 2015, the White House released to the press a one-minute video, shot on board Air Force One, in which President Obama announced that the Department of the Interior had developed a new fifteen-year management plan for the Arctic National Wildlife Refuge in Alaska. The plan, he said, calls for managing as wilderness the coastal plain of the refuge, the use of which the 1980 Alaska lands act left to Congress to decide; the coastal plain is potentially rich in oil. The president called upon Congress to officially designate the coastal plain as protected wilderness. Oil industry spokespeople, Alaska political leaders, and resource development lobbyists have repeatedly urged Congress to open the coastal plain to exploratory oil drilling. Congress has voted on the issue five times since 1980, failing to muster a sufficient majority for development on four of the votes; the fifth vote was positive but was attached to a budget bill and for that reason vetoed by President Clinton.

The same day as President Obama's statement, the Interior Department issued a press release announcing revision by the US Fish and Wildlife Service, which manages the refuge, of the Comprehensive Conservation Plan and the Environmental Impact Statement for the refuge. Seven million acres of the 19-million-acre refuge already are congressionally designated wilderness. The revision calls for wilderness designation for the other 12.28 million acres. On January 26, the *Washington Post* reported that, "according to individuals briefed on the plan," the Interior Department intended also to place off limits to oil drilling biologically sensitive areas of the Arctic Ocean off Alaska's north coast and would likely impose additional limits on oil and gas production in National Petroleum Reserve–Alaska, which is also on Alaska's North Slope.[1]

Alaska's political leaders reacted angrily to these announcements, charging that the Obama administration was trampling on the state's sovereign rights. "What's coming," the state's senior US senator, Lisa Murkowski, stated, "is a stunning attack on our sovereignty and our ability to develop a strong economy that allows us, our children and our grandchildren to thrive. It's clear this administration does not care about us, and sees us as nothing but a territory. . . . But we will not be run over like this."[2] Alaska's long-serving congressman Don Young said, "Simply put, this wholesale land grab, this widespread attack on our people and our way of life, is disgusting." The state's new governor, Independent Bill Walker, said he'd had an hour-long phone conversation with Interior Secretary Sally Jewell during which he'd expressed "strong disappointment." "I need to send you an invoice for the cost of doing business in Alaska," he reported telling Jewell, "because you are taking away our ability to earn a living."[3] State legislators reacted strongly as well, condemning the president's action by resolution, one state senator using doggerel poetry to warn Obama that Alaskans would not accept his actions peaceably. "While Alaskans might look sweet," he wrote, "they might be packin' heat."[4]

Alaska is a vast and beautiful land. With its rugged, majestic mountains tracked by Dall sheep and brown bears; its untamed rivers coursing through great valleys populated by caribou and moose; and its magnificent forests with old-growth stands 500 years old dominating coastal waters teeming with salmon, crab, and sea otter, it holds pride of place in American environmental consciousness. It is America's last wilderness, teasing the imagination of any who have reflected on the character of the natural world and its place in human endeavor. Huge in area—equal to 20 percent of the land area of the contiguous United States, with more coastline than the contiguous states combined—and stupefying in its diversity, Alaska stands as a beacon, a statement that there is yet in the world a place of permanent, natural magnificence. It is at once a physical and a mental refuge from modernity and civilization, a preserve of natural earth—what it was, is, and may be.

Much of Alaska, its natural wonder and especially its wilderness, is protected today by federal ownership and management. Sixty percent of the state, 225 million acres, is in federal ownership. More than two-thirds of the federal land is in congressionally established conservation units; half of those are formally designated wilderness, amounting to half of all designated wilderness in the country.

Though the United States purchased the region from Russia in 1867, Congress long delayed a definitive disposition of Alaska's lands because of ignorance, confusion, and overwhelming challenges, which included policy considerations regarding the region's indigenous people—12 percent of the total population—and the vexing question of where to find a balance between environmental protection and economic development, between wilderness and frontier. Three forces combined to compel Congress finally to act on what to do with Alaska: Alaska statehood; Alaska Native land claims, driven by the discovery of North America's largest oil deposit at Prudhoe Bay on Alaska's North Slope; and the rise of modern environmentalism and subsequent congressional legislation. Congress found it necessary to assign significant portions of Alaska land to each: to the new state, created in 1959; to Alaska

Natives in the landmark Alaska Native Claims Settlement Act (ANCSA) of 1971; and to federal environmental protection and preservation in the Alaska National Interest Lands Conservation Act (ANILCA) of 1980. Today, of Alaska's 375 million acres, only about 72 million are unassigned, managed, as are most undesignated US lands, by the Bureau of Land Management (BLM).

The story of these dramatic episodes has been told. It is a story of the shaping of modern Alaska, in all three instances a story of intense idealism tempered by political maneuvering and economic reality. Along with the state's unusual economy, that story sets the context of today's Alaska. Aspects of that story, however, need reexamination. Alaska's role in the evolution of an ecological understanding of environment and in the subsequent refashioning of environmentalism and the formulation of the Wilderness Act of 1964 is not well known. Initially, visionaries such as George Collins and Olaus and Margaret "Mardy" Murie, through their advocacy of an Arctic wilderness in Alaska, were central to defining what modern environmentalism might mean, as understood by the most ardent and effective spokespersons for environmental protection and those who acted on its behalf—such as Howard Zahniser and David Brower—and also those who opposed them. Later, pragmatic necessities in developing the landmark Alaska lands act of 1980 presaged a redefinition of wilderness and the wilderness idea among environmental scholars, a definition more cognizant of the constancy of human presence in wilderness. Finally, Alaskans, particularly the state's political leaders, have persistently fought environmental protection and regulation in the state while at the same time embracing virtually any economic development project that holds the promise of jobs and alternative contributions to the state's economy. Alaska's economy is uniquely dependent on exploitation of the state's natural resources because the economy is isolated, remote, narrow, and dependent. Congress made accommodations to Alaska's economic circumstances in the 1958 statehood act and later in the Alaska lands act of 1980, maximizing Alaska's access to lands with mineral and other economic potential. Many state leaders have interpreted those accommodations as permanent commitments by the federal government. This interpretation has led to a reflexive resistance to federal actions regarding public lands in Alaska that is significantly greater than is found in other western states, where conflict between federal and state notions of public landownership and management is common. In Alaska, which holds what have been called America's environmental crown jewels, exaggerated antistatism puts state leaders and

spokespersons at odds with federal environmental regulators whose responsibilities are to protect the land from development and despoliation. This
book addresses these aspects of the relationship between Alaska and modern environmentalism and between Alaska and the federal government and
does so within the larger context of the unique characteristics that define and
explain Alaska today. Because of its unusual pattern of settlement and development, Alaska historically has been a battleground between economic
development and environmental protection. This remains as true today as it
ever was.

This book is primarily a work of interpretation and analysis. The details of
the fights over the establishment of the Arctic National Wildlife Refuge, permitting the Trans-Alaska Pipeline, and passage of the Alaska lands act, especially the role of the US Congress, have been reconstructed in several excellent
accounts. But none place these battles within the unique economic and political structure of Alaska itself. Since the arrival of an appreciable non-Native
population in the territory, resident Alaskans have identified with the notion
of a developmental frontier. Ernest Gruening, territorial governor from 1939
to 1953 and US senator from Alaska from 1958 to 1968, a vigorous and effective advocate for statehood, characterized Alaska as a modern manifestation
of "the westward trek of peoples in search of greater freedom and greater
economic opportunity."[1] Like settlers on the American far west frontier, immigrant Alaskans subscribed to an atavistic belief in their democratic right
to harvest any and all resources the land provided, without let or hindrance.[2]
They were persuaded of the inexhaustible nature of Alaska resources, a conviction exacerbated by the small number of people, 224,000 at the time of
statehood in 1959, in so vast an area. Alaskans of that era subscribed to what
Stewart Udall later labeled the myth of superabundance.[3] For these Alaskans,
frontier meant development, a pushing back of nature, a conquest. Wilderness was an affront, evidence of challenges yet unmet. Alaskans viewed any
restraint on development as unwelcome, unwarranted, and unfair. From early
in the settlement experience it has been habitual for Alaskans to interpret
environmental regulation as an assault on their economic opportunity and
independence.

But this view of their environment, not different from similar convictions
held by many residents of western states, is augmented by Alaska's unique
economic and political structure. The state's economic context colors the way
most Alaskans view the environmental community, which has stood behind

federal land regulations since the 1950s. At that time a holistic, ecological concept of environment came to define environmentalism, and environmentalists came to understand Alaska's vulnerability to development and environmental despoliation, even as opponents to regulation came to understand Alaska's vulnerability to environmental constraints on economic development. This book adds an understanding of Alaska's unique structure and its effects on environmental battles.

"Environmentalism," as used here, is an expansive term that includes a host of ideas and values, including such pragmatic considerations as clean air and water; such scientific concepts as ecosystem; the preservation of a permanent legacy to hand off to future, uncounted generations; and such transcendent ideals as the integration of all species of fauna and flora in an interdependent whole as well as a level of spirituality deemed essential to completion of the human psyche.[4] The battles related here deal both with those ideas and values and with their individual and organizational representation and pursuit. A majority of Alaskans were among those who found environmentalism as so described to be, at best, hopelessly romantic, impractical, and economically threatening and at worst a conspiracy directed against their most cherished freedoms, which they identified with American tradition. An idealized view of nature as pristine and unmanipulated by humans was complicated in Alaska by the presence of a vigorous indigenous population inhabiting the land and harvesting its subsistence resources to sustain itself. Congress executed no treaties with Alaska Natives, so there were no traditional reservations that restricted their movement. Alaska Natives were free to harvest resources from lands and waters across the territory. Within federal regulations, which before statehood were often applied with wide latitude, non-Native Alaskans also inhabited and harvested from lands to which later federal law would severely limit access or place off limits. These conflicting ideas coupled with the unique political economy that has generated antistatism and antienvironmentalism in the state have made Alaska America's premier environmental battleground.

In the clash over ANILCA in Congress in the late 1970s, environmental lobbyists engendered in national consciousness a sense of ownership of America's "environmental crown jewels," a phrase that would be repeated frequently in congressional debate and in the press. Environmentalists wanted Alaska's unique and grander environmentally significant regions preserved and protected because of their national value—not just Alaskans' but the nation's nature, the nation's wildlife habitats and recreational plantations. The principal impetus for saving Alaska was conservation for the sake of the philosophical, even spiritual, value attributed to those of the region's natural areas seemingly unmarked by human manipulation. Perhaps captured in John Muir's assertion that "the clearest way into the Universe is through a forest wilderness" or in Wallace Stegner's plea for the preservation of nature as an alternative to living in a human-built environment, the primary reason for preserving Alaska was to save nature, not to use it.[5] Although Alaska's mountains and forests might house resources that could contribute to long-range sustainability, environmentalists eschewed the notion of ever using them. For modern environmentalism, the place of Alaska's environmental crown jewels was simply to be there, unmolested by extraction, exploitation, or other development. The fear that Alaska's pristine natural areas might soon be lost to manipulation, articulated forcefully by the wilderness activist Robert Marshall after his fifteen-month sojourn in Alaska in 1929–1930, motivated many who joined the battle for Alaska lands preservation.[6]

Few outside the elite conservation community knew much about Alaska's wilderness mountains, valleys, forests, and wildlife when Marshall, Aldo Leopold, and others formed the Wilderness Society in 1935. Even as late as 1963, when the executive council of the Wilderness Society first met in Alaska, the extent and character of the Alaska environment was still largely a mystery to most who professed and supported wilderness values.[7] Identifying and learning about Alaska's crown jewels was an important first step in waging the fight to save them.

In terms of geography, Alaska suggests a giant appendage protruding off the northwest quadrant of the North American continent between the Arctic and North Pacific Oceans, separated from Asia by the Bering Sea and from Russia by the 56-mile-wide Bering Strait. The land of the peninsula is so huge and variegated as to defy description, its scale dwarfing the frames of reference used to describe and grasp land areas in the contiguous states. At 375 million acres, it's not just that Alaska is more than twice as big as Texas in land area; of the nearly 90 million acres of national park land in the United States, 55 million are in Alaska. Twelve percent of America's national forest land, about 22 million acres, is in Alaska, and that includes the two largest, the Tongass and Chugach National Forests. Four federal agencies administer most of the federal land in the state: the National Park Service (NPS), US Forest Service (USFS), US Fish and Wildlife Service (FWS), and BLM.

In reality as in imagination, Alaska is perhaps dominated by the extraordinary Denali, North America's highest peak[8] (20,310 feet) and anchor of the 650-mile-long Alaska Range, which lies in a north-pointing arc across the center of the region from the White Mountains and the Pacific Ranges at the Canadian border in the southeast to the long and rugged Alaska Peninsula and the Aleutian Islands in the southwest. A dozen major glaciers flow from Denali and its sister mountains' various flanks, and its snows give rise to four major rivers. Today, three federal conservation units protect parts of the Alaska Range: Wrangell–St. Elias National Park and Preserve (13-plus million acres), Denali National Park and Preserve (roughly 6 million acres), and Lake Clark National Park and Preserve (more than 4 million acres).

North of the Alaska Range, the Arctic Brooks Range, which elicited rhapsodic descriptions by Marshall and Adolph, Olaus, and Margaret Murie, stretches across Alaska 700 miles from the Canadian border in the east to the Arctic Ocean coast in the west. With peaks of 9,000 feet, the range is uninhabited but for two Native villages and four small non-Native communities. Three different massive caribou herds cross the range in various places. Today, the Arctic National Wildlife Refuge (more than 19 million acres) and the Gates of the Arctic National Park (nearly 8.5 million acres) protect spectacular peaks and river valleys in the Brooks Range.[9] The Arctic National Wildlife Refuge alone, more than 7 million acres of which is designated wilderness, spans 5 sub-Arctic and Arctic ecological zones and includes 45 species of land and marine mammals and 150 species of birds.

The Chugach Mountain Range, the Wrangell Mountains, and a portion of the St. Elias Mountain Range rise for over 700 miles along the coast of the Gulf of Alaska in Southeast Alaska, subgroups of the Pacific Coast Ranges. Mt. St. Elias in the St. Elias Range is over 18,000 feet; Mt. Marcus Baker in the Chugach Range is over 13,000 feet; within the Wrangell Mountains, Mts. Sanford and Blackburn are over 16,000 feet and Mt. Wrangell exceeds 14,000 feet. The Chugach National Forest includes the Chugach Range; Glacier Bay National Park lies wholly within the St. Elias Range, the Alaska portion of which today is protected by Wrangell–St. Elias National Park and Preserve, which also protects most of the Wrangell Mountains.

The mountainous, 300-mile-long Alexander Archipelago, consisting of 1,100 coastal islands, comprises Southeast Alaska, the Panhandle, along with a narrow stretch of the mainland. The 17-million-acre Tongass National Forest encompasses virtually all of the Alexander Archipelago, which includes the largest remaining stands of old-growth timber in the United States, about 5 million acres; all but half a million acres of that are included in wilderness areas and cannot be logged. Nearly 6 million acres of the total forest are today designated wilderness, protecting a number of unique and endangered species of flora and fauna. Several relatively large communities lie in the archipelago, including the state capital, Juneau, and Ketchikan, Wrangell, Sitka, and Haines.

Southwest Alaska is the largest area of the state not dominated by significant mountain ranges. It is a vast wetland that is home to scores of species and millions of individual migratory waterfowl. Three major rivers bisect the region: the Yukon, Kuskokwim, and Nushagak. Bristol Bay, which comprises the Bering Sea coast of the region, is the most prolific salmon-producing fishery in the world. Several US Fish and Wildlife refuges protect areas of the region today, including Togiak, Yukon Delta, and Innoko.

Other federal conservation units protect vast reaches of tundra and wetlands of Alaska, including the Yukon-Charley Rivers National Preserve, Lake Clark National Park, Glacier Bay National Park, Alaska Marine National Wildlife Refuge, Yukon Flats National Wildlife Refuge, and many others, including wild and scenic river designations.

Together these lands comprise an incomparable American legacy for the future. Because of Congress's failure to provide for a comprehensive disposition of Alaska lands through the first century of US ownership, when modern environmental lobbying organizations began to focus on Alaska's pristine natural areas, they were largely unprotected by government regulation and thus were regarded by those organizations as exposed and in danger. Most Alaskans, however, did not accept that characterization of Alaska's wild lands. The confrontation of the two fundamentally different views of Alaska's environment has made the state a consistent philosophical, environmental, and political battleground. This work reexamines four specific environmental battles that gave form to the emerging and maturing modern environmental movement while at the same time helping to shape modern Alaska.

First, in December 1960, shortly after the electoral victory of John F. Kennedy but before President Dwight Eisenhower had left office, Secretary of the Interior Fred Seaton by executive order established the Arctic National Wildlife Range in far northeast Alaska, bounded by the Arctic Ocean on the north and Canada on the east. Creation of the Arctic range partially realized a dream Robert Marshall had articulated as early as 1938, that Arctic Alaska should be kept a wilderness, an area of land that might reflect life the way the human race had known it before "the strangling clutch of civilization."[10] Senator Gruening, testifying against the proposal to establish the range, asserted that if created, it would be set aside "not for the benefit of human beings, but to satisfy some theoretical conceptions of distant men unfamiliar with Alaska."[11] This was a common theme in Alaska territorial politics, but instead of diminishing it, statehood exacerbated it, as is explained in chapter 1. Others expanded Marshall's vision to mean a pristine wilderness of complete ecosystems left intact without human manipulation or imprint, a vision Gruening and other opponents thought a fantasy, one that would deprive Alaskans of their rightful control over their landscape. Subsequent events would intensify this debate, which continues intractably today. Yet while Alaskan leaders opposed creation of an Arctic wilderness with familiar arguments and rhetoric, supporters of the withdrawal did not initially encounter the vehemence and uncompromising adamancy that characterized Alaska's opposition to regulation that developed after statehood. Olaus and Mardy Murie and others were able to persuade Alaskans that the Arctic wilderness they proposed could be defined so as to be compatible with the state's character. The battle over establishing the Arctic National Wildlife Range was tame compared to the clashes to come.

Second, signed by President Richard Nixon on November 16, 1973, the Trans-Alaska Pipeline Authorization Act sanctioned construction of the Alaska pipeline from Prudhoe Bay on Alaska's North Slope to the warm-water port of Valdez on Prince William Sound on the Gulf of Alaska. The vast Prudhoe Bay oil field lay exactly adjacent to the western boundary of the Arctic National Wildlife Range. The pipeline was, as historian Peter Coates writes, "alien in principle" to environmentalists' image of northern Alaska.[12] William Ransom Wood, president of the University of Alaska, called opponents of the pipeline "anti-God, anti-Man and anti-Mind." Supporters of the project argued that its impact on wilderness Alaska would be negligible and that the oil would make America energy-independent and guarantee the security of the nation's supply.[13] Environmentalists might be said to have lost the battle over the pipeline, though environmental lawsuits forced a redesign of the project that made the line far more environmentally secure. Oil drilling in the National Petroleum Reserve–Alaska (NPR-A), adjacent to Prudhoe Bay on the west, and in the Beaufort Sea, north of Prudhoe, is yet embroiled in controversy.

Third, upon leaving office in 1980, President Jimmy Carter called the Alaska National Interest Lands Conservation Act the most significant legislation passed during his tenure as president. Establishing 104 million acres of new federal conservation units in Alaska, ANILCA has been hailed by environmentalists and historians as the most momentous conservation measure ever enacted.[14] Senator Ted Stevens of Alaska called ANILCA the congressional action he most regretted in his forty years of service in the US Senate and the greatest betrayal of Alaska. ANILCA reshaped the interior map of the state, and battles continue over the meaning and implementation of the act regarding subsistence harvest of traditional resources by indigenous and other rural residents and over access to lands it includes.

Fourth, as Congress debated the Tongass Timber Reform Act of 1990, Timothy Egan, the *New York Times* stringer in Seattle, wrote that the US Forest Service was selling 500-year-old-growth trees in the Tongass for less than the price of a McDonald's Big Mac.[15] Environmental critics of US Forest Service policy for the Tongass argued that compromise provisions inserted into ANILCA forced a level of timber sales far beyond an amount that could be sold and that the level of harvest threatened the last stands of old growth in the United States. Supporters insisted that the sales were necessary to satisfy the requirements of existing fifty-year logging contracts and to provide jobs that would keep the towns of Ketchikan and Sitka, the location of the two pulp mills on the forest, economically viable. Their owners unable or unwilling to comply with environmental constraints, the pulp mills have since closed. The towns continue to be viable, but controversy endures over Forest Service policy for timber harvesting and over the forest's inclusion in the national forest roadless policy.

In addition to analyzing each of these contests and examining their role in the rise of modern environmentalism, this book contextualizes these environmental battles with an exploration of Alaskans' persistent resistance to federal environmental constraints in the name of necessary economic development and states' rights. The study also includes a review of representative new battles over coal development intended for a global market; the extraordinary Pebble Mine prospect, the very large and potentially hugely profitable porphyry copper, gold, and molybdenum deposit in the headwaters of streams flowing into Bristol Bay, which hosts the largest wild salmon fishery in the world; and a proposal to construct a road through Izembek National Wildlife Refuge, designated wilderness, in the far west of the Alaska Peninsula.

Given Congress's delay in addressing land disposition in Alaska, it was probably inevitable that Alaska should emerge as America's premier battleground for the clash between development and preservation and the far more complex dialogue over the meaning and implications of modern environmentalism. This study adds to that conversation the importance of Alaska's unique economic isolation, its influence in the rise of the ecological understanding of environment, and an explanation of its persistent and virulent antistatism.

CHAPTER 1 ANTISTATISM IN ALASKA

In her reaction to President Obama's call in spring 2015 for Congress to designate the coastal plain of the Arctic National Wildlife Refuge a wilderness area, Alaska's senator Lisa Murkowski charged that the president's action constituted an assault on Alaska's sovereignty. The senator's assertion is representative of a widespread and tenaciously held conviction among Alaskans that the federal government exceeds its constitutional authority in implementing federal policy in Alaska, particularly in regard to the management of federal land in the state and especially in regard to environmental regulation. Complaints about what locals label "federal overreach" are frequent. When asked by a reporter how the federal government's relationship to Alaska's state sovereignty is different from that with other states, Murkowski averred, "We're just a little more sensitive to it."[1] In this the senator was correct, while perhaps implicitly acknowledging that there is no constitutional difference, for Alaskans are much more sensitive to perceived attacks on their state's sovereignty than are other states' citizens. Moreover, politicians often argue that the manner in which the federal government manages its land and resources in Alaska violates promises made at statehood, which came late to Alaska, in 1959. Such protest is not uncommon in the western states, but in Alaska unique historical, economic, and social circumstances exacerbate the sense of injustice and persecution felt by many, perhaps a majority, of the state's citizens.[2] Analysis of the state's political reaction to President Obama's 2015 announcement helps to explain Alaskans' long history of resistance to and condemnation of federal management of Alaska's resources.

This book attempts to explain the vehemence of Alaskan antistatism, the resistance to federal activity in the state, and the conclusion by many Alaskans that Alaska has been subjected to more federal oversight and coercion than other states. Although there are tangible artifacts of Alaska's antistatism, the subjectivity of its intensity and how it is felt by the resident population and Alaskan political leaders obviates any conclusive or definitive finding. Nonetheless, analysis of the phenomenon is useful, for it helps to identify and explicate the unique factors of Alaska's history and political economy that do set it apart and give its residents their claim to exceptionality. Resistance to federal management of Alaska lands long predates statehood, reaching back at least to the years immediately following the Klondike and Alaska gold rush at the end of the nineteenth century, when the first appreciable number of non-Native migrants arrived in the territory.

Although Senator Murkowski's claim of federal trampling of state sovereignty is of particular interest, the claim that the federal government has reneged on promises made at statehood is more specific and, in the frequency with which it is used as evidence of the claim, unique to Alaska. An examination of both contentions is revealing. Theoretically, these claims rest on the compact theory of American government, the idea that the states formed the federal government through the ratification of the 1787 constitution and therefore have the authority to impose limits on the exercise of federal power. Contract theory, the idea that the nation, dating from the 1776 Declaration of Independence, is older than the states and in actuality created them and therefore has authority over them, save for such powers as the US Supreme Court has found are reserved to the states, seems the more dominant explanation of the nature of the American founding.[3] Practically, most references by Alaska politicians are to what is often called the "statehood compact," a supposed binding agreement between Congress and the new State of Alaska that limits what either party can do without the approval of the other.[4] This notion is based primarily on a plebiscite mandated by Congress in 1958 that asked whether Alaska voters approved the Alaska Statehood Act; the measure passed by a vote of 40,452 to 8,010. Subsequently, in 1969 the attorney general of Alaska issued a formal opinion holding that, based on the results of the plebiscite, "the federal government may not unilaterally amend the Statehood Act."[5] That opinion, however, has not prevailed in federal court cases, most critically in *Alaska v. U.S.*, filed in 1993 and decided in 1996, in which the state sued in the US Court of Federal Claims specifically for violations of the "statehood compact."[6] This case is discussed in detail in chapter 7. The court found against the state, the judge ruling that only one portion of the statehood act can be viewed as unilaterally unalterable—namely, the grant of state title to 104 million acres of Alaska—but that other portions cannot, and the act as a whole cannot be so understood.[7] The Ninth Circuit Court of Appeals upheld the decision; the US Supreme Court declined to take up the case. But that has not prevented state leaders from repeatedly and reflexively invoking the "statehood compact" as if it were an entity with the force of law that should guide the state in its relations with the federal government.[8]

Alaska leaders protesting federal actions in Alaska also often argue that they violate explicit promises made at statehood. Usually they note that Congress intended that Alaska use the land and resources of the state to support itself through economic development. Article VIII of the state constitution, concerning the state's natural resources, states explicitly that "it is the policy of the State to encourage the settlement of its land and the development of its resources by making them available for maximum use consistent with the public interest."[9] Moreover, the same article states that "wherever occurring in their natural state, fish, wildlife and waters are reserved to the people for 'common use.'" This reservation is unique among the fifty states. Section 6 of the Alaska Statehood Act grants the land for the purpose of providing economic support for the state.[10] Before Congress approved Alaska statehood, many members of Congress expressed concern that the territory did not have a sufficient tax base to support the costs of state government.[11] Both Senate Majority Leader Lyndon Johnson and House Speaker Sam Rayburn of the Eighty-Fifth Congress had expressed reservations about the region's economic future, as had many others. Alaska's congressional delegate E. L. "Bob" Bartlett had persistently worked for the inclusion of a generous grant of land for state title with the expectation that mineral development on such land would provide both state revenue and jobs.[12] To ensure that the land grant would be used for that purpose and not to enrich private owners, Congress forbade the new state to sell or otherwise dispose of the mineral land given to it.[13] The state can only lease exploration and production on such lands; it must retain ownership. Walter J. Hickel, who served as Alaska governor from 1966 to 1970 and again from 1990 to 1994, turned this provision to positive advantage in calling Alaska an "owner state," meaning that, unlike other states, Alaska retains ownership of the natural resources on its lands. With the discovery and development of the Prudhoe Bay and associated North Slope oil fields, Alaska has fared well as an "owner state."

Alaska leaders' complaints about federal activity in Alaska must be placed in the broader context of American and Alaskan exceptionalism. The story of America is most often told as the triumph of individual freedom and equal economic opportunity over strong central authority, authority justified in the name of security and restraint of human licentiousness. Property, contract, and freedom of expression are understood as the constitutional framework that facilitates the free market, an active civil society, and democracy. It's a story of self-reliance, voluntary associationism, free labor, and the free market, all of which release human creativity, ingenuity, and initiative, which in turn nurture the full realization of human potential and happiness. It is an article of national, cultural faith that no other political system so encourages freedom, equal opportunity, individualism, and the realization of human potential. It is a celebration of national exceptionalism.[14]

The story begins with classical liberalism, the assertions of Enlightenment liberals, most particularly John Locke and Adam Smith, who posited the fundamental equality of all; the self-evident right to life, liberty, and property; the sanctity of private property; and the necessity of a free market. The founders of the American republic, Louis Hartz wrote in 1955 in *The Liberal Tradition in America*, were all "Lockean liberals." American exceptionalism, Hartz contended, was the product, as William Novak summarized, "of a persistent preference for society over polity, individual initiative over collective action, and private competition and voluntarism over public regulation and state direction."[15] Early celebrants of American exceptionalism include J. Hector St. John de Crevecoeur, Alexis de Tocqueville, and, above all, Thomas Jefferson. From these beginnings American historians such as Hartz, Daniel Boorstin, and Arthur Schlesinger, Jr., among many others, fashioned a tale that praises American individualism and the self-made man and glorifies his unaided conquest of nature and construction of a modern civilization in which government plays at best, and grudgingly, merely a supporting role. A good deal of Frederick Jackson Turner's frontier thesis has found its way into the story, the absence of government and amenities on the frontier necessitating the ingenuity and individualism Turner took to be the essence of the new American man, perfectly capable of fashioning a society and a culture without the guiding, heavy hand of the state. Politicians from Andrew Jackson to Ronald Reagan made themselves heroes of a vocal, aggressive antistatism. The problem with government, they said, is government.

It's an ascensionist story, uplifting and noble. But it is, as any number of perceptive scholars have pointed out, mostly a false one or, at best, one representing only one aspect of a complex cultural identity.[16] It flies in the face of a national history of strong central government with "broad interventionist, regulatory and coercive power at home as well as abroad." The American government has always been "powerful, capacious, tenacious, interventionist and redistributive," a fact poorly recognized by many American historians and barely at all in the imaginative reconstruction of their history taught to and embraced by most of the nation's citizens.[17] Among others, Hannah Arendt pointed out that the objective of the new US Constitution in 1787 was not to limit power but to create it, much to the consternation of the anti-Federalists.[18] In the early national period, as Americans defined in practice what democracy might mean, the federal government put in place a comprehensive structure of administrative law and bureaucratized basic public functions such as the postal service, the telegraph, and later the telephone. The Civil War and its aftermath saw a remarkable growth of government intervention, from the abolition of slavery and management of the money supply to engagement in intercontinental railroad construction and the curtailment of labor unionization, the latter culminating in the *Lochner* decision in 1905, which, ironically, relied on the authority of the federal judiciary to protect the "right and liberty of the individual to contract." The substantial expansion of governmental power at the federal and state levels is a familiar motif of general US histories, an expansion accelerated by America's involvement in World War II. One of the enduring political conversations since the 1980s has been the widespread resistance to the power and reach of government. Contrary to President Clinton's proclamation in his 1996 inaugural address, the era of big government is not over; it is part and parcel of the practical administration of American life, as it has been since the beginning of American national government.[19]

But the mythology of a limited American government, constrained in favor of the nourishment of individual initiative and private enterprise, persists as the national identity narrative.[20] That narrative fuels the antistatist rhetoric so prevalent in American politics over the past thirty-five years. "Running against Washington" has become a staple of contemporary journalism, as has the conservative attack on "federal overreach."[21] One of the more familiar quotations in American discourse is from Ronald Reagan's first inaugural address: "Government is not the solution to the problem; government is the problem." Such formulations rest on the underlying assumption that the government is acting inappropriately and ahistorically, that the current exercise of government power is unique, a departure from both the intentions of the framers and the manner in which that government has been administered in the past. It is a convenient fiction that flatters individual capability and an economy free of constraint and justifies attacks on virtually all government regulation.

Antistatism characterizes Alaska's self-identity to an exaggerated degree. The state's governors and legislators and its congressional delegation maintain a persistent plaint of persecution by an overweening, abusive use of federal power in the state that illegitimately usurps state sovereignty while it threatens personal freedom. The expressions of discomfiture in Alaska over President Obama's recent announcements on managing the Arctic Refuge, NPR-A, and offshore drilling are only the latest in a long history of such protests. In Alaska there is a symbiotic relationship between several substantive historical factors and the tenacious grievance that constitutes the framework of daily conversation and political discourse. First is the set of physical conditions that describe Alaskan daily life: separation from the contiguous states by 1,500 air miles and by another sovereign nation; the vast size of the state together with its sparse population; the long, dark, and somewhat cold winters with permanent snow on the ground that necessitate extra effort for daily activities. All of these contribute to a sense of both isolation and exceptionalism and encourage the notion of a personal pioneer experience. As Americans are convinced of the exceptionalism of their country, so Alaskans are even more persuaded of the exceptionalism of Alaska, even though 70 percent of the population is urban and has unencumbered access to the material norm of contemporary American culture and most of its amenities. More than half the total population lives in the general area of the largest city, Anchorage.

The second factor is a mischaracterization of the state's history. In a perceptive essay on Alaska exceptionalism written a generation ago, historian Jeannette Paddock Nichols warned of the dangers of embracing a false history.[22] Forging a false history inflates and distorts identity; it occludes a realistic and usable vision of the future. But much historical treatment of Alaska has favored heroic tales of resilient individualism; has adopted the interpretation that Alaska was disadvantaged by its long territorial history because of insensitive federal management; and, somewhat paradoxically, has embraced the idea that the federal government neglected Alaska when it should have nurtured the region's development.[23] A more realistic history of Alaska acknowledges the essential and continuing role of federal support for a population without a self-generated economy that demanded all the services and amenities of contemporary American culture.[24]

There were few Americans in the territory before the Klondike gold rush in the winter of 1897–1898. A few hundred flocked to Sitka immediately after the purchase in 1867, hoping to be in the vanguard of a new western economic boom. They were soon disappointed, for no economic base developed, and what little resources the earliest settlers brought with them were soon exhausted. The climate was not conducive to surplus agricultural production, and even if it had been, any market was too far distant. Furbearers were not plentiful in accessible areas. Only with the discovery of gold in 1880 at what became Juneau did anything resembling a modern economy begin to develop, dependent on corporate investment from San Francisco businesspeople to fund development of the largest gold stamp mill in the world. But the several thousand attracted by the new jobs created easily imagined themselves as pioneers, pushing back the frontier and throwing up an outpost of civilization. In the meantime, a few hundred intrepid souls did brave the harsh conditions of the interior river basins to trap furbearers; prospect the mountains for mineral riches; and establish among the indigenous peoples, upon whom they were heavily dependent, tenuous footprints of American culture. Both of these groups of immigrants to Alaska freely harvested the game resources; took possession of the minerals, which the indigenous people could not legally do because they were not citizens; and manifested an individualist's sense of ownership and right. They were, however, dependent upon the US Army for exploring the land and cataloging its resources and providing aid and comfort in times of emergency and on the federal territorial system for establishing security by enforcing and adjudicating basic law.

The US Census in 1900 counted 30,000 non-Natives, people who had been attracted to the territory by the Klondike gold rush, the same number as the enumerated indigenous people. Nearly all of the immigrants had settled in new towns in the territory, most of which were funded by absentee investors in various mineral prospects and most of which were short-lived. These second-wave non-Native immigrants also treated the land as their own, harvested its resources without let or hindrance, and thought of themselves as self-reliant and self-sustaining.[25] Yet the federal government provided communication (federally financed and operated telegraph connection to the contiguous states), transportation (federally constructed, owned, and operated railroad), public safety (US Army; federal court system and constabulary), health care (federal hospitals, circulating medical and dental staff), education (federally funded non-Native and indigenous schools), civil administration, and eventually a federally authorized bicameral legislature. Federal expenditures continued in Alaska during the Great Depression, including a creative rural rehabilitation project in the Matanuska Valley. During World War II, 300,000 military personnel served in the territory. As one Alaska historian cataloged their impact, the federal government serviced localities with airfields, radio stations, hospitals, maps, coastal surveys, roads, housing, utilities, and schools.[26] Significant military spending continued through the Cold War years as well. Federal spending is one-third of Alaska's current economic base, which is discussed later in this chapter. It comes in funding of the military establishment, in conservation-unit management, in the provision of Native services, and in basic infrastructure.

One of the elements of Alaska's past used to justify the mantle of victimhood is the region's long territorial apprenticeship. When the founders of the American republic approached the question of frontier settlement, they determined that newly developed areas should eventually come into the union as states and that new states constitutionally should be on an equal footing with existing states. However, the founders were not confident that every new area would stay populated, nor were they confident that settlers unrestrained by the traditional social and political institutions of American life would acquit themselves responsibly of their civic responsibilities. So they established a system of civic tutelage for newly acquired, sparsely settled areas, codified in the Land Ordinance of 1785 and the Northwest Ordinance of 1787, both adopted by the Articles of Confederation congress—the latter while the constitutional convention was meeting next door in Philadelphia.[27] Both ordinances were subsequently adopted by the first Congress elected under the new constitution. Congress devised the policies for both land and governance through its authority provided in Article IV, Section 3 of the Constitution. Article IV conveys upon Congress the power to govern the territories, that is, the newly acquired lands before those lands were made states, and to create new states. The provisions in the two ordinances became the general pattern for organizing virtually all the newly acquired lands of the United States, including Alaska and Hawaii.

The Land Ordinance provided for an orderly survey of newly acquired lands and their sale by an executive agency, the General Land Office, on a schedule approved by Congress. The governing template was laid out in the Northwest Ordinance; it provided that initially Congress would name the territory and establish its political boundaries; Congress would also confirm the appointment of a governor and such other civil officials as it might, including judges, marshals, and clerks. In the 1787 ordinance, when the territory achieved a population of 5,000 free, white, adult males, Congress might authorize the biennial election of a bicameral territorial legislature and a territorially elected delegate to Congress to sit in the US House of Representatives. The manifestation of Congress's lack of trust in territorial citizens came in the additional provisions that Congress could disallow any legislation passed by the territorial legislature and that the delegate had no vote in Congress. In the 1787 ordinance, when the territory achieved a population of 60,000, otherwise undifferentiated, the territory could apply for statehood or Congress could initiate statehood. Nearly all the US states after the original thirteen entered the Union by this general pattern, later ordinances of similar design being crafted for the various territories by Congress.[28]

Various of the states were held in territorial status, with an appointed governor and federal judges, for varying lengths of time, depending on political circumstances and the vicissitudes of congressional mandate.[29] Alaska had a long tutelage as a territory. The United States acquired Alaska by purchase in 1867. Though some federal officials expected a rapid migration of pioneer settlers to the new territory, that did not happen. Only the coastal areas adjacent to the Pacific Ocean were well-known and understood, and those were heavily forested, for the most part. Alaska's agricultural potential was unknown, and although there were expectations of significant mineral deposits, suspected mineralized lands had not been surveyed. Exploration of the interior would wait until it was undertaken by the US Army in the 1880s, and full cataloging of the region's arable land would not occur until after 1900.[30] Congress did not authorize the organization of civil government until 1884, then providing for the appointment of a governor, a judge, and a marshal.[31] Authorization of the territorial legislature did not come until 1912, two years after the US decennial census showed that the gold-rush population of 30,000 non-Natives was permanent.[32]

From before the beginning of the twentieth century, most non-Native Alaskans did not live a frontier experience in the wilderness. A very high percentage were urban residents, living in towns such as Ketchikan, Juneau, Sitka, Cordova, Seward, Kodiak, Anchorage and its environs, Fairbanks, and other communities where most people worked for wages; lived in framed houses in platted subdivisions; and had access to all the goods, services, and amenities of modern American material culture.[33] The towns and the jobs that supported them were essential to non-Native migration and residence; without them, most non-Native Alaskans would not have remained in the territory. They had not come to Alaska to homestead or imitate characters in the fiction of Jack London or the poetry of Robert Service; they had come to advance themselves economically and for the novelty and perhaps adventure of living in a remote colony.

Only with the advent of World War II did the number of non-Natives in the territory begin to increase beyond gold-rush levels. The second world war transformed Alaska, remaking the region's economy and bringing new non-Native immigrants, including, after the war, many veterans who brought with them high expectations for the territory's development and for equal status with other citizens of the United States.[34] The war experience in Alaska brought territorial residents closer to mainstream America. The Japanese bombed the town of Dutch Harbor at the far west end of the Alaska Peninsula in June 1942 and invaded and captured islands at the far west end of the Aleutian Islands chain at the same time. A separate army theater, the Alaska Defense Command, was based in Anchorage, which was also the headquarters of the territory's federal railroad, the Alaska Railroad. Military and other federal personnel brought with them to Alaska all the assumptions and expectations associated with American mainstream material and social culture.[35] Fraternization led residents to adopt the same assumptions and expectations and to chafe at limitations that marked them as second-class citizens, such as nonrepresentation in Congress and no participation in the selection of their governor.[36]

These limitations and others led to a burgeoning statehood movement immediately after World War II. The Alaska statehood campaign of the 1950s effectively demonstrates Jeannette Nichols's point about Alaska's false history. That campaign began with a territorywide referendum on the question of seeking statehood in 1946. Though the result was less than a resounding endorsement, with 40 percent voting against, statehood advocates pushed ahead with confidence and determination.[37] Advocates expected that statehood would generate new population, new investment to develop Alaska's natural resources, and new and lasting prosperity. Territorial governor Ernest Gruening was a former newspaper reporter and editor of *The New Republic*; he was a strong and aggressive statehood advocate. Assiduous in his dedication to the cause, he made three substantial contributions to the campaign that had enormous impact.

Franklin Roosevelt appointed Gruening, who guided Alaska through World War II and pressured the territorial legislature into revising the tax structure and other reforms directed toward greater control over their affairs for Alaskans, including the territorial referendum on the question of statehood in 1946.[38] But the election of Republican Dwight Eisenhower as president in 1952 ended Democrat Gruening's governorship. The statehood campaign was in full swing, and the former governor immediately set about completing a new history of Alaska, which he published in 1954. The former publicist cannily and ostentatiously titled it *The State of Alaska*, not knowing whether such an entity would ever exist. The book echoed previous histories that had developed the theme that the federal government had held Alaska in tutelage for the economic benefit of a few absentee corporations, mostly in the Pacific canned-salmon industry, which took riches from Alaska for their shareholders' benefit while leaving nothing for Alaskans and, worse, prevented Alaskans from profiting from their own resources.[39] Utilizing the records of various congressional committees and executive agencies, Gruening added to this already well-worn story a legislative history of the federal government's dealing with Alaska, which he represented as at once neglectful and also abusive and oppressive. The federal government, he charged, had thwarted the territory's economic development, had denied Alaskans their rightful control over their own destiny, and had complicated their ordinary affairs with competing jurisdictions, which confounded common sense and the legitimate progress of the territory's citizens. This was familiar ground; throughout the saga of westward expansion virtually every territory seeking statehood had made the same arguments. But Gruening could argue more effectively that Alaska's noncontiguity and its unusual physical circumstances—vast geographic size, almost no roads, isolated and roadless indigenous villages, sparse population—made it unique and prevented federal officials from understanding the effects of their directives. The lack of control over their own affairs for these people who were otherwise comparable to US citizens, he insisted, constituted an untenable anomaly in the mid–twentieth century. Gruening intended the book for the reading public and for the broad national audience attentive to civil and political affairs, and particularly for members of Congress who would vote on Alaska statehood.[40]

Statehood advocates had decided early on that rather than wait for enabling legislation from Congress that would authorize the territory to prepare for statehood, they would jump-start the process by drafting a state constitution in advance of Congress taking up the issue.[41] A number of other states had followed the same course. Accordingly, the territorial legislature authorized an election for delegates to a constitutional convention that was held at the University of Alaska campus in Fairbanks during the winter of 1955–1956. As his second initiative, Gruening delivered the keynote address for the convention.[42]

Again he focused attention on Alaska's dependence on federal civil management, painting it in a highly negative context: the cumbersome and insensitive federal bureaucracy thwarting Alaska development and Alaskans' initiative. But he sharpened this interpretation significantly with the charge of US colonialism in Alaska. The American government, he argued, held the territory as a colony, an entity that benefited the holders and their economic clients with great and unconscionable disadvantage to the intrepid and courageous souls who had braved the elements, endured separation from their forebears, and sacrificed many of the conveniences of modern life to forge a new civilization in the Alaskan wilderness. This was on the face of it a preposterous claim, for the federal government, as noted, had from the purchase forward facilitated Alaskan development, protected Alaskans' safety and health, established planning mechanisms for the territory's future, and distributed uncounted federal funds in support of the region and its people.[43] But for many Alaskans, as Gruening intended, the address and its arguments became, and remain, a touchstone of Alaska's history and collective identity. For countless residents of the state, public life plays out as a daily contest between freedom-loving Alaskans and an overreaching federal government that remains insensitive to the true conditions of life on the "last frontier." Gruening had the address delivered to all members of Congress as part of the statehood campaign, but its primary audience was the Alaskan public. He understood the necessity of building as great a majority in support of statehood as possible if the campaign were to be successful, and he portrayed Alaskans as victims of an enduring power that could be broken only by statehood.

But it was not just the federal government that oppressed Alaska, according to Gruening and other purveyors of the victimhood myth. There were also the members of the rapacious, ruthless Pacific canned-salmon industry, who were the most ubiquitous absentee corporate investors in the Territory. The first salmon cannery had operated in Alaska in 1878, and by the turn of the twentieth century Alaska salmon canning had become a huge economic engine for cannery owners based mostly in San Francisco and Seattle. In 1900, 42 canneries packed 1.5 million cases of salmon. In 1917, 118 canneries packed 6 million cases, valued at $46 million.[44]

Resident Alaskans indeed profited little from this bounty. The salmon packers brought their own labor force to the territory each summer and operated for the most part as self-contained, isolated units, impacting the local people and their environment little save for the appropriation of the abundant and highly remunerative salmon resource. Soon after the turn of the twentieth century, innovators introduced a new technology that significantly increased the efficiency of the salmon harvest: the fish trap. This device consists of surface-to-seafloor netting extending as much as a half-mile into the ocean perpendicular to the shoreline, placed so as to interdict migrating salmon heading toward their home stream to spawn. The core of the trap proper is essentially a closed net box into which the anadromous fish are driven as they swim along the extended netting, becoming trapped in the core, from which they can easily be transferred to scows that move them to the cannery. The fish trap is perhaps the most efficient method for harvesting salmon ever devised, as it can catch virtually all the fish heading toward a particular spawning stream or streams.[45] Recognizing the potential destructive capability of traps, Congress mandated as a conservation measure in the 1924 White Act that 50 percent of the returning fish in a designated fishery must be allowed to escape into their spawning waters. However, enforcement was problematic due to insufficient funding for policing of trap operations. Alaskans and others charged that the poor funding was deliberate, a covert subsidy of the canned-salmon industry resulting from collusion between the federal government and the canners.[46] Alaskans testified aggressively and frequently against the use of traps.

For Gruening, the fish trap was a perfect symbol of Alaska's exploitation by Outside[47] interests who exploited Alaska's abundance and frustrated resident Alaskans' attempts to develop and profit from their own resources. With the charge of collusion, it could stand for victimization by either absentee corporate interests or the federal government, or both.[48] Gruening was not interested in analyzing the potential usefulness of fish traps, which, if properly managed, may be the most economical and efficient technology for harvesting salmon. Nor was he interested in analyzing Alaskans' potential as investors in the salmon fishery, which, given the limited resources extant in the territory, was minimal. Nor did he suggest how the new state might regulate the traps to ensure the mandated escapement and generate revenue. What he wanted was a symbolic representation of Alaska's victimization, one easily comprehensible and accessible.[49] Fish traps were tangible: they could be photographed and represented in schematic drawings. Models could even be made so people could see how they worked to decimate the salmon resource.[50] So successful was the trap as a representation of Alaska's exploitation that in 1958, when Alaskans voted on accepting the statehood act adopted by Congress, the territorial legislature included on the ballot a proposition to prohibit their use in the state; the measure passed 19,712 to 2,624.

The statehood campaign succeeded; Congress passed the statehood bill in July 1958. The success came against what might be considered major odds.[51] Alaska's population in 1958 was barely 224,000; the territory was noncontiguous with the existing states; because Alaska's governor and congressional delegate were liberal Democrats, southern Democrats in the US Senate feared Alaska's senators would be liberal and a threat to their successful opposition to civil rights legislation. Statehood was achieved through persistent, insightful lobbying organized behind a simple idea: given the demonstrable responsible civic character of Alaska's people, there were no grounds for denying statehood, with the possible exception of a slim economy and an inadequate tax base to support the costs of state government, as noted earlier.[52]

Ironically, Alaska's modern antistatism began with the success of the statehood movement. First, statehood did not generate the prosperity advocates had expected and promised, and Alaskans fell easily into their habit of blaming the federal government. Soon afterward, Native land claims began to compete with Alaska's selection of its immense statehood land grant, leading in 1966 to a federally imposed halt to the selection process after barely 10 percent of the grant had been selected. Capitalizing on national civil rights consciousness, Alaska Natives won an immeasurable victory that included title to 44 million acres of Alaska land, which Native corporations were permitted to select ahead of the state. But settlement of Native claims did not clear the way for continuation of state selections, for Alaskans were forced to watch as the national environmental lobby mobilized against construction of the Alaska pipeline, the bonanza that held the promise of economic emancipation for the state. Developers finally won that battle for Alaska, but the victory seemed somewhat Pyrrhic, for Alaska's land selection remained enjoined while Congress fought for eight years over vast new conservation withdrawals in the state. Only when the monumental Alaska lands act passed Congress in 1980 were state selections allowed to proceed. Those selections had been designed to provide the state with economic stability, and even though it was the Alaska pipeline that afforded largesse, at least for the short term, by 1980 Alaskans felt sorely abused and aggrieved, and they looked to environmentalism and federal prerogative as the enemies that had kept them in bondage and had denied them, as many thought, their statehood birthright. The deep and lingering sense of betrayal and maltreatment felt by many Alaskans was still plainly evident well into the twenty-first century.

Statehood did not generate a surge of migration or investment. Rather, after the transition from territorial to state government was virtually complete, the new state legislature faced a jump in anticipated expenses from the last territorial budget of $18 million to the 1962 state budget of over $55 million, with little substantial increase in revenue sources.[53] As one analyst wrote, the finance committees in the legislature found the prospect "disturbing."[54] It wasn't long before commentators began casting about for someone to blame. The federal government was the favorite target. Both gold mining and canned-salmon packing, which with federal spending on the Alaska military establishment formed the backbone of the economy, had reached a low ebb at the end of the 1950s. The government had frozen the price of gold during the Great Depression and then had suspended gold mining as a "nonessential" activity during World War II. The industry never recovered, and territorial officials held federal policy responsible.[55] At the same time, the Alaska salmon industry reached the nadir of its productivity in the 1950s. The 1953 pack was so low that President Eisenhower declared some portions of the Alaska coast disaster areas so local residents could secure emergency funds. Again, many in the territory believed there was an unofficial policy in the US Commerce Department not to enforce the escapement provisions of the 1924 White Act—50 percent escapement to insure perpetuation of the fishery—which led to overfishing and depletion of the annual salmon runs. The reason for the supposed government policy was to maximize profitability of the canning corporations' investments while offsetting their high costs of harvesting the resource.[56]

But the federal government was not the reason for the new state's fiscal woes. Alaska's principal challenge was development of a natural resource base that would generate tax revenue. Since 1940 Alaska had relied heavily on federal spending, which during World War II and then the Korean War had brought unprecedented money into the territory. With the close of the Korean War in 1953, military spending was curtailed, though Cold War installations ensured that it would not atrophy completely. But, aside from its long-term unreliability, it was not enough. With economies of scale defeating profitable manufacturing and commercial agriculture in the territory, natural resource development was the only alternative. But the sad truth was that resource development depends on market, which could not be artificially generated and over which, in any case, Alaskans had little if any control. By the mid-1960s this fact had become sufficiently clear to many Alaska leaders that they began to question whether the state should even select all of the land to which the statehood act entitled it. Land ownership brought with it a host of costs that the state could not afford in the 1960s. Robert Atwood, the publisher of the state's largest-circulation newspaper, the Anchorage Daily Times, listed some of them as he lamented the burden represented by the land grant:

> lands and minerals officers, forestry and range officers, administrative officers, cadastral engineering officers, land office managers, adjudicators, registrars, draftsmen, secretaries, stenographers, clerks, surveyors, truck drivers, airplane pilots, helicopter pilots, fire fighters, smoke jumpers, fire superintendents, police inspectors, patrolmen. These men and women would need salaries, offices, staff costs, health insurance, per diem, travel expenses and the tools of their trades, from typewriters to telephones, from pens to pencils to parachutes and plumb bobs. All this expensive staff and stuff to administer land that may remain worthless.[57]

Bleak as the state's financial circumstances appeared, there was one resource already under development that went far toward saving Alaska from bankruptcy: oil. In 1957 oil had been discovered on what soon would be state land on the Kenai Peninsula. The peninsula was prime moose habitat in the early and mid–twentieth century, and heavy harvesting pressure had reduced the animals' numbers substantially.[58] For their protection, in 1941 President Roosevelt, on the recommendation of US Fish and Wildlife Director Ira Gabrielson, established the Kenai National Moose Range, managed by the US Fish and Wildlife Service. Governor Gruening reacted angrily to the president's proclamation, accusing Gabrielson of attempting to prevent oil exploration on the peninsula. Later Gruening would label the director "the principal factor in Alaska's plight and problems, past, present and future."[59] Gruening needn't have been so exercised; Fish and Wildlife had normally allowed oil exploration on its refuges. But the governor, soon to become deeply engaged in the Alaska statehood campaign, understood Alaska's need for resource development as the region's economic foundation. He also had already begun to develop his strategy of justifying statehood by blaming the oppression of Outside constraints for inhibiting Alaska's economic opportunities.[60]

Consistent with long practice, Fish and Wildlife did grant numerous oil leases on the new Kenai refuge, including a number held by a group of Anchorage businessmen. But in 1953 Interior Secretary Douglas McKay, perhaps reacting to rising interest in postwar America in protecting the nation's unbuilt environment, banned all oil exploration and leasing on all refuges, pending a study of the effect on wildlife.[61] The secretary could grant exceptions and would do so in the moose range. But that did not prevent more reaction in Alaska. The moose range lay 50 miles directly south of Anchorage, now the territory's largest city, and Anchorage businessmen joined with Gruening in attacking McKay and also Gabrielson, who had retired from the FWS to become president of the nonprofit Wildlife Management Institute. As it happened, within a year, Richfield Oil Company filed an application for new leases on the moose range. When these were granted, Richfield top-filed some of the leases already held by the Anchorage businessmen, that is, obtained leases for the same plots of land.[62] Richfield subsequently made the 1957 Kenai oil discovery on leases it had obtained from the Anchorageites. Though small in relation to the later Prudhoe Bay and North Slope deposits, the Kenai find was enough to stave off complete insolvency in the mid-1960s.

Far more significant in explaining Alaska's antistatism is a conflict inherent in the statehood act itself. The deep origins of the conflict lay in Congress's failure to address the question of land distribution in Alaska for nearly 100 years. At the time of statehood, withdrawals Congress and the president had made included Mt. McKinley National Park; Katmai National Monument; Glacier Bay National Monument; Chugach National Forest; National Petroleum Reserve No. 4; several military installations; and a number of education reserves, mostly around mission stations and most comprising limited acreage. The total of these withdrawals was about 54 million acres. The remainder of Alaska, over 320 million acres, lay in uncertain status, waiting for Congress and the president to determine its use, managed in the meantime by the Bureau of Land Management. Section 6 of the statehood act included the grant of over 104 million acres for state title, which the new state was to select within twenty-five years from "the public lands of the United States in Alaska which are vacant, unappropriated, and unreserved at the time of their selection."[63]

As soon as the state could mobilize its Department of Natural Resources, the selection process began. It did not take long, however, for a grave and unsettling problem to arise to complicate the selections. Section 4 of the statehood act dealt with Alaska Native claims, which had previously been a problem for Alaska planners. As written in that section of the statehood act, Alaskans "do agree and declare that they forever disclaim all right and title to any lands or other property (including fishing rights) the right or title to which may be held by any Indians, Eskimos or Aleuts (hereinafter called natives)." No one knew in 1958 which lands those might be. But in 1941 the US Supreme Court had confirmed the validity of "aboriginal title" to US lands. Aboriginal title is title to land indigenous people once utilized and occupied, whether they continue to utilize and occupy it or not, unless said title has been formally extinguished by the US Congress.[64] Such title had been formally extinguished in the contiguous forty-eight states, mostly by the various Indian treaties, all of which included extinguishment of aboriginal title outside the designated treaty lands. There had been no treaties with Alaska Natives because they appeared to be self-sufficient, if only at the level of subsistence, and because of the federal government's failure to undertake comprehensive land disposition. Neither through treaty, then, nor any other legal mechanism had there been any formal extinguishment of Native title, a fact that provided Alaska Natives with a unique opportunity to claim land in Alaska as their own.

As elaborated in fuller detail in chapter 3, the issue of Alaska Native claims had come up before. Southeast Alaska Natives had formed a Native advocacy organization in 1912 and had pursued a claim for ownership for all of the land in the Alexander Archipelago, their ancestral homeland. In 1935 they persuaded the US Congress to pass an act authorizing them to bring suit for that claim in the US Court of Federal Claims. The US Forest Service opposed the claim; 90 percent of the land in the archipelago comprised the Tongass National Forest. The regional forester did not think Alaska Natives had any claim to land title in Alaska. Neither did Gruening, who vigorously opposed the notion that Natives had claim to any land except that on which their houses and villages stood.

Such views help explain why in 1958, when Alaskans voted to accept the Alaska Statehood Act as passed by Congress, very few people in Alaska understood the contradiction over competing land rights between Sections 4 and 6 of the act. Despite the US Supreme Court's finding for aboriginal title in 1941, virtually no one expected that the courts of the United States would award title to vast areas of Alaska to Alaska Natives.[65] The western conception of private property, an individual interest, militated against it. So did the western use of land for economic development. The Native notion of collective use of the land and traditional harvest of its subsistence resources, such as moose and caribou, and the traditional, aboriginal, animistic interdependence between land and human was foreign to most non-Native Americans. The traditional US Indian policy had been acculturation and assimilation of Native people; the indigenous view of the land as sacred and sublime in its natural state seemed at best primitive and quaint and not to be taken seriously in civilized and cultivated circles.[66] It was in this frame of reference that the state began selecting its land entitlement soon after statehood became official on January 3, 1959.

Alaska Native communities and individuals were as uninformed about the contradiction and implications of the conflict between Sections 4 and 6 of the statehood act as were non-Natives in the state. And there was considerable confusion over what the disclaimer actually might mean, that is, exactly which lands might be subject to aboriginal title. But over a few years immediately after statehood, as the Alaska Department of Natural Resources began to make the state's selections, several developments helped to raise Native awareness and then resistance. Donald Craig Mitchell, former general counsel and vice president of the Alaska Federation of Natives (AFN), has reconstructed the evolution of raised Native consciousness and subsequent steps taken by Natives and their allies to advance their claims to Alaska's undisposed land.[67] First, the nonprofit Association on American Indian Affairs (AIAA) became involved. Comprising men and women across the country knowledgeable about American Indians and their circumstances, including former federal government officials from the Interior Department and the Bureau of Indian Affairs (BIA), the AIAA was committed to publicizing and mitigating unmet needs on Indian reservations and among Indians in urban areas. The organization's leadership learned about the threat to potential Alaska Native land title while investigating a planned test of a low-yield nuclear device by the US Atomic Energy Commission (AEC), set in a remote area of far northwest Alaska in the late 1950s. The test was to involve an aboveground detonation.[68] The AEC had ignored Native concerns in its selection of a site and in planning for the test. The AIAA stepped in to help affected Native villagers protest such use of land they considered their own. The protest gave rise to a new Native organization among Eskimo people along Alaska's Arctic coast. At the same time, drawn together by the impending threat to their land claims represented by Alaska statehood and inspired by the civil rights movement in the contiguous states, a new generation of Alaska Native leaders emerged. They took the lead in establishing several new regional Native advocacy organizations to raise Native awareness and to protest the state's selections on the grounds of the Section 4 disclaimer. Also recognizing the threat to Native land rights, the regional office of the BIA began to counsel Native groups on the necessary bureaucratic procedures for protesting the state's land selections. Through the philanthropy of Henry S. Forbes, the AIAA funded publication of a Native weekly newspaper, Tundra Times, which, in the era before the Internet, served as the primary vehicle for sharing information and for generating Native unity.

Procedurally, once state officials identified an area for selection, the state filed an application with the regional office of the BLM for transfer of title from the federal government to the state. Before Natives fully appreciated the threat to their claims represented by the selections, the BLM routinely approved the applications and issued a tentatively approved title to the selected land. But before the end of 1959 Native leaders organized a conference on Native rights and publicly issued a statement of policy, calling on Congress quickly to settle Alaska Native claims. Soon afterward Natives began to file official protests to BLM's transfers of title, citing the Section 4 disclaimer. When they learned of the protests, state leaders reacted vigorously, and the BLM office denied the protests. At that point the regional office of the Bureau of Indian Affairs began to counsel Native petitioners on the process for appealing the denials to the Interior Department in Washington, DC. Both because some sympathetic personnel in the Interior Department were in no hurry to process the appeals and because the bureaucrats had no clear policy direction on how to handle them, which they argued needed to come from Congress, the appeals languished in Washington, much to the consternation of Alaska state officials. Seeing that no action was forthcoming, the state felt constrained to put its selection agenda on hold temporarily.

In 1962 President Kennedy's secretary of the interior, Stewart Udall of Arizona, and Governor William Egan, Alaska's first state governor, jointly selected a Native affairs task force to examine the situation and make a recommendation. After traveling that state, the members suggested that individual Natives be titled to the land under their homes and fish camps, that Congress establish a tribunal to hear broader claims, and that the secretary withdraw land around villages to ensure their further development. But the task force found that grants of large amounts of acreage were "not in the best interests of the state." This was the first of many recommendations by many groups for a settlement of Native claims. At one point a group of young Native leaders crafted draft legislation for Congress that provided that the Court of Federal Claims be directed to "award to Alaska Natives legal title to all federal land subject to Native aboriginal ownership whose legal title was still owned by the federal government."[69]

Seeking a path out of the confusion and contradiction surrounding the state's selection process, in 1963 the official in the Interior Department who oversaw both the BLM and the BIA convened a meeting in Alaska attended by Native, state, and federal officials. The attendees reached an agreement that the state should continue its selections and Natives their protests and that the BLM should process both and prepare a tentative title transfer but that no actual transfer should take place until either Congress should have provided legislation or the secretary issued specific instructions.

This was clearly a stopgap measure, for although it rationalized the contradiction between Sections 4 and 6, it resolved nothing and made no guarantees to any group. Gruening, now elected one of the new state's two US senators, articulated the state's primary concern: that the state's land selection process had effectively been placed on hold. Alaska's "economic development is frustrated," he told a congressional committee, "and opportunities for commerce and industry in such fields as mining, lumbering, agriculture and recreation, which would benefit Native citizens together with others, are lost to Alaska." The situation produced "economic and social paralysis in the state," he continued. In a sentiment that would echo repeatedly in Alaska in the years and decades ahead, he argued that the hold "constitutes a repudiation by the fiat of an executive agency of provisions of the Statehood Act enacted by the Congress."[70]

As Natives continued to organize and protest, and as the state continued to agitate, pressure for a solution mounted. Although BIA officers in Alaska were sympathetic to Native claims, their superiors in Washington were generally indifferent. BLM officials, however, were skeptical that Natives had viable claims and were hostile to the idea of large conveyances to Natives, collectively or individually. In addition to having conveyed about 12 million acres to the state before the 1963 agreement, the BLM continued to arrange mineral-lease sales on Alaska lands.[71] In September 1966 the BLM announced an oil-exploration lease sale for 4.3 million acres in far northwest Alaska. By then, however, North Slope Natives had established a regional Native organization, Arctic Slope Native Association, and quickly protested the sale. The BLM announcement and an Arctic Slope Native Association protest put Secretary Udall squarely in the middle of the Alaska land conundrum. Congress had shown no inclination to take up a bill to solve Alaska Native claims, and allowing the BLM to proceed with the lease sale would signal the Interior Department's sanction or disregard of the issue. Udall was sympathetic to Indian issues and served in the administration of a liberal president at the height of the modern civil rights movement. He was also an environmentalist. Counseled by his staff to do something "bold and daring," in December the secretary issued an order indefinitely suspending the lease sale.

It was a singular moment in the Alaska lands drama, and a number of people understood its import. Gruening immediately sent a telegram demanding reversal of the order, which, he said, would deprive Alaska of $18.2 million in rebated federal mineral-lease revenue. Another was Walter J. Hickel, who in November 1966 had been elected to succeed William Egan as Alaska's governor. Soon after his election Hickel directed his attorney general to file suit challenging the legality of Udall's order.[72] Not long afterward Udall expanded his initial action; he announced a suspension of federal lease sales anywhere in Alaska. He also ordered that the BLM not approve any applications from the State of Alaska for transfers of federal land title to the state; the Native claims issue had to be dealt with first, he said. Observers soon gave the name "land freeze" to Udall's actions. The secretary had concluded that halting title transfers to the state would force Congress to address, and solve, Alaska Native land claims. But unless and until the courts should invalidate Udall's order, Alaska would be prevented from exercising its right transmitted in the statehood act of gaining title to the remainder of its 104 million acres of land. The hostility many Alaskans still feel toward the federal government dates from the imposition of Steward Udall's 1966 land freeze.

Udall had two more years to serve as secretary of the interior before the election of Richard Nixon as president at the end of 1968. During that time the secretary voiced publicly his concern that justice be done to Alaska Native people in regard to their land claims. He was convinced that if Alaska secured title to lands that might be subject to aboriginal title, the years of litigation and expense required for Natives to regain title would militate against their ever getting the lands back. For him it was as much a moral issue as a legal or an economic one. When various attempts to fashion a compromise solution and to persuade Congress to act failed, as he was leaving office in December 1968 Udall issued a public order formally withdrawing all unreserved federal land in Alaska, which was nearly all of Alaska, thereby protecting whatever Native rights might be confirmed and preventing the state from obtaining any title to it. At the same time Alaska's governor, Walter Hickel, who was outspoken, often bombastic, and a reflexively decisive individual, also interpreted the freeze as a moral issue. He was adamant in his belief that the freeze violated Alaska's basic rights, denying Alaskans control over their own affairs and the independence promised by statehood. For Hickel, as for Gruening, statehood was to have been the antidote to exactly the kind of dominance by Outside actors and forces represented by Udall's land freeze. When Alaskans reflected that statehood did not bring the economic bonanza its advocates had promised, it was easy to link that disappointment with Native land claims and the manner in which the Interior Department had frustrated Alaska's economic development. To many Alaskans in 1968, statehood ten years earlier seemed a failure—one for which they held the federal government directly responsible.

Alaska Native claims would not be settled until congressional passage of the Alaska Native Claims Settlement Act in December 1971. Unprecedented in its scope and provisions, the act titled 44 million acres of Alaska land, an area equal to the size of the state of Washington, to twelve regional Native economic development corporations chartered to operate under the laws of the State of Alaska. It extinguished aboriginal title to all other Alaska land and awarded $962.5 million to Natives in compensation. All Alaska Natives living in 1971 became shareholders in one or another of the corporations, which were capitalized with the compensatory award and which have a fiduciary responsibility to generate profit to be distributed annually to shareholders, or as the shareholders sanction. The act identified 211 Alaska Native villages, all of which were entitled to form village corporations; 50 percent of the compensatory award to any one region was divided among however many village corporations were established within the region. The regional corporations hold the other 50 percent of the capitalization and all the subsurface estate for the entire region.

Discovery of the Prudhoe Bay oil field on state land on the North Slope in 1968 generated enormous pressure on Native groups, the state, and Congress to resolve the claims challenge, for the only economically feasible way to move the oil to refineries and to market included an oil pipeline across land in Alaska that was potentially subject to aboriginal title. Details of the relationship between the oil discovery and the passage of the act are related in chapter 3. State and community officials and leaders and prominent journalists persistently complained publicly that titling a large acreage of land to Natives would inhibit if not preclude economic development. But the industry's need to clear impediments to construction of the pipeline, together with the state's desire to restart its land selection program, forced industry, state, Native, and federal personnel to search for enough common ground to fashion a settlement. The various parties found that they needed to work together, however uncomfortable that might be, in order to achieve any of their goals. In addition, Alaskans' views of minorities were as transformed by the civil rights movement as were those of people in the rest of the nation. By the late 1960s, when Congress took up the claims issue and the parties began serious negotiations, Congress had passed the 1964 civil rights act; the march on Selma had galvanized the nation; the 1965 voting rights act had become law; and in 1968 Martin Luther King, Jr., had been assassinated. The 1964 Economic Opportunity Act had brought new money and a host of activist volunteers to Alaska bush villages, especially through the Rural Community Action Program, which had helped to empower Alaska Natives and to change collective perceptions of Native capability. For Alaska leaders, opposition to Native land claims became increasingly morally unpalatable and even somewhat politically risky.[73]

The parties worked throughout Nixon's first presidential term to craft a resolution that was fair, just, and workable for each. The settlement went far toward meeting that objective. Along with statehood and the Alaska lands act of 1980, ANCSA is one of the principal formative documents that contextualize Alaska. But the loss of 44 million acres of land that might have generated revenue for the State of Alaska under either federal or state title rankled many who understood the implications; to some it seemed an assault on Alaska's state sovereignty. When the final pieces of the settlement act were put in place, these Alaskans would insist on their day in court.

The deepest root of Alaska's extreme antistatism lies neither in Alaskans' sense of exceptionalism nor in the state's long territorial apprenticeship nor in the conflict between Native claims and land entitlement. Rather, the explanation lies in persistent aspects of the region's political economy that form a fundamental foundation on which those factors rest, constituting a systemic rigidity that circumscribes both policy and perception. Not many Alaskans understood the fundamental structure of Alaska's economy: very narrow, heavily based on commodification of the state's natural resources, and highly isolated. Because of the state's remote location—1,500 sea miles and 2,500 land miles from Seattle—and its small population—737,000 in 2014—as noted, economies of scale defeat commercially profitable manufacturing or agriculture. The cost of transportation of materials needed for any manufacturing venture, the high cost of labor, and high infrastructure costs for such things as heat and light require a higher volume of production for sustained profitability than Alaska can absorb. Moreover, the transportation costs alone just to get a finished product to market render any Alaska-made product noncompetitive outside the state. With the unusual growing season, short but featuring twenty hours of daylight at the height of summer, a number of crops can be grown in Alaska. But again, the cost of importing such necessities as fertilizer and packaging, added to transportation costs, necessitates a volume of production beyond the capacity of the Alaska market. When placed on market shelves, manufactured goods and agricultural products from outside Alaska are cheaper in Alaska than those produced in state. That explains why exploitation of natural resources is the only element on which an economy can be built. Furs, gold, copper, fish, and forest products were the primary resources developed before oil became the dominant element in the regional economy, which it quickly did with the construction of the Alaska pipeline between 1974 and 1977 and with the beginning of throughput in the pipeline in 1977. Moreover, there are no neighboring economies to help Alaska absorb a downturn in its economy. The population of neighboring Yukon Territory is a mere 36,500, the least population of any Canadian province or territory.

The 70 percent of Alaska's population that is urban today is consistent with Alaska's history since the beginning of the twentieth century.[74] Though the US Congress passed a homestead act for Alaska in 1898,[75] few people were interested in trying to coax an agricultural crop from a land frozen most of the year; often forested; and with thin, rocky soil. The US Agricultural Experiment Program early in the twentieth century found that the two areas of the state most suitable for agricultural development could support limited crops under difficult conditions. Neither of these has developed substantial production.[76] Non-Natives did not migrate to Alaska until there were jobs that would give them the wherewithal to allow them to live in a built environment familiar to them and to purchase the material norm of American culture. Investment in resource development from outside Alaska created the jobs, which created the communities. Douglas and Juneau were the first towns established, by the discovery of significant gold deposits near tidewater. Fairbanks was a gold town as well. Today oil is the major resource under development: one-third of Alaska's economic base comprises oil production, state taxes, rents and royalties on oil, and oil-patch servicing.[77] Between 80 and 90 percent of state revenue comes from oil taxes, rents, and royalties.

As noted, from the beginning of America's possession of Alaska, the federal government continually nurtured Alaska non-Native settlement and development, and the Native population, through investment in basic services, military presence, transportation, and communication. Anchorage came into existence as the construction, then administrative and operating, center of the federal Alaska Railroad. From 1940 to 1970 federal spending was the primary driver of the Alaska economy, with, as noted, Anchorage the headquarters for military in Alaska, during both World War II and the ensuing Cold War. Alaska today leads the nation in per capita federal spending. With the funding of Native services, conservation-unit management, military, and basic infrastructure (highways, ports, etc.), today federal spending is one-third of Alaska's economic base, with oil another one-third.[78] All other economic activity makes up the remaining third, including commercial fishing, tourism, mining, forest products, and all the commercial activity that serves the population.

This unusual economic profile is not only narrow, isolated, and remote; it is also highly dependent. Alaskans have little control over what decisions are made by the oil-company investors in Alaska; those decisions are made in the boardrooms of the industry players, primarily British Petroleum, ConocoPhillips, and Exxon/Mobil. Moreover, oil-industry activity in Alaska is linked to the world supply and demand for oil and to world oil prices. Higher prices and high demand translate into more jobs in Alaska, and the contrary. In addition, the federal portion of the state's economy leaves Alaska at the mercy of the vicissitudes of the congressional budget process in any given year. These circumstances keep job anxiety high in Alaska. If there is contraction in oil production or exploration, it is manifested immediately in furloughs and layoffs. These conditions take on a critical character unlike that in other dependent economies that are less isolated. For example, in 1986 world oil prices fell precipitously in a matter of months by over 50 percent, from around $27 dollars a barrel to less than $10. Severe contraction in oil activity led to a net migration loss of 25,000 people (of a population of 540,000) over the two years 1987 and 1988.[79] Home values fell dramatically, leaving many people with negative mortgages. Nine of the sixteen public financial institutions in the state failed.[80] The crisis in the state budget led to a significant contraction in state employment.

Given these factors and the state's volatile economic history, it is unsurprising that any prospect for diversifying the Alaska economy, any promise of new economic development, is heartily endorsed by the state's leadership. Nor is Alaskans' reflexive response to anything that threatens economic development surprising, including the prospect of environmental despoliation. Since the 1960s and 1970s, Alaskans have felt sorely aggrieved and abused by the continuing postponement of their selection of resource lands that they hoped and imagined would generate new investment, settlement, and prosperity. The natural targets of their anger and outrage are the federal government and the national environmental lobby, whom they hold responsible for their past frustration and present anguish. This book analyzes and interprets the sources and evolution of Alaska's persistent antistatism in the context of the rise of modern environmentalism.

CHAPTER 2

THE ARCTIC NATIONAL WILDLIFE REFUGE

The Klondike and subsequent Alaska gold rushes brought the first major increase in official population figures, from 5,000 non-Natives in 1890 to 30,000 in 1900, with about the same number of Natives. The population of both groups would stay about the same until the outbreak of World War II. Thirty thousand immigrant Alaskans spread over a land area 20 percent the size of the continental states would seem too few to have any significant impact on the environment. But they were not evenly spread; for the most part they were concentrated where there were economic opportunities that would allow them to approximate the material norms of the American culture of their day, including framed housing with modern furnishings; packaged food; access to medical care, education, and legal services; and entertainment that, while less frequent, was nonetheless on a par with that available in most of small-town America. As noted, this meant that most of the immigrants lived in town.

Popular imagining of gold-rush Alaska does not conform to this picture, and in fact much gold-rush activity did not; individual prospectors fanned out across the Alaska landscape to try their luck on virtually any mountain stream that federal surveyors had identified as potentially rich in mineral deposits. But the gold rush was an aberration and in any case was over by the end of the first decade of the twentieth century.[1] By then, the placers and easily accessible lode deposits had been found and worked. Increasingly, because of the deep expense necessary to develop important deposits, industrial mining replaced the lone prospector in the gold fields. Where investors, virtually all from outside Alaska, supported development, towns sprang up, though many were short-lived because the deposits played out. Candle, Iditarod, and Sleetmute are examples. Where the deposits were more substantial, the towns lasted longer and sometimes found alternative economic support, which allowed them to survive the gold rush; Fairbanks is the quintessential example.

Other towns formed around fishing processors, such as Ketchikan and Wrangell in the southeast and Kodiak. Juneau formed around the extensive, low-grade lode gold deposit that was developed by its San Francisco investors and mined industrially. Its population dwarfed any other community in the territory, and in 1899 Congress designated it as the territorial capital. Anchorage was the construction and then operating headquarters of the Alaska Railroad, construction of which Congress authorized in 1914. During construction the federal expenditures for constructing this railway in the wilderness, 470 miles from Seward to Fairbanks, cost 10 percent of the total national budget, $72 million.[2]

Game resources were quickly depleted in areas near Alaska's towns, and popular guiding operations depleted areas farther afield. Acting on their conviction of the inexhaustible nature of Alaska resources, fur hunters took inordinate numbers of fox, beaver, lynx, and other pelts, and trophy hunters threatened the brown bear population in several areas. In fact, Alaska's game and fish were not inexhaustible, as scientific data gathered in the interwar period would show. The biotic properties of most of Alaska do not support large populations of animals; the growing season is short, and the corresponding long winter limits food supplies. Conservationists knowledgeable about Alaska worked to extend to the territory federal legislation that limited the harvest of such species as brown bear, Dall sheep, and other big game and a number of birds that nested in Alaska, including swan, geese, brant, duck, snipe, oyster catchers, curlew, and grouse.[3] Legislation included the Lacey Act, Migratory Bird Act, Alaska Game Law, Migratory Bird Hunting Stamp Act, and Walrus Act, all of which limited the harvest. These regulatory provisions and a shift in Alaska's immigrant population from transient to permanent helped to curb the growing appetite of Alaskans for unfettered harvesting. Some long-term residents did show interest in maintaining a sufficient game and fur population to meet their personal needs. Congress passed regulatory legislation specifically for Alaska in 1902 and 1908, reflecting the new national interest in conservation, but neither act included adequate enforcement provisions. Many Alaskans chafed under the limitations, nonetheless, and both acts were violated with regularity. A familiar gambit was to list on restaurant menus an item labeled "hunter's steak"; it was code for illegally taken game. One governor, championing the complaints of locals, lobbied for territorial rather than federal authorization for the enforcement of all game laws. Congress thought otherwise and in 1925 created the Alaska Game Commission, comprising professional game managers and including a workable enforcement structure. Historians who have evaluated its functioning rate it a generally positive success at establishing a balance between accessibility for harvesters and perpetuation of species.[4]

Such was not the case with the Alaska canned-salmon industry, which migrated north from the Columbia River and Canadian fisheries in the 1880s. Virtually all the canneries in Alaska were owned by companies and investors from outside the territory, mostly in Seattle and San Francisco. Primitive fish regulations, poorly enforced, led to wanton overfishing, and the appropriation of Native fishing sites, by large cannery operations.[5] Harvests at the turn of the century amounted to 30 million fish annually and in the next decade 60 million, aided by the invention of the fish trap. The allied governments purchased Alaska salmon during World War I, and harvests topped 100 million. The poorly funded and enforced 1924 White Act did little to control successive destructive harvests. By the 1950s the Alaska salmon fishery was on the verge of collapse, the harvest falling to just over 34 million in 1957 and barely over 25 million in 1959, the year Alaska became a state. The industry was ripe for Ernest Gruening's highly successful campaign against fish traps as symbolic of Outside industrial exploitation of Alaska. His campaign also stands as an example of Alaska's vulnerability to environmental destruction, one that had a telling effect for environmentalists in the battles over preservation of Alaska's pristine nature. In a remarkable success story, the salmon fishery recovered under state management after statehood.

In game resources, the balance established in the interwar period changed dramatically with the arrival of the allied forces at the beginning of World War II. Of the 300,000 military personnel who served in the territory during the war, the greatest strength at any one time was 150,000. The military also employed thousands of civilians who came north for the good jobs, and the resulting boom economy attracted thousands more. During the early part of the Cold War, before American defense reliance on satellite reconnaissance and land and submarine-launched nuclear missiles, Alaska was of critical strategic significance. By 1950 the non-Native population neared 100,000, and by 1960 the total population had reached the 224,000 counted at statehood. Potential pressure on harvestable resources became enormous.

Yet though the threat to harvestable resources was significant, the non-Native population, because concentrated in the few cities and towns, generally trod lightly on many of Alaska's environmentally sensitive areas. Vast stretches of Alaska's natural landscape bore light evidence of permanent human manipulation, even though many areas that would later be designated wilderness were, and are, utilized by Natives in their traditional harvest of subsistence resources. Least impacted were areas north of the Arctic Circle, beyond Robert Marshall's Gates of the Arctic; the North Slope west of Naval Petroleum Reserve No. 4;[6] north of the Yukon River drainage in the east, the area that would be included in the Arctic Range; and also certain areas of western and southwestern Alaska, along the Arctic Ocean and the Bering Sea coast. In some other areas, though, human impact was significant. The fifty-year leases for pulp mills on the Tongass National Forest, authorized by Congress in 1947 (to be discussed later), had led to major logging operations there. Long-term industrial mining left ugly scars. In other regions, Alaska had escaped immense potential impacts, from a planned but unbuilt high dam on the Yukon River, for example, and the proposed atoms-for-peace construction project in the northwest on the Arctic coast. Alaskans supported these major economic development plans—in the Tongass Forest, on the Yukon River, and on the coast of the Arctic Ocean—even though the environmental impacts were potentially immense and likely to be permanent.

Robert Marshall was not an ecologist, even though he once described himself as one.[7] Nor did he imagine an unpeopled wilderness. In fact, he thought that wilderness experience was what was most lacking in modern civilization. With many others early in the modern environmental movement, he thought the encounter with wilderness in early America had been a critical element in forging the American character of individualism, ingenuity, and self-reliance. In the conclusion to *Arctic Village*, the sociological survey he wrote of the people of the village of Wiseman on the south slopes of the Brooks Range, where he spent thirteen months from September 1930 to October 1931, he asserted that the people there had their economic destiny in their own hands instead of being subject to economic forces over which they had no control.[8] This gave them an independence and freedom unknown to most people in the country and produced a personal happiness that Marshall thought exceeded the level of satisfaction with life of any group of people he had known. The kind of wilderness he imagined when he proposed that all of Alaska north of the Arctic Circle be set aside as a permanent wilderness was one free of the mechanistic attributes of modern civilization that he thought enslaved the majority of Americans and that, if brought to Alaska, would destroy the country's last wilderness where people could see and experience the land as the first pioneers had seen and experienced it. Alaska should be kept free of development, he argued, such as roads and tourist lodges, a view he articulated in a minority report to the US Natural Resources Committee assessment of Alaska in 1938.[9] Marshall, then working for the US Forest Service, did not encourage migration to the territory; he wanted it left alone, with only a few intrepid souls to enjoy it.[10]

It was quite different for George Collins and Lowell Sumner. Collins was a National Park Service planner; Sumner was an NPS regional biologist. When the NPS undertook a comprehensive study of Alaska's recreational potential in 1951, Collins, as senior project leader, headed the study. From 1951 to 1953 he visited 147 areas in Alaska to determine their suitability for recreation, historical importance, or scientific research.[11] As he expressed in a paper many years later, having spent an entire career with the NPS, he appreciated the spiritual value of wilderness as fully as Robert Marshall but developed a non-utilitarian, integrated, ecological view of nature, one that, while viewing humans as interdependent with nature, respected the biological integrity and evolutionary character of whole ecosystems.[12] As a result of the survey, Collins became convinced that the eastern Arctic, the northeast corner of Alaska, was a unique, spectacular landscape. It included remarkable mountains and extraordinary valleys, vast herds of caribou roving through the north-flowing rivers, ocean lagoons that filled with fresh water in spring and supported fish that migrated with the snowmelt, and millions of migratory birds that returned in spring to summer in the Arctic. He developed a firm conviction, he said in a 1978 interview, that if the NPS had a duty "to have within the scope of the national park system representative types of all the landforms, the landscapes, the history, the earth and life science interests that are outstanding in the nation, then there was an obligation to do something there in the Arctic."[13] His was a national, public perspective. The lands he was surveying were of national interest, the public's lands that should be a legacy for all Americans. This was a perspective diametrically different from that of the Alaskans who assumed a special right, simply by virtue of their having made the trek to Alaska, to avail themselves of any and all of its resources for their personal benefit.

What most distinguished Collins's view of nature and wilderness from Marshall's was the role Collins accorded science. In his survey he studied the geological genesis of the landforms and the relationships among various species and between fauna and flora. Lowell Sumner shared Collins's ecological understanding of natural systems and his enthusiasm for Arctic Alaska, especially the eastern Brooks Range and adjacent coastal plain. But Sumner's conception of nature was even more expansive than was Collins's. As historian Roger Kaye explained, Sumner's thinking progressed beyond a simple anthropocentric-biocentric dichotomy in managing wilderness. He believed wilderness had its own intrinsic value beyond any human use or appreciation. He may have been the first in the NPS to propose limitations on the types of recreational use for natural areas. He also understood that part of the aesthetic of nature lay in "knowing the land is free from human interference, and that the natural processes of its genesis continue."[14] He would share this view with conservationists in the NPS and in the national conservation organizations, particularly Olaus Murie, the veteran Alaska outdoorsman who had come to the territory in 1920 with the Bureau of Biological Survey and from 1937 served on the Wilderness Society council. Collins and Sumner became partners in their admiration of the eastern Arctic, working together and formulating a proposal for preserving it. For Collins, especially, preservation of this portion of the Arctic would represent an alternative to the pioneer conviction of the right of conquest, control, and domination of nature.

In an internal NPS report of their findings in 1952, Collins and Sumner proposed the reservation of northeast Alaska as a protected area.[15] This was the starting point for eight years of battle in Alaska between the new environmentalism and the traditional, pioneer, exploitative view of the land. The new reservation would be bounded on the north by the Arctic Ocean but would not include islands and island formations that lay more than 3 miles offshore. The eastern boundary was the Canadian border, though Collins and Sumner included the idea of an international park in the title of their report. The southern boundary was about 100 miles south of the Arctic Ocean. On the west, the two surveyors selected the Canning River. John Reed, Arctic expert in the US Geological Survey, had told Collins that there was little prospect of oil and gas deposits east of there.[16] The area Collins and Sumner proposed is essentially that portion of the current Arctic National Wildlife Refuge that is designated wilderness, and also the coastal plain (area 1002) study area, which Congress has not designated wilderness. The proposal listed all the ideas the two had discussed between themselves and also in conversations with Olaus Murie and his wife, Mardy, and others. First and foremost was the unique scenic and biological character of the area. It would, they wrote, serve as a laboratory for the study of Arctic natural processes. They called attention to the vast caribou herds, comparing them with the nearly extinct buffalo herds of the Great Plains. Should the area be lost to development, they noted, the last Arctic wilderness would be gone. Over the next eight years Collins and Sumner, and then others, mostly nongovernment personnel, would hone and refine the proposal and fight for its realization as a federal reserve.

But the proposal for an Arctic wilderness did not come entirely from the NPS. As early as 1951, the Wilderness Society, by resolution at its annual meeting in the Great Smoky Mountains, had endorsed Collins and Sumner's idea for a protected wilderness in Alaska.[17] Olaus Murie was elected Wilderness Society president in 1950. Even before Collins and Sumner submitted the formal proposal, the Sierra Club Council also endorsed the Arctic wilderness idea.[18] Other conservation organizations followed suit beginning in 1953.

Kaye has reconstructed the campaign waged for what became the Arctic National Wildlife Range, established by executive order in 1960.[19] Once the proposal became public, Collins and Sumner could not lobby for it as employees of the NPS. In late 1953 they met with Murie and with Howard Zahniser, then editor of the Wilderness Society magazine, *Living Wilderness*. Zahniser was about to embark on his nearly decadelong campaign with David Brower of the Sierra Club for the congressional passage of the Wilderness Act of 1964.[20] But in 1954 Zahniser was helping with the fight against the Bureau of Reclamation plan to dam the Colorado River at Echo Park in Dinosaur National Monument, part of the bureau's Colorado River Storage Project. Reflecting the new environmental consciousness Collins and Sumner shared, which was developing rapidly in affluent America after World War II, the two conservation organizations argued that if a dam could be built in a congressionally established conservation area, no landscape in the country was safe from development, from manipulation by humans.[21] The proposal for an Arctic wilderness reflected the same values that were at stake in the Echo Park fight. Also attending the meeting in late 1953 were Richard Leonard, an attorney who had just been elected president of the Sierra Club, and A. Starker Leopold, professor of zoology and forestry at the University of California at Berkeley and active in both the Sierra Club and the Wilderness Society; Leopold was the son of Aldo Leopold, acknowledged as perhaps the foremost promoter of ecology in mid-twentieth-century America. In December the Wilderness Society began an active campaign for the Alaska preserve.

Zahniser was an effective lobbyist and a brilliant political operative; the Wilderness Act is a testament to his remarkable capabilities.[22] So, also, is the compromise finally agreed to between environmentalists and Congress regarding the Echo Park dam. Congress eliminated that dam from consideration in exchange for the conservation organizations ceasing to protest a dam across Glen Canyon, above the Grand Canyon, and a promise that Congress would authorize no further dams in national conservation units. Though later rued by most conservationists, the compromise was the beginning of an unprecedented and unequaled two decades of significant environmental legislation, culminating in the Alaska lands act of 1980.

Throughout 1955 and 1956, Zahniser and Brower, now the acknowledged leaders of the new environmental movement, pursued the campaigns for the Arctic wilderness and against the Echo Park dam simultaneously, and the tactics of one became the tactics of the other. Zahniser had used articles and photographs in Living Wilderness to bring the Echo Park dam to the Wilderness Society membership and beyond, a tactic he had used previously with threats to Mount Rainier and Olympic National Parks in Washington State as well as to generate support for establishing such withdrawals as Big Bend, Death Valley, the Everglades, Black Canyon of the Gunnison, Organ Pipe, Joshua Tree, and other new conservation units.[23] Brower had done the same with the Sierra Club Bulletin. They adapted this tactic to proselytizing for an Arctic wilderness. Another tactic was publication of a first-person account of a trip through the proposed withdrawal, together with photographs of its more spectacular aspects. These were intended primarily to generate a political base to give heft to the more direct work of lobbying Congress; they were an integral accompaniment to building legislative awareness and, eventually, action. The lobbying effort was supported also by a vigorous grassroots letter-writing campaign involving thousands of volunteers in many states.

The Wilderness Society/Sierra Club campaign was a success. In early 1956 Congress passed the Colorado River Storage Project with the Echo Park dam deleted and with the promise to keep dams and reservoirs out of national parks and monuments.[24] Roderick Nash wrote that this "finest hour" of the environmental movement gave leaders and members the confidence and momentum to launch the subsequent campaign for the Wilderness Act. The Echo Park success also gave inspiration to supporters of the Arctic wilderness. If a major project by such a congressionally revered agency as the Bureau of Reclamation could be stopped, then environmental causes such as the Arctic preserve might generate enough political support to become reality. Kaye wrote that the Echo Park campaign became a model for the Arctic crusade.[25]

In 1926 Olaus and Mardy Murie had hiked and camped near the southern part of the area selected by Collins and Sumner for the Arctic wilderness. As part of the 1950s campaign, they made plans to go back with a film photographer to develop a first-person narrative that could be used to show the unique character and irreplaceable value of the region. Delayed temporarily, they made the trip in 1956, accompanied by a filmmaker and several others. The Wilderness Society, the Conservation Foundation, the New York Zoological Society, and the University of Alaska sponsored the expedition. Rather than fly to various sites in the proposed withdrawal, they decided on a thorough survey of the centrally located Sheenjek River valley. Though the principal reason for the journey was to gather material to publicize the proposed reserve, expedition members spent two months gathering research material and notes on the geology, ecology, and fauna and flora of the valley, treating the trip as a summer field survey, an opportunity to show the area's scenic and spiritual significance as well as its scientific importance. Expedition members spent two months hiking, climbing, collecting, and analyzing virtually every accessible aspect of the landscape they explored.

The result of the publicity side of the effort was a cascade of publication, including two short films, one of which was narrated by both Olaus and Mardy Murie. The articles that appeared in magazines, newspapers, and professional journals extolled the virtues of the caribou, bears, and wolves of the proposed reserve as well as the idea of nature unmanipulated by humans. They also asserted the advocates' belief in the restorative power of a visit to the preserve for those burdened by their persistent need to negotiate the mechanistic urban topography of most readers' lives—the idea Marshall had championed in first proposing an Arctic wilderness. Over the four years between the Sheenjek River odyssey and executive withdrawal of the Arctic Range, articles in popular magazines, conservation organization organs, and professional journals continued to appear. Then, in the spring of 1957, at the Sierra Club's biennial conference in San Francisco, delegates adopted resolutions endorsing congressional enactment of both a wilderness preservation bill and the creation of the Arctic wilderness.[26] In addition, several people with national reputations joined the cause. Supreme Court Justice William O. Douglas, already famous as a defender of the environment, joined the Sheenjek expedition for part of the time and later wrote of his reverence for it in his autobiographical *My Wilderness: The Pacific West*, published in 1960.[27] Herb and Lois Crisler filmed in the Brooks Range for Walt Disney; their footage comprised the bulk of the popular *White Wilderness*, released in 1958. In that same year, Lois Crisler published *Arctic Wild*, her account of raising wolf pups in the Brooks Range. Both works exalted the significance of wilderness to the human spirit and endorsed preservation of an Arctic wilderness. In *Arctic Wild* Lois Crisler wrote, "In civilization there is a vast, overwhelming whimper to be secure, sheltered, cared for. But if you refuse danger too much, you refuse life. . . . Either you must cover every chance, or go free, not tethered like Gulliver and the Lilliputians by a thousand threads of caution."[28] It was a paean that again echoed Robert Marshall's celebration of the primitive life in nature in his conclusion to *Arctic Village*.[29]

The notion of pristine, nonhuman nature as spiritual inspiration was an expression of praise for an idea only some Alaskans could relate to from their personal experience; most could not. For most Alaskans, nature was practical, an everyday experience characterized by work and daily difficulty, often threatening and sometimes cruel. They appreciated its beauty, but they also knew firsthand its challenges. They did not conceive of it as human-free. For many, harvesting its resources was a normal part of everyday life. Opposition to the idea of an Arctic reserve grew quickly in Alaska soon after Collins and Sumner made their formal proposal and the public learned of the idea. In October 1953 the territorial Alaska Development Board, established by the territorial legislature after World War II at the urging of Governor Gruening, contacted Collins about the projected reserve. The board wanted a full survey of area resources before any work should be undertaken on a withdrawal. Soon a Fairbanks newspaper carried a story about Collins and Sumner's proposal that elicited a stream of letters in opposition to it, fewer in support.[30] Opponents deplored any restriction on hunting or prospecting and mining. They also objected to the federal government determining what the status of Alaska land might be, which would increasingly become the default Alaska position whenever environmental withdrawals were discussed. One protester labeled the proposed wilderness "a land grab without precedent in the long history of withdrawals in Alaska."[31] These were the first of a continuing flow of letters propounding the notion of abuse of Alaskans' freedom by federal regulators willing to disregard the moral rights of hardworking, independent settlers sacrificing to develop the territory. Anchorage was a particular source of attack on the idea of an Arctic withdrawal. Robert Atwood of the *Anchorage Daily Times* through the 1950s pursued a persistent editorial rebuke of the wilderness proposal. "Restrictions on game hunters are an affront to the cherished utilization of the American frontier," he wrote at one point, "threatening not just people's livelihood but a long cherished and valued way of life."[32] To Atwood and many others, federal land withdrawals in Alaska were anathema, an abnegation of the pioneer spirit that had forged American freedom and prosperity.

From the beginning the Muries understood that the idea of an Arctic withdrawal would need support within Alaska. Following the Sheenjek expedition they traveled to all the towns along Alaska's rail belt from Seward to Fairbanks, where most of the non-Native population lived, to show their slides and film of the proposed reserve and to explain their view of the need to preserve at least one piece of unspoiled wilderness. The reception was often unwelcoming, but Olaus in particular was low-key in his approach, letting his visible emotional attachment to nature and his long career of trekking the territory, together with the images he and Mardy showed their audiences, contextualize the appeal.

The Tanana Valley Sportsmen's Association (TVSA) of Fairbanks was a group whose support the Muries considered essential. This collection of hunters and hikers included interior Alaska businessmen and politicians as well as numerous outdoorsmen scattered across undeveloped portions of Alaska wilderness. Many members resented the fact that notice of the proposal had been first published in the Sierra Club Bulletin without Alaskans having been consulted. They felt they were being taken advantage of by people who had no direct knowledge of Alaska or Alaskans. The TVSA was influential in resource-policy formulation for Alaska. Murie himself had once been a hunter of significant reputation, and he regarded hunting as a legitimate extension of man's historic relationship with the natural world, so long as the hunting did not include high-powered rifles and airplanes. This attitude somewhat eased resistance to his appeal for support for the proposal. He met with association members in Fairbanks in the spring after the Sheenjek expedition and, through quiet persistence and a nonconfrontational manner, persuaded them to draft a petition to the US Fish and Wildlife Service for an Arctic wildlife range. In a tribute to Murie's powers of persuasion, the association did adopt a resolution of support. It included reference to the preservation of such features as ecologically undisturbed landscapes unimpaired by human development. It also provided that hunting, fishing, and trapping should be permitted, and also prospecting and mining, but subject to preservation of the surface estate. It included a broad delineation of uses and thus achieved authenticity as an endorsement from a knowledgeable aggregation of Alaskans. Their view of the reserve was a harbinger of the practical integration of the human and nonhuman elements of nature that would characterize the later Alaska lands act. It contradicted both the uncompromising resistance of Alaskans farther removed geographically from the proposed reserve and the unrealistic view of environmentalists who excluded humans from their definition of wilderness.[33]

It is unlikely that the Fairbanks group would have been so ready to accept the idea of the reserve if its members had thought there was a significant likelihood of commercially developable mineral deposits within the proposed areas, particularly oil and gas. Thus, John Reed's earlier counsel to Collins that there was little possibility of such deposits in the lands east of the Canning River proved very helpful. Reed's was the assumption, also, of the Fairbanks Chamber of Commerce, which subsequently endorsed the proposal.[34] Oil geologists had concentrated on Naval Petroleum Reserve No. 4, far to the west, where the US Navy had undertaken a major drilling program in 1944. That program had not been successful, except for sufficient natural gas to provide heating energy for the community of Barrow, and the navy suspended the program in 1953, which also helped assuage potential opposition. Oil geologists maintained their interest in Alaska's North Slope as a potential oil source, but few imagined there would be oil as far east as the proposed wilderness reserve.

The most significant endorsement of the proposal came from another veteran Alaska hand, Clarence Rhode, regional director of the FWS in Alaska, which managed the Alaska Game Commission. Rhode could support a reserve that permitted sportsmanlike hunting, and he became an ardent advocate. Not long after the Muries met with the TVSA, Rhode flew an assistant secretary of the interior, Ross Leffler, around the proposed reserve. Following his tour, in Fairbanks Leffler announced that Fish and Wildlife endorsed the proposal. Fish and Wildlife had initially rejected the idea, but the growing statehood campaign through the mid-1950s helped to change that position, and to awaken other land agencies as well to a looming danger: state selection of potential mineralized lands. The state constitutional convention met on the campus of the University of Alaska in Fairbanks during the later stages of the Arctic wilderness campaign, and in 1957 Alaskans elevated their lobbying of Congress on the statehood issue. The various Alaska statehood bills that Congress debated all included the grant of land to the proposed state, which Alaska would use to advance economic development. With only 54 million acres of Alaska's 375 million yet formally designated and withdrawn,

Alaska's vast stretches of land that environmentalists imagined as unmanipulated might come under state title. Officials of Fish and Wildlife and other land management agencies with jurisdiction in Alaska began to consider which lands they might wish to keep under federal title, anticipating that state protections of environmentally valuable lands likely would be less restrictive and more development-friendly than federal ones.[35] Collins and Sumner had expressed similar reservations about the state's capacity to develop environmentally valuable lands.

Leffler's endorsement, which had the approval of Secretary of the Interior Fred Seaton, dramatically changed the campaign. It was not a guarantee of creation of a reserve, but now the most important executive branch of the federal government in regard to natural resources would put its weight behind creation of the Arctic reserve, lobbying others in the executive branch and the Congress and briefing the national press. Rhode also showed the proposed wilderness to the secretary, and in 1958 Seaton wrote an article for *National Parks Magazine* endorsing it. Later he testified for it before the House Committee on Fisheries and Wildlife Conservation.[36]

Seaton was a shrewd if transparent politician. He had been elected to the Nebraska legislature and appointed to fill the vacated seat of one of Nebraska's US senators before President Eisenhower selected him to head the Interior Department. In 1943 President Roosevelt had withdrawn all of Alaska north of the Brooks Range for use of the military, which barred use by civilians, including hunting and mineral exploration. The North Slope was the area of Alaska that petroleum geologists thought most likely to hold significant deposits. The order had continued in force after the war, partly because of the ensuing Cold War. Alaskans had lobbied unsuccessfully for rescission of the withdrawal, and enforcement had been lax.

Knowing well what the political reaction would be in Alaska to his withdrawal of the new wilderness reserve, Seaton tempered the impact of his endorsement by pairing it with an order rescinding the wartime military withdrawal of the area between the proposed wilderness withdrawal on the east and the national petroleum reserve on the west, the very area petroleum geologists thought most likely of any part of Alaska to have significant oil deposits.[37]

Nevertheless, the secretary's embrace of the reserve idea raised the ire of Alaska's lone delegate to Congress, E. L. "Bob" Bartlett, who was widely respected in Congress. Though born in Seattle, Bartlett was a graduate of the

University of Alaska and had worked as a *Fairbanks Daily News-Miner* reporter before becoming secretary to the Alaska congressional delegate. Later he served as the presidentially appointed secretary of Alaska, effectively the territorial governor's chief of staff, before being elected delegate himself. With the transfer of focus from Alaska to Washington, DC, Bartlett would lead the opposition to the Arctic wilderness proposal, including convening hearings intended to discredit the idea and prevent congressional approval. His chief concern was Alaska's economic development.

Congress passed the Alaska statehood bill in the summer of 1958, and the new state became official on January 3, 1959. The first two US senators elected were Bob Bartlett and Ernest Gruening; Ralph Rivers, former mayor of Fairbanks, was elected congressman. All were Democrats. In May 1959 legislation to establish an Arctic wildlife range was introduced in both the Senate and the House. There would be hearings in both bodies. The introduction of the bills generated a new storm of opposition and criticism in Alaska. The new Alaska legislature resolved that all possible action be taken to discourage establishment of the "arctic wildlife refuge" in northeast Alaska.[38] Other officials of the new state government wrote to Secretary Seaton and to the congressional committees working up the bill to complain about the lockup of Alaska land and its inhibition of industrial development. Some argued that the bill would move Alaska in the wrong direction, away from settlement and potential tourism. Mining interests across the state wrote to protest possible restrictions on mining they found in the bill. The bill provided that prospecting and mining would be subject to regulations promulgated by the Interior Department, and it prohibited patents of the surface estate.[39] The Alaska Constitution, adopted by Alaska voters before statehood became official, included its unique article on natural resources and also an aggressive statement of resource policy: "It is the policy of the State to encourage the settlement of its land and the development of its resources by making them available for maximum use consistent with the public interest." The article further called on the legislature to "provide for the utilization, development and conservation" of all the state's natural resources "for the maximum benefit of its people." These statements were ambiguous at best, but they clearly signaled the founders' intent that the land and resources be developed, albeit within a context of conservation, though that context was not defined.

Perhaps unnerved by this forceful expression of the development philosophy in the state constitution, and deeply concerned that the new state would not have sufficient revenues to defray the costs of state government, Congress moved to counter the possibility that the state might give away its resources without ensuring an appropriate return: as noted, the state is prohibited from alienating its land; it cannot patent mining claims but must lease the right to mine and share in whatever revenue may be generated.[40] Congress also moved to protect Alaska fish and game. The statehood act included a provision that the federal government would retain jurisdiction over the management of fish and wildlife resources until such time as the secretary of the interior should be satisfied that the state legislature had made adequate arrangement for their management and conservation "in the broad national interest."[41] It was an expression of how committed a majority of Alaskans were to statehood that the plebiscite to approve the statehood act as written with this and other limitations on state sovereignty passed with the overwhelming majority that it did.

These provisions cut deeply against the grain of the freedom of movement and independence of action most Alaskans celebrated as the essential difference between Alaska and the lower forty-eight states. Bartlett commented on several occasions that freedom from federal control over Alaska's natural resources was a major source of support for the statehood movement.[42] Despite the solid vote approving the statehood act, there was considerable protest that citizens were still being held in second-class status by the federal government. Some miners noted the irony that on the state's lands they were now prohibited from the entry and placement regime applied to federal lands under the 1872 Hard-Rock Mining Act that had applied to Alaska before statehood.

Having been elected Alaska's senior US senator, Bartlett chaired all the Senate hearings on the Arctic bill, which were held in Washington, DC, and in Ketchikan, Juneau, Cordova, Valdez, Seward, Anchorage, and Fairbanks. Gruening, as senator, was the first to testify. He and Bartlett had decided on several strategies to defeat the bill. The first was to emphasize the change the proponents had made in the justification for federal conservation withdrawals. In their various statements they correctly captured the evolution of the concept of nature conservation from the classical utilitarian, multiple-use notion to the Aldo Leopold–inspired idea of preservation of an ecosystem based on a scientific appraisal of the ecological nature and significance of a natural area wedded to an appreciation of its scenic and spiritual value. By 1959 virtually all the proponents offered one or another version of the new environmentalism as their rationalization for preservation of the proposed reserve. Gruening demurred; a refuge, he insisted, should be set aside for the benefit of human beings. Bartlett seconded this idea in his questioning, saying he had "trouble with this word 'ecology.'" Gruening argued that the withdrawal the supporters sought was a fantasy, an act of preservation for a theoretical construct based on a view that subordinated human beings to nature.[43] What the advocates had in mind, Gruening insisted, was not a refuge that would protect wildlife but an inviolate and sacred wilderness. As such it would eliminate the area's economic potential and in so doing diminish Alaska and its residents and make the work of subduing the frontier yet more difficult. More tangibly, the former governor also argued that the withdrawal would cost the new state money, for the annual allocation of federal highway subsidies was based on a formula that included the amount of undesignated and unreserved land in the state; the greater the amount of unreserved land, the greater the subsidy.

The Washington, DC, hearings provided Interior Department officials and others in the federal bureaucracy with an opportunity to defend the initiative, now identified with the department as much as with anyone who had actual experience in Alaska. Their testimony was uniformly favorable. Among the Washington witnesses was Ted Stevens, later to be Alaska's premier US senator but in 1959 working in the solicitor's office in the Interior Department. Stevens supported the preserve, partly because he thought its creation would give the environmentalists a victory that would silence them and also because he thought the trade-off with the rescission of Public Land Order 82 (the 1943 military withdrawal) a good one.[44]

Opponents did testify in Washington or had their remarks added to the record by Bartlett; these included the Western Association of State Fish and Game Commissioners and the International Association of Game, Fish and Conservation Commissioners, with overlapping membership, who adopted resolutions supporting Alaska jurisdiction over fish and game in the state. The Alaska Department of Fish and Game opposed the reserve unless it should be under state jurisdiction.

Taking advantage of their opportunity, opponents testified on numerous points at the various Alaska hearings. Some attempted to elucidate Alaska's land-disposal history. Alaska had been subjected to a series of federal withdrawals, they asserted, all of which created a hardship for Alaskans. No federal withdrawal was in Alaskans' interest; all trampled on the state's rights to manage its own destiny. Others thought the reserve premature, or that it set aside an area far too large for its stated purposes. Members of the Alaska Miners Association appeared at every venue in Alaska, protesting that permitting for exploration and leasing under the interior secretary's regulations would inevitably be cumbersome. Several miners asserted that the regulations would be so burdensome as to inhibit any mining and wondered if that wasn't in fact the department's intention. Phil Holdsworth, former territorial mines commissioner and now the state's commissioner of natural resources, echoed Gruening, maintaining that "mining" and "wilderness" were diametrically opposed concepts. A particularly colorful opponent was miner Joe Vogler, who would in later years become an outspoken advocate of Alaska secession from the United States. He noted that after World War II the federal government had initiated a program to advertise Alaska's virtues for new settlers and to encourage discharged veterans to avail themselves of Alaska's opportunities. But this new federal energy, he suggested, was closing out the "last frontier" with its rules and regulations, stifling the freedom represented in the idea of "frontier."[45] Alaska's two senators hoped opponents' testimony would persuade enough members to block the bill.

Bartlett and Gruening had a second grand strategy. Congress has a long tradition of not approving a measure confined to a single state over the opposition of the congressional delegation from that state. But despite Bartlett's long service in the House of Representatives (from 1944 to 1958), with his election to the Senate the burden in the House fell to Alaska's lone congressman, Ralph Rivers. Before his election to the US House, Rivers had served only one year in the Alaska Territorial Senate. In the House, where the bill had been sent to the Merchant Marine and Fisheries Committee, that committee voted it out to the full body unanimously with a "do pass" recommendation. Within weeks the full House voted for the bill, a huge victory for the proponents. Legislative management of the proposal now passed to Bartlett and Gruening. Determined to quash the reserve idea and confident that they could defy the federal bureaucracy, they worked to prevent any further action on the bill in the 1959–1960 congressional session. In the end they were successful, managing to table the bill in committee. With no action having been taken by the end of the second session of the Eighty-Sixth Congress, Bartlett and Gruening apparently had won: the Arctic wilderness bill was dead.

But there was still Secretary Seaton; he could recommend that the president withdraw the proposed reserve by the authority of the Antiquities Act, a 1906 measure that authorized the president to withdraw public lands for specific uses over his signature alone. Congressional legislation would trump executive action, but history had shown that when Congress was unable to produce public lands legislation, the Antiquities Act was a viable alternative. Both proponents and opponents looked to Seaton to validate their view of the reserve proposal. Alaska's popular governor, William Egan, wrote to the secretary proposing that the preserve area be titled to the State of Alaska as part of its 104-million-acre entitlement under the statehood act. The state would manage it, Egan averred, without compromising the wildlife and wild-land values so prized by supporters of the proposal.[46] The offer was so transparent that Seaton seems not to have dignified it with a reply.

Supporters had two advantages that may have persuaded the secretary to establish the reserve. First, the publisher of the *Fairbanks Daily News-Miner*, C. W. Snedden, was a good friend of Seaton; the two had worked together on the statehood campaign. During the late 1950s Snedden had written a number of editorials supportive of the Arctic preserve, provided it should be open to mining. The other advantage supporters of the proposal had with the secretary was the support of the wilderness writer Sigurd Olson. Famous for his advocacy for and defense of the Boundary Waters Canoe Area in northern Minnesota, Olson worked with the Wilderness Society's Howard Zahniser on writing the Wilderness Act. Both Olson and Zahniser were members of the Interior Department's Advisory Committee on Fish and Wildlife, to which Olaus Murie had shown his slides and film of the 1956 Sheenjek expedition; Murie had persuaded the committee to advocate for the Arctic proposal.[47] Olson lobbied Seaton for establishment of the reserve.

But as the end of 1960 approached, Seaton had taken no action. In November John F. Kennedy was elected president and soon announced that Stewart Udall of Arizona would be his secretary of the interior. Not wanting to pass the proposal to his successor, Seaton acted. A month after the election, on December 7, Seaton announced the creation of the Arctic National Wildlife Range by executive order, 9 million acres between the Canning River and the Canadian border and the Arctic Ocean and the Brooks Range.[48] It was a signal triumph for modern environmentalism. Northeast Alaska would now be preserved from development. It is significant that the secretary's order did not mention ecology or science. The withdrawal, over which the Fish and Wildlife Service would have jurisdiction, was for the purpose of preserving "unique wilderness, wildlife and scenic values." Mining was prohibited but not mineral leasing. The secretary could permit the taking of game animals, birds, and fish and the trapping of fur animals, all of which would be subject to the his prescriptions, administered by the FWS.

Furious that they had been thwarted, Bartlett and Gruening in the Senate were able to stifle any attempts by the bureaucracy to fund management of the range. Not until after Bartlett's death in 1968 and Gruening's defeat for reelection the same year did the FWS secure funds for a range manager and equipment. The *Anchorage Daily Times* decried Seaton's actions as the further "lock-up" of Alaska land and the trampling of frontier values. Governor Egan wrote to the secretary to protest the "unfortunate treatment" of the new state and its opportunities for settlement and development.

For their part, Howard Zahniser of the Wilderness Society and David Brower of the Sierra Club were energized by the secretary's action.[49] They viewed the campaign as a momentous success, an augury of a positive outcome of their years of work on a wilderness act. The Muries particularly, but other proponents also, had used the political tactics still being developed by environmental advocates. These included the personal narrative of journeys and fieldwork in the proposed area, recounted for countless audiences, accompanied by photographs, drawings, slides, and film; thousands of letters written by supporters to congressmen, but also to newspaper editors and civic groups; testimony before congressional committees as well as appearances before civic groups not regarded as supporters; and coordination between government and private officials. As the fight against the Echo Park dam was instructive and inspirational for the campaign for the Arctic National Wildlife Range, so was the wildlife range fight instructive for the campaign for the Wilderness Act, each campaign reinforcing the conviction and strategies of the other, as in a true symbiosis.

At the same time, the Arctic wilderness campaign represented a maturation, an evolution, of the wilderness idea. In 1951 and 1952 George Collins was struck by the arresting scenic power of the eastern Brooks Range, the Sheenjek and other river valleys, the vast Arctic coastal plain, the enormous migrating herds of caribou, and the hordes of birds arriving in spring from all over the North and South American continents. On the survey trips he made with Lowell Sumner in 1952 and 1953 and after, both he and Sumner began to develop their understanding of the geology of the area and of the interrelated character of the myriad species of land, fauna, and flora. For Collins especially, it was a transformative experience. From their investigations the two came to appreciate the science of ecology as it was manifest in the lands of the proposed reserve, particularly its evolutionary nature, the fact that any one day represented simply a snapshot of processes that were continuing to develop, to change. They grew in their conviction of the worth of seeing a dynamic system, an ecosystem, that did not depend on humans and that had a past, a present, and a destiny all its own, separate from humans and indifferent to them. In a word, they became environmentalists. For Zahniser and Brower, too, and others in the postwar environmental movement, Alaska was a maturing epiphany, for in the wilderness of northeast Alaska they saw a near perfect example of the ecosystems Aldo Leopold had written of and taught, which came to define modern environmentalism. Far from human influences strong enough to alter it, the area came to be seen as the "living wilderness" that had enraptured the Muries in 1926 and captivated William O. Douglas and others thirty years later.

Of all the advocates of the Arctic preserve, only a few, Collins, Olaus and Mardy Murie, and Bartlett, seemed to regard the Native people of northeast Alaska as interested and involved parties whose sensitivities demanded attention. Early in the campaign advocates had debated who should have jurisdiction over the proposed reserve and how it should be named. Collins rejected the idea of a national park partly because of his respect for the Natives. Nomadic Inupiaq (Eskimos) had inhabited the coastal plain of the area since time immemorial and had traded with Inuit from Canada and later with Arctic whalers at what came to be called Barter Island (now Kaktovik, population about 250). On the south flanks of the eastern Brooks Range lay the Athabascan (Gwitch'in) community of Arctic Village (population about 150), whose people were dependent on migrating caribou as their primary food source. Collins said he wanted the Natives in the area to have their traditional subsistence economy undisturbed.[50] On their 1956 Sheenjek expedition the Muries and their companions had met a trio of Arctic Village hunters looking for wolves, for which the territory paid a bounty of $50. This prompted the visitors to consider both the history and the future of Alaska's indigenous people, to whom they did not begrudge their use of the land and its resources.[51] Bartlett had argued unsuccessfully at the Alaska Constitutional Convention in 1956 for formal recognition of Alaska Natives. When queried about input from Natives in the region at the Fairbanks hearing, Bartlett said he'd be happy to talk with anyone to whom he might be directed.[52] Several people, including Natives whom historian Roger Kaye asked about consultation, reported that everyone in Alaska in the 1950s assumed the Bureau of Indian Affairs spoke adequately for Alaska Natives.[53] As will be seen in the next chapter, this attitude toward Alaska's indigenous people would change dramatically over the following decade.

The contest to establish the Arctic National Wildlife Range was the first in Alaska with major national implications, the first that involved a sustained exchange of views and intentions between proponents and opponents within Alaska and between Alaskans and national environmentalists and their antagonists in the lower forty-eight states. When compared with the later battles to be described in this book, it was reasonably docile. Although all the arguments offered in personal accounts and narratives, letters written by various parties in the effort, editorials in the press, and testimony in public hearings would be repeated in future struggles over withdrawing Alaska lands, those from the campaign of the 1950s are calmer and less vociferous than those that would be seen later. That is probably because the Arctic range was indeed one of the more remote areas of Alaska, known to only a handful of people who could speak with full knowledge about it. Also, there was much confusion about what in fact was being proposed. The term "range," settled on by the proponents in order to reduce opposition, and particularly its inclusion of the rights of mineral prospecting and hunting and trapping, did deflect what would later be far more concerted opposition; only experienced miners and hunters understood that permitting by the secretary of the interior meant that FWS personnel would likely move to highly constrain both activities. In addition, few in the general public in the 1950s were yet familiar with the science of ecology and the concept of ecosystem, an esoteric concept of natural systems still limited mostly to specialists in biology and a few defenders of the natural world. Most significant, the state had yet to experience the postponement of its entitled land selections contained in the statehood act, a postponement and curtailment that seemed to many Alaskans to fully justify their complaints of unfair treatment by the federal government.

The nature and status of the Arctic range would surface again in the great dispute over ANILCA in 1980. But before then, circumstances wholly unforeseen and unprecedented would throw Alaskans, both Native and non-Native, and environmentalists and developers as well as millions in the American general public into protracted debate and argument over Alaska's resources, a debate none were prepared for and that had significant implications for America's environmental and economic future.

CHAPTER 3

NATIVE CLAIMS AND ALASKA STATEHOOD

While the advocates and opponents of the establishment of the Arctic National Wildlife Range directed their focus and energies toward that seminal challenge, at the same time other Alaskans were deeply engaged in the epic campaign for Alaska statehood. Like most of the figures involved in the range contest, many Alaskans had not given much thought to Alaska's Native people and how they and their interests might impinge on the statehood battle and on the new state, once established. When the capability and power of Alaska Natives became clear, many Alaskans were chagrined and uncertain how to react.

Many of Alaska's Native people—the Eskimos, Aleuts, Athabascans, and Pacific Northwest Coast Indians—today lead lives fully integrated into Alaska's wild lands. Of the 720,000 people currently living in Alaska, about 115,000, something over 15 percent, are indigenous. However, 45,000 Alaska Natives are now permanent urban residents. Of the 211 villages identified in ANCSA, about 150 are roadless, accessible only by plane or boat, with travel between by snowmachine in winter and all-terrain vehicle or boat in summer. Many of these have populations of 150 to 250 residents. There are few jobs in those villages: perhaps a few people to run the airport, a village public safety officer, a health aide, some people working for the village government and the village development corporation and perhaps the local village store; not much more. Subsistence harvest of traditional food resources sustains many of these people, making up the bulk of their family, and thus the village, economy. Moose and caribou, seal or whale, fish, berries, and other natural products—these are the primary food sources, and because there are few alternative economic sources, acquiring sustenance and processing it constitutes the daily activity of most of the adults.

Alaska Native cultures are rich in philosophy (cultural mores), art, and social relationships. Though it is difficult to generalize across people of diverse ethnicity who live in very different environments, have disparate histories and ancient traditions, and define themselves distinctively in terms of those traditions, Alaska Natives do share an attachment to the land quite different from western notions of landownership. Because they have relied on the land for survival for millennia, their attachment to it lies at the core of their sense of identity. In these cultures, the land is not convenient for life; it is essential to life. Though the first European contact with Alaska Native people came early in the eighteenth century, the integration of western lifeways with Native life did not come for most until well into the twentieth century, earlier for the Pacific Northwest Coast people (Tlingit and Haida Indians) and Aleut Islanders than for Eskimos (Inupiaq speakers in the north and Yupik and Cupik speakers along the west coast) and the interior Athabascan groups.[1]

As noted earlier, because no reservations had been established in Alaska, Alaska Natives were never reservation-bound. The US Congress halted treaty-making in 1871, four years after the Alaska purchase, before any treaties were made with Alaska's indigenous people. Nor did tribal organization on a model familiar in eastern Iroquois, Plains Indians, or other North American groups characterize Alaska Native social units. For most, the village was the primary social unit. For example, Pacific Northwest Coast people were organized as exogamous clans, a village consisting of the houses of several different, competitive clans. Aleuts' social and economic organization was defined by their access to sufficient maritime resources. Most interior Athabascan people were seminomadic. Though the Pacific Northwest Coast people's organization was more socially and economically sophisticated than that of other Alaska groups, even among them there was no political leader with whom visitors could conduct negotiations, despite the repeated attempts of Europeans to find or designate one.[2]

Congress's long delay in addressing Alaska land disposal left the question of Native title to land unclarified and ambiguous. The purchase treaty provided that Natives should not be disturbed in their use and occupation of their land, but confusion over the status of Natives and cultural assumptions at the time regarding Indian capacity left the issue of land title unaddressed and undecided.[3] The 1941 US Supreme Court case that confirmed the validity of aboriginal title did not provide sufficient clarification of what that title might encompass, only that it existed.[4] Even so, the decision is considered the leading legal statement on extinguishment of Indian land title. It would play a significant role in Congress's disposition of Alaska land.

In 1912 Alaska's Tlingit, Haida, and Tsimshian leaders formed a highly successful regional advocacy association, the Alaska Native Brotherhood

(ANB), and in 1915 a companion association, the Alaska Native Sisterhood, both still in existence today, to pursue integration, justice, and equality for all Alaska Natives. Though a regional body, the ANB spoke for all Alaska Natives; there being no other, it was the group to which federal (BIA) and territorial officials turned to learn the Native position on policy questions. In the mid-1950s, when statehood advocates launched a concerted, well-structured campaign and Congress for the first time appeared seriously interested in the matter, the ANB made its support of statehood contingent on the inclusion of the explicit disclaimer in the statehood act of any right or title of Alaskans to land that might be subject to Native title, the already discussed Section 4 of the act. As explained, the disclaimer put Alaska Native land claims at odds with the State of Alaska. The claims settlement act legitimized Alaska Native people as did nothing else in the modern era, made the regional development corporations that were established under the act major economic players in Alaska, and facilitated broader options for Alaska Natives than were and are available to most American indigenes. Alaska Natives generally have the option of staying in their ancestral villages or living in one of Alaska's urban centers on equal terms with the non-Native residents there. Today, every village has a village school, a satellite receiving dish, a public safety officer, a community health aide, several kinds of village administration, and a retail store of one kind or another; most have an airplane strip. Nonetheless, because of lack of employment opportunities and confusion for young people over whether to leave their village and culture behind or forgo urbanity, there is a dark side to village life. School completion rates are low, alcohol abuse is prevalent, domestic violence is endemic, and the teen suicide rate is one of the highest in the world.[5] Alaska Native for-profit corporations function well, and most pay annual dividends, but their primary responsibility is to generate profit, not to provide social and economic services to the villages. Aspects of the long campaign to achieve the settlement are described later.

For those who remain in the villages, and even for those who do not, the role of the land in identity and psyche continues; what has occurred is not a replacement of western culture for Native culture but a syncretic integration probably more complete than for most indigenous people in the contiguous states. Many Alaska Natives live comfortably in their villages, though the challenges are substantial. Many travel to Alaska's cities for medical care, for special events such as the annual state basketball tournament or the annual Alaska Federation of Natives convention,[6] or to see relatives. Many of those who have migrated to Alaska's cities and towns retain a deep sense of identity with the cultures of their origin but feel fully at home in their western city homes and places of work. Many return to the villages to see relatives, to hunt or fish, and to renew their spiritual and cultural ties to the land. Thus, Alaska Native quest for title to ancestral lands in Alaska did mean opposition to economic development or the state's pursuit of it in its defense of its grant of land in the statehood act. Though traditional Indian reservations had not been established, there were a number of education reserves. Oil had been discovered under one of these, which lay across Cook Inlet from Anchorage, during exploration subsequent to the Kenai Peninsula oil find in 1957. When oil companies sought leases on the Indian education reserve, the secretary of the interior ordered that the proceeds of the lease sales belonged to the Indians who lived in the education reserve at a village named Tyonek.[7] The Tyonek community council received $12 million, which it used to upgrade conditions in the village, putting in a modern airstrip and constructing single-family houses and water, sewage, and electricity systems. It also invested in businesses, the profits from which flowed back to the village for maintenance and sustainability. Native leaders and Alaska state officials lauded Tyonek as a demonstration of Native capability and the economic benefit of a fair settlement of Alaska Native land claims.[8]

It was not axiomatic that Alaska Natives would support the environmental protection of Alaska's pristine natural areas proposed in the 1960s and 1970s. If environmental withdrawals meant loss of access to traditionally used lands, or if they meant curtailment of traditional Native lifestyles, Native support was problematical. Further, Native communities were aggressive in defining and pursuing specific economic opportunities arising from public and private economic development that might affect them. That did not necessarily mean Alaska Native leaders opposed environmentalism. But it did mean that effective and permanent guarantees for Native subsistence use and specific development opportunities would have to be included in any legislation that might be fashioned for settling Alaska Native claims and later for determining which Alaska lands would be federally designated as conservation withdrawals. The framers of the 1971 claims settlement act had these considerations firmly in mind when they wrote into the legislation the provision for economic development corporations whose shareholders, and beneficiaries, would be the Alaska Native population of Alaska. The ANB had rejected the idea of reservations for Alaska when the Interior Department and others proposed it in the 1930s and 1940s as a way of protecting whatever Native land rights might eventually be confirmed, both because of the paternalism associated with reservations and because reservations would isolate and separate Alaska Native people from the main currents of Alaska social, economic, and political life. This was a major element in the design of the claims settlement act.[9] Although the state's political leaders may have been sympathetic to the advance of Alaska's Native people, they initially opposed any land claims settlement that threatened in any way to restrict economic development. The Tyonek example should have suggested that Natives were as interested in economic development as anyone else in Alaska and that federal resolution of the issue of land disposition and distribution in Alaska was essential to the state's economic and other interests. But the state's first reaction to Secretary Udall's land freeze was litigation. Only over time were Governor Hickel and others persuaded to support a settlement that included 44 million acres of Alaska assigned to Native ownership.

Alaskans did have reasonable complaints about federal regulation of Alaska land. Most Alaskans viewed federal mineral leasing protocols as needlessly complicated, slow, and restrictive. Under state ownership, boosters were confident, Alaska's mineral-rich lands would be opened to rapid and comprehensive exploration and development, which would lead to industrialization with its accompanying jobs, new settlement, and prosperity. In particular, Alaskans expected development of deposits of bauxite, lead, zinc, and copper as well as oil and gas. US Geological Survey reports from the early twentieth century described numerous sites where there might be commercially viable occurrences of these elements. It did not seem to concern advocates that few of these had been studied sufficiently to ensure their viability, particularly in regard to market conditions and world prices. Statehood advocates simply assumed that state control and state development policies would be more progressive and more productive than federal management. The first statehood bill Alaska's delegate to Congress Bartlett introduced in 1946 would have granted the new state 200 million acres of land, over half of Alaska, in state title. Freeing this land from federal constraints would guarantee Alaska's economic future, advocates averred.[10]

Another condition viewed as a federal impediment was a Seattle firm's monopoly on shipping to Alaska, protected by the federal Maritime Act of 1920, the "Jones Act," which mandated that freight to Alaska be shipped only in American-flagged vessels manned by American crews. Alaskans expected that statehood would bring lower transportation costs, which would encourage potential investors in Alaska projects. Still another obstruction was federal management of Alaska's salmon fishery.

"Opening Alaska" became a mantra for statehood advocates, and for none more than Ernest Gruening. Using language reminiscent of previous environmental battles in the western states, Gruening proclaimed repeatedly that statehood "will unlock Alaska's industrial potential."[11] Gruening leaped on any development idea that came along, no matter what its consequences might have been, sometimes remarkably unrealistically. An example is the Project Chariot fiasco in the late 1950s. The project was never brought to fruition, but it had the remarkable unintended consequence of generating a deeper understanding for national conservation leaders of the biocentrism that lay at the heart of modern environmentalism. In 1957 the Atomic Energy Commission announced its program to investigate possible peaceful uses of explosives. Chariot was the primary construction proposal. It involved simultaneously detonating two 1-megaton and two 200-kiloton nuclear explosions over a site 110 miles north of the Arctic Circle on Alaska's northwest coast, near Cape Thompson, to blast out a shipping harbor and entrance channel. The site was chosen for its isolation, far from any towns, and for what the AEC called the "barren character" of the land. AEC officials noted that the potential practical use of the harbor was only a secondary consideration of the plan, though they claimed it would open far northwest Alaska coal deposits to development—a claim difficult to credit because the deposits to which they referred were hundreds of miles away over a mountain range. Rather, it was to be an experiment in construction technique, to test the feasibility of nuclear explosions as tools for large-project excavation.[12]

In 1959 the AEC commissioned a series of environmental and biological studies of the projected fallout zone; several of the contracts went to researchers at the University of Alaska in Fairbanks. Among other findings, the university scientists demonstrated that radioactive fallout would contaminate lichens in the region that were a primary food for migrating caribou in the area. Although there were no white towns nearby, the AEC had quite taken for granted two Native villages: Point Hope, 32 miles away with 324 residents, and Kivalina, 40 miles away with 142 residents. The Natives in the two villages consumed on average 200 pounds of caribou meat annually, harvested from the herd that migrated through the Cape Thompson area—meat that, after the Chariot blasts, would be heavily saturated with carcinogenic radionuclides.

Before these links in the biological chain became known, support for the Chariot project was high in Alaska, though not unanimous, and in fact, there was enough skepticism when the plan was first promulgated that the AEC undertook an extensive sales campaign to explain what the economic benefits for Alaska would be: initially hundreds of construction jobs and then major industrial mineral development. Early to sign on was the state chamber of commerce, followed by most of the municipal chambers and shortly thereafter the territory's major urban newspapers. George Sundborg, previously director of the territorial development board and author of a study on the benefits of statehood, but in 1958 editor of the *Fairbanks Daily News-Miner*, extolled the appropriateness of centering world scientific attention on Alaska just at the time it was transitioning into statehood. Soon after being established, the new Alaska State House of Representatives passed a resolution in support. Governor Egan was cautious, but his concern was states' rights, not the human or biological aspects of the proposal: he wanted state oversight of the experiment, despite the fact that the Interior Department had already approved the AEC's request to withdraw 1 million acres from the public domain around Cape Thompson. Senator Bartlett was uncertain; he liked the idea of experimentation with nuclear devices in Alaska, but he thought there were more practical applications—a waterway through the Alaska Peninsula, for example, to shorten the sea route from Seattle to the Bering Sea coast. But *Anchorage Daily Times* editor Atwood was enthusiastic. So was University of Alaska president William R. Wood, who argued that the AEC should be trusted: if it said the project was good for Alaska, it was good for Alaska. Gruening, too, was initially keen on the project, but as criticism grew, he lamented that the AEC had chosen the wrong site in Alaska; he recommended a truly uninhabited Alaska island, which the AEC shortly did settle on for a later, fully different kind of nuclear experiment.[13]

There had been criticism even before the results of the environmental studies became known. It was very unclear whether the harbor could ever be used. The Bering Sea at Cape Thompson was frozen nine months of the year. There was no transportation link from there to the coal deposits touted by the AEC. Olaus Murie, deep into the last thrust of promoting the Arctic wilderness preserve, wrote to protest that the land at Cape Thompson was not barren at all, that there was a subtle and permanent beauty in the mostly unmolested land-scape that should be protected and preserved. In early 1959 both the Wilder-ness Society and the Sierra Club adopted resolutions against proceeding with Chariot.

It was its impact on Alaska Natives, however, that stopped Project Chariot. The villagers at Point Hope and Kivalina organized to protest the withdrawal of their land. In November 1961 Natives at Barrow, assisted by the Association on American Indian Affairs, assembled a regionwide meeting of Arctic Inu-piat people, Inupiat Paitot (Eskimo Heritage). Among other resolutions, the meeting condemned the land withdrawal for Project Chariot, calling it a viola-tion of recognized aboriginal land rights, and demanded that it be revoked. As it happened, in 1963 the AEC closed its application for the land, and BLM restored the area to the public domain.

But aboriginal land rights, about which the AEC was as skeptical as were Alaska political leaders, did not persuade the AEC to kill the project. Rather, Chariot contributed to rising national consciousness of the public health and safety threat represented by atmospheric fallout from nuclear testing. Perhaps more significant, through a pathway few Alaskans could have anticipated, the project generated an epiphany regarding biocentrism among some important national thinkers, leading them to understand and become converts to mod-ern environmentalism. In January 1959 a group in Alaska concerned about fallout, including a manager of one of the few dairies in Alaska who wor-ried about strontium 90 contaminating milk, formed the Committee for the Study of Atomic Testing in Alaska. The group quickly established a relation-ship with the national Committee for Nuclear Information (CNI), founded at Washington University in St. Louis, an organization of scientists, doctors, and others whose bulletin, Nuclear Information, had become a major source of objective information on the implications of global nuclear testing and had attracted broad attention. Alerted by Alaska's Committee for the Study of Atomic Testing, Nuclear Information published several reports on Chariot. Drawing on the work of the University of Alaska scientists, Barry Commoner, a professor of plant physiology and one of the founders of CNI who would go on to become an indefatigable publicist for environmentalism and resource sustainability, wrote in Nuclear Information explaining in accessible detail the linkage between radioactive fallout, lichen, caribou harvest, and contamina-tion of Alaska Native villagers. Other scientists followed with additional in-formation on the health hazards of the AEC project. Commoner, whom one

historian describes as "the prophet and leader of the environmental movement,"[14] wrote that Project Chariot was his personal introduction to ecology
and the beginning of his career as an environmentalist.[15] It was through study
of the direct linkage between radionuclides and strontium 90 levels in Alaska
Natives that Commoner, and through his writings and lectures many others,
came to understand biocentrism.

At its annual meeting in 1960 the Wilderness Society went further than
simply protesting the AEC's planned detonation. The society adopted a resolution calling the DeLong Mountains, the western end of the Brooks Range
not far from Cape Thompson, part of "the last great non-tropical wilderness on the planet." In the same year, Alaskans concerned about Chariot and
other environmental issues formed the Alaska Conservation Society (ACS);
membership included many of the University of Alaska scientists who had
researched Chariot and also Olaus and Mardy Murie as well as others who
would be active and visible in the coming struggles over wilderness preservation in Alaska.[16] A widely circulated ACS newsletter, given over entirely to
Project Chariot, also explored in detail the biocentric linkage between fallout
and Alaska Natives.[17] Soon national publications such as *Outdoor Life* and the
Sierra Club Bulletin published similar articles. Later in the year villagers from
Point Hope and Kivalina sent a letter directly to President Kennedy. "We know
about strontium 90," they wrote, and they knew the danger to their health;
they called on Kennedy to suspend the project. Then, in April 1962, *Harper's
Magazine* published a long critique of the project.[18] At the same time, critics
noted that justification for the venture seemed unconvincing, either for the
harbor, for which there seemed little if any real use, or as a demonstration
of the peaceful uses of the atom, especially given the potential threat to the
lives of the Native villagers. Later that year the AEC threw in the towel and
canceled Project Chariot. Remarkably, Atwood complained that the demise of
the project represented the "victory over atomic science by Alaska Eskimos,"
implying that the Natives were unsophisticated Luddites standing in the way
of erudite technological advance.[19]

Under Barry Commoner's tutelage, *Nuclear Information* became the magazine *Environment*. In his subsequent book *The Closing Circle*, Commoner popu-
larized biocentric environmentalism. There he laid out his four laws of ecology in simple, manageable terms: everything is connected to everything else;
everything must go somewhere; nature knows best; there is no such thing
as a free lunch.[20] As had the Muries in their advocacy of the Arctic National

Wildlife Range and Wallace Stegner in his "Wilderness Letter," Commoner argued that humankind needed an alternative to the highly technologized character of modern life. But he would go much further, as had Rachael Carson in *Silent Spring*, published in 1962, arguing that in increasingly complicated technology lay the unintended and often unrecognized destruction of humankind. The role Alaska and Project Chariot played in shaping his ideas was not insubstantial, as he acknowledged later in interviews. Nor was the involvement of the new Alaska Conservation Society and, nationally, the Wilderness Society and the Sierra Club. Both national organizations had become more aware of Alaska by virtue of their work with Olaus and Mardy Murie and George Collins and Lowell Sumner and the campaign for the Arctic wilderness. Project Chariot raised that awareness further, though Mardy Murie observed that the national organizations were slow to grasp the full extent of the threat to Alaska's wilderness represented by statehood and Alaska's increasing population. In addition, in his reconstruction of the Project Chariot debacle, historian Peter Coates argued that the biological and environmental studies served as a model for Congress's later mandating of environmental impact studies in the National Environmental Policy Act of 1969.[21] Certainly there had not previously been such extensive biological studies associated with federal projects that might significantly alter the environment.

By 1962 it was becoming clear not only that the economic leap anticipated by statehood advocates was not going to happen but also that the state was deeply enmeshed in an economic crisis. For all practical circumstances, by that year the State of Alaska was broke. Not only had the economic boom failed to materialize but there was as yet very little federal mineral lease revenue collected in Alaska, 90 percent of which Congress had committed to the state. When a state economist published a pessimistic assessment of Alaska's present and the prospects for its future, there was even talk that statehood had been a mistake.[22] Even though the Cold War continued, defense priorities shifted with the advent of satellite surveillance capability and submarine-launched multiple-entry nuclear missiles, and after 1957 defense spending in Alaska fell sharply. The military population in the territory declined 30 percent from 1957 to 1959, when everyone's attention was riveted on the statehood campaign. Over the decade of the 1950s construction employment had fallen by one-half.[23] The salmon fishery was on the verge of collapse. The small oil deposits discovered on the Kenai Peninsula were too modest to provide much state revenue, partly because the state production tax at the time was but 3 percent. Only the proceeds of the sale of exploration leases in Cook Inlet, offshore from the Kenai Peninsula discovery, kept the state afloat financially.

But in the midst of these disturbing statistics a new economic development project arose, one much more enthusiastically endorsed by Alaska's political leadership than Project Chariot, and by none more than the aggressive Gruening. In 1954 the US Army Corps of Engineers began work on a proposal for a high dam on the Yukon River, one of America's great rivers, over 1,200 miles long from its sources to its mouth, free-flowing, and draining much of interior Alaska. The dam, which would be in a 100-mile-long natural gorge 400 miles from the Canadian border, would flood an area 200 miles long and between 40 and 90 miles wide; it would create a reservoir with a surface area greater than that of Lake Erie. It would be the largest high dam ever built. It would produce far more power than could be used in Alaska, but proponents argued that supply should precede the need; it would be available when Alaska's development caught up with it.

To some extent the proposal represented the corps's contest with the Bureau of Reclamation to become the dominant dam builder in the American West, which Marc Reisner outlined in Cadillac Desert in 1986.[24] Floyd Dominy, commissioner of the Bureau of Reclamation, was critical of the Rampart dam idea, proposing instead a smaller dam in Devil's Canyon on the Susitna River. The Rampart dam would produce more power than could be utilized in Alaska for generations, and the cost of transmitting it to the contiguous states would be prohibitive. From that standpoint, it could not be cost-effective. The Fish and Wildlife Service also found the Rampart proposal unrealistic. In summer the area teemed with migratory waterfowl that depended on the open lakes for food and for breeding. Predictably, opposition came also from the newly formed Alaska Conservation Society. Perhaps surprisingly, it also came from the popular outdoors magazine Alaska Sportsman. One and a half million ducks fed in the Yukon Flats area above the dam site, which would be flooded by the huge reservoir; the magazine's letter writers found the endangerment of this area intolerable. The waterfowl thrived because of the thousands of small lakes in the region, which they needed for nesting. Also critical of the dam were the residents of six Native villages that would be drowned, forcing relocation with its attendant disruption. In 1963 the new Native newspaper

Tundra Times published the results of a poll taken in the Yukon River villages; the villagers overwhelmingly opposed the dam, fearing the consequences of having to move.[25]

In the face of this criticism, what is remarkable is the tenacity with which the dam's proponents clung to the notion that Alaska's development was being retarded by fainthearted federal bureaucrats and misguided conservationists. In its initial analysis the Corps of Engineers suggested that the dam would attract light-metal and alloy industries that would utilize copper, lead, and zinc deposits in the vicinity, as well as some forest products development, cement production, and agriculture. Later most analysts found these expectations too optimistic at best, beyond likelihood at worst. Without a rail connection to the contiguous states, and even with it, the costs of production and transportation would defeat profitability. But proponents fixed upon these potentialities as justification for their support of the project. Gruening in particular promoted the dam as the key that would unlock Alaska's growth and development into an unseen future. Such was his irritation at having Alaska's future retarded and perhaps lost that he had little patience with environmental concerns. More than once he ascribed criticism of the dam to "fanatical conservationists" who put ducks ahead of humans, preferring, in his view, protection of the animals and their habitat to economic development that would provide jobs and the material infrastructure and commercial activity necessary to supply and sustain thousands of new Alaskans.[26] Territorial development board director George Sundborg also dismissed the natural setting. In his view, it would be greatly improved by being under 400 feet of water. He and Gruening concluded that given the primitive circumstances of the Native villages in the area, the villagers' lives would be measurably improved by being moved.

Proponents held a conference at Mt. McKinley National Park in the fall of 1963; it was attended by several hundred participants, including most of Alaska's political leaders. They adopted the name Yukon Power for America, calling attention to the hope that the excess power produced by the dam would be transmitted south and marketed in the lower states. The principal organizers were the publisher/editors of the two major urban newspapers, Atwood and Snedden. In editorials in their papers the two injected Alaska patriotism into support for the dam so heavily that a *Washington Post* reporter observed that they had raised the economic symbolism of the dam to a mystical level.[27] Schoolchildren were invited to join the organization for a nominal membership fee of 25 cents. The Alaska legislature not only voted a resolution in favor of the project but appropriated annual funds to help defray Yukon Power's expenses. Both former president Wood and new president Terris Moore of the University of Alaska joined Yukon Power and made statements of endorsement, arguing that the only opponents were zoologists and nature lovers and that their number was small.

Although the efforts of Yukon Power raised expectations in Alaska, they had little effect outside the state. In May 1965 the *Atlantic Monthly* ran a critical article titled "The Plot to Drown Alaska." The author, Paul Brooks, saw no recreational or economic benefit to the project, which he called an ecological disaster. Gruening responded, arguing that the Yukon Flats area had no measurable value, which he offered as good reason for inundating it. Ten months later the Natural Resources Council (NRC) of America published a highly negative report, suggesting that Alaska's power needs should rather be met by Cook Inlet natural gas, then being brought on line, and elsewhere along the rail belt between Anchorage and Fairbanks. Then, in April 1966, the *New York Times* weighed in, praising the NRC report and endorsing its findings.[28]

The final decision on Rampart lay with Interior Secretary Udall. Given his environmental sympathies and his concern for Native land and other rights, few expected him to give his approval to the project, and he did not disappoint. In June 1967 Udall recommended against the project, noting the other, more realistic sources of power for Alaska and the environmental costs of building the dam. Ultimately the Corps of Engineers itself also recommended against the idea, citing the lack of an Alaska market for the power that would be produced. Rampart dam was done for the moment. But Gruening could not let go of it. Right up to his defeat for reelection in 1968 he continued to attack environmentalists and to argue that Rampart represented Alaska's economic sustainability.

Understanding well Alaska's economic vulnerability as a remote, distant province where economies of scale militated against a diversified economy and natural resource development was the only economic fuel, Gruening knew also that the funds to develop any of the resources—minerals, including oil and gas; fish; and timber—did not reside in the territory, that they must come from Outside. That was why he and other Alaska leaders were so eager to support any prospect for economic development at virtually whatever cost, environmental or human. With his departure from politics in 1968, Gruening represented the passing of an era, for the discovery of the great Prudhoe Bay oil deposit in December 1967, confirmed in spring 1968, took Alaska into a new economic, social, and political dispensation of unimagined and unprecedented dimensions. Remarkably, it was a new reality much as Gruening had envisioned the one to be wrought by development of the Rampart dam. But the aggressive Alaska booster watched the beginnings of that transformation from the sidelines. Defeated for reelection, he died just as construction of the Trans-Alaska Pipeline project got under way in June 1974.

Historian Peter Coates noted that Samuel P. Hays wrote that the watershed between conservation and environmentalism was the decision by the US Supreme Court to prevent the building of a high dam in Hells Canyon on the Snake River in Idaho in 1967.[29] There the Supreme Court placed environmental integrity and quality of life ahead of economic development. Coates argued that Rampart is an even better watershed, for there were no villages that would have been inundated on the Snake River. In the case of Rampart, the dam was not built because of concern both to retain the environmental integrity of the Yukon Flats migratory waterfowl breeding area and to preserve the six Native villages that would have been flooded.

The battle over the Trans-Alaska Pipeline can be said to have begun with Congress's passage of the Alaska statehood act in the summer of 1958, long before oil was discovered at Prudhoe Bay on Alaska's North Slope, west of the Arctic National Wildlife Range. The issue of Alaska Native land claims had to be addressed before Congress could enter into any disposition of Alaska land, including the grant of land to the new State of Alaska—or so logic would suggest. However, in 1957 and 1958, when Congress was debating the Alaska statehood bill, not many Alaskans seem to have understood the coming conflict between Alaska Native land claims and state land selections. That was because, despite the US Supreme Court's finding in *United States v. Santa Fe Pacific Railroad* in 1941 for the validity of aboriginal title, it was unclear how that finding might apply to Alaska lands. One of the most important leaders of the Alaska Native Brotherhood through the three decades from 1920 to 1950 was William Lewis Paul. He was the first Alaska Native to be admitted to the Alaska bar and the first to be elected to the Alaska Territorial Legislature.[30] Paul had studied Indian law and in 1951 brought an Alaska Native land claims case before the US Court of Claims: *Tee-Hit-Ton Indians v. United States*.[31] Paul wanted compensation for the loss of his clan's property in Southeast Alaska in the establishment of the Tongass National Forest in 1905. The court found against Paul but in so doing acknowledged that aboriginal title existed in Alaska, which had not yet been formally recognized by the US government. This was the first formal and legal acknowledgment of the existence of Native land claims specific to Alaska. One could infer from the court's finding, later upheld by the US Supreme Court in 1955,[32] that much of Alaska might be subject to aboriginal title. Subsequently, a central council representing all Indians in Southeast Alaska filed a suit, *Tlingit and Haida Indians v. United States*, seeking validation of their aboriginal title. In 1959 the US Court of Claims found that these Indians did have such title. It was a landmark finding, for by implication, so did the rest of Alaska Natives.[33]

Alaska leaders had always been prepared to recognize Indian title to land their homes stood on, and perhaps a small portion of adjacent land, but very little more.[34] The US Forest Service had been authorized by Congress in 1947 to sell timber leases on the Tongass Forest to support pulp mills with which the Forest Service was authorized to execute fifty-year contracts. A forest industry in the Tongass Forest had been the careerlong dream of B. Frank Heintzleman, USFS regional forest director in Alaska from 1937 to 1953.[35] He had projected that five pulp mills could be established within the boundaries of the forest, providing 5,000 direct jobs and supporting 60,000 people. During hearings on the Tongass Timber Act of 1947, both Gruening and Heintzleman asserted that from their points of view, Gruening for the Territory of Alaska and Heintzleman for the USFS, the Tlingit and Haida Indians had neither aboriginal nor what were then being called possessory rights, that is, rights to some quantum of land adjacent to their villages. Alaska's territorial attorney general, Ralph Rivers, who later would serve as the new state's first US congressman, declared that "the only rights [Alaska Natives] have remaining would be to places like home sites and village sites for particular Indians or village groups—not rights to *areas*."[36] Gruening wrote that for forty years the people of Alaska had hoped for the establishment of a pulp and paper industry, but just as the prospects were brightest, "they are in danger of being shattered by the cloud of 'aboriginal rights' over the title to all land in the Tongass National Forest—practically all of which has been claimed by or for the Indians—and unless dispelled will prevent any successful negotiations between the Forest Service and possible pulp and paper manufacturers."[37]

Gruening and Heintzleman based their opinion regarding the absence of aboriginal rights on an Alaska District Court decision, upheld by the Ninth Circuit Court of Appeals, that held that any title the Tlingit and Haida Indians might have had had been extinguished by the Treaty of Cession of Alaska to the United States by Russia in 1867.[38] Because the decision was precedent, finality would need to wait for a ruling from the US Supreme Court, but Gruening and Heintzleman did not wait. There was a national newsprint shortage after World War II, and Heintzleman had persuaded several potential pulp-mill owners to invest in Alaska's Tongass Forest, which they were willing to do only if the question of Native land title should be cleared first. With others, Gruening and Heintzleman persuaded the Interior Department to submit legislation to Congress to deal with the problem. It was a novel bill, designed to quickly eliminate the potential obstacle to economic development in Alaska. After hearings and reshapings, it would emerge from Congress as the Tongass Timber Sales Act of 1947. The Forest Service would be authorized to enter into the fifty-year contracts, to hold timber sales, and to lease land for the pulp mills. The money collected would be put into escrow, pending finality on the question of aboriginal title, and paid to the Natives for extinguishment of that title should the Supreme Court find for such title.[39]

In hearings on this unusual arrangement, which was prejudicial to the Natives because they would have no determinative role in the disposition of the resources on land that the court might decide had been theirs before the extinguishment of their title, one committee member commented that at the time Congress did not recognize any Native land right at all, agreeing with Gruening and Heintzleman.[40] The bill manifested Gruening and Heintzleman's, and their Alaska constituents', view that what was most important for Alaska was economic development. Subsequently, there would be two pulp mills established on the Tongass National Forest, one at Ketchikan in 1956, the other at Sitka in 1962.

For Gruening and others this consideration also overrode the prospect of environmental degradation resulting from logging and the operation of the pulp mills. In 1947 the principal periodical organ of the canned salmon industry, *Pacific Fisherman*, worried that "unless the logging and manufacturing of timber is carefully planned and administered it can impair and perhaps destroy the priceless salmon fisheries of the region."[41] The editors went on to say that the timber of Southeast Alaska could be developed without damage to the fishery, but in 1956 a former executive director of the Alaska Game Commission, Frank Dufresne, wrote that by that time already the pulp industry in Alaska was a menace, "a destroyer of essential timbered watersheds, polluter of clean waters so necessary to the life cycle of the salmon, enemy of all wildlife, and ruthless despoiler of a nation's recreational heritage."[42]

For most Alaskans, the fight over the Tongass Timber Act and the question of aboriginal land rights receded into the background, if it had ever been in the foreground, during the campaign for Alaska statehood in the 1950s. As with most political issues in Alaska's history, the primary focus of that campaign was Alaska's economic development. Statehood would remove impediments to the underdevelopment of Alaska's natural resources, which in turn would encourage new settlement. When Gruening argued that statehood would "unlock Alaska's industrial potential," he meant large-scale mining, forest products, and fishing, that is, industrial development of Alaska's natural resources.[43] Gruening also hoped the Rampart dam on the Yukon River would create thousands of jobs during construction and hundreds in operation. And as noted, it was axiomatic among Alaska leaders at the time that the greater independence accompanying statehood would generate an economic boom and new settlement, that the state control and leadership would create opportunities the federal agencies could or would not.[44]

But whether understood or not by most Alaskans (many of whom were new settlers) during the campaign for statehood, the question of aboriginal claims had the potential to derail the economic development embraced and expected by statehood advocates. Senator Hugh Butler of Nebraska, at the time an ardent foe of Alaska statehood, had written in 1950 that Native land claims "are an almost complete barrier to the development of the resources of the Territory."[45] It is easy to imagine that those who might have had some notion of the problem took refuge in the all-too-human phenomenon of not dealing with the uncomfortable unknown.

Delegate Bartlett was not among these. Following the successful referendum vote on statehood in 1946, Bartlett introduced the first of what would be several statehood bills in the postwar period. When hearings were held on the bill, an attorney representing Alaska Natives pointed out to committee members that the bill lacked a disclaimer of the new state's right to lands that might be subject to aboriginal title, such as had been included in previous statehood bills in the modern era. As noted, this potentially could have been most of the land in Alaska. Without such a disclaimer, the attorney suggested, Alaska Native and national Indian organizations would oppose the statehood bill.[46] Over the course of the next several years Bartlett and other territorial leaders struggled to craft language for a disclaimer that would protect Alaska's economic development from the threat of Native land claims. The final statehood bill, introduced by Bartlett in the House in 1955, included the disclaimer, Section 4 of the Alaska Statehood Act.[47]

But getting the disclaimer into the statehood act had been neither inevitable nor easy. Under substantial pressure from the canned-salmon industry, the Forest Service, the Alaska Miners Association, and prominent businessmen in Alaska who did understand the threat of Native claims to economic development, Bartlett, the lone representative from Alaska in Congress, consented to its removal on several occasions. Historian Peter Metcalfe wrote that it was primarily threats from the Alaska Native Brotherhood to withhold support for statehood that moved Bartlett to keep the disclaimer in the bill that became law and fight to keep it there.[48] At their annual convention in 1950, the Grand Camp meeting, ANB delegates adopted a resolution calling on Delegate Bartlett to work to restore the disclaimer that at that time had been stricken from the statehood bill he had introduced in 1947.[49] If this should prove impossible, delegates counseled that the ANB should work to defeat the statehood bill. Soon after the convention, the Indians' attorney wrote to every US senator to convey the ANB's attitude and action. The 1951 convention adopted an even stronger condemnation of any statehood legislation that did not provide adequately for Native land claims. Historian Metcalfe wrote that Bartlett and Gruening came to understand from such resolutions the necessity of generating Native support for Alaska statehood.[50]

The disclaimer that is Section 4 of the Alaska Statehood Act provides that the

State and its people do agree and declare that they forever disclaim all right and title to any lands or other property not granted or confirmed to the State or its political subdivisions by or under the authority of this Act, the right or title to which is held by the United States or is subject to disposition by the United States, and to any lands or other property, (including fishing rights), the right or title to which may be held by any

Indians, Eskimos, or Aleuts (hereinafter called natives) or is held by the United States in trust for said natives.[51]

Again, that might have been most of the land in Alaska under the concept of "aboriginal" that the US Supreme Court had upheld in the 1941 aboriginal title case. The ANB, and Bob Bartlett, had won a comprehensive and foundational victory for Alaska Natives despite the opposition of Alaska's territorial governor, the canned-salmon industry, the USFS, the Alaska Miners Association, and numerous businesspeople across Alaska.

But in 1959 more than a century of national Indian policy confirmed for the few who attended to the issue that the US government would never give Alaska Natives title to any vast amount of Alaska land. That century of policy was predicated on the premise that acculturation and assimilation were the Indians' only practical and reasonable future. Reservation history did not inspire confidence that large grants of land or money served either Indians or the nation. In 1887 the Dawes general allotment act codified acculturation. Large land grants to Indians ran counter to most national politicians' ideas of Indian policy.

But the question of title to land for Alaska Natives had puzzled officials in the Interior Department and the Bureau of Indian Affairs since the 1930s, when Congress had passed a jurisdictional act permitting Tlingit and Haida Indians to bring their land claims case before the US Court of Claims. And even though the later *Tee-Hit-Ton Indians* case had suggested there was aboriginal title in Alaska, Congress had seemed determined not to recognize it. In the early 1940s the secretary of the interior had created two new large reservations in Alaska's eastern interior in areas sparsely settled by Natives, one on the south boundary of the area that became the Arctic National Wildlife Range and one still farther south, not far from the Canadian border. Though the ANB had through most of its history been opposed to reservations, the fight over inclusion of the disclaimer in the statehood act persuaded some ANB leaders to agree with the Interior Department that reservations might be the only way to certify at least some land as Native, a concession to the determination of state leaders such as Gruening that no significant amount of land should be titled to Natives.[52] As a manifestation of the difficulty in Congress, Senator Butler had at one point introduced legislation to prohibit the secretary of the interior from establishing further reservations in Alaska, though Congress never passed the proposal.

Another reason many did not imagine the federal government would title large acreages to Alaska Natives was the inclusion in the statehood act of the vast grant to the new state. Section 6 of the act provided that the new state would be "granted and shall be entitled to select, within twenty-five years after the admission of Alaska into the Union, not to exceed one hundred and two million five hundred and fifty thousand acres from the public lands of the United States in Alaska which are vacant, unappropriated, and unreserved at the time of their selection." With the addition of some acreage in the national forests and some other lands to support state mental health services, the total grant came to over 104 million acres. Though only 28 percent of Alaska's total land area, it was an area larger than the total area of California. The grant had been included in the various statehood bills from 1954, initially at the request of Senator Butler.[53] Congress was specific about the purpose of some of the land; it was "for the purpose of furthering the development of and the expansion of communities."[54] Testimony and discussion in committee and on the Senate floor at final passage of the act indicated that the land without other specified purpose would be used for mineral leasing and other development that would contribute to the state's capability to support the costs of statehood. This was consistent with the natural resources article of the Alaska constitution, which provided for the development of Alaska's resources. It seemed illogical to many Alaskans that Congress would provide land for development and then deny the state title to vast amounts of land on the basis of Native aboriginal title.

Alaska statehood became official on January 3, 1959. Within weeks state planners in the Department of Natural Resources began mapping the areas from which the state would select its 104 million acres, directed toward three categories: settlement, resources, and recreation. The work of filing applications for selected areas went slowly. The growing number of Native appeals slowed the process even more. Among the few people who knew and understood the implications of the contradiction in the statehood act and the fact of BLM conveyance of some land title to the state were officials of the Bureau of Indian Affairs in Alaska. Others who understood the implications included officers in the Association on American Indian Affairs, the influential national nongovernmental organization on Indian matters. Sensitive to Native interests, the BIA worked with the AAIA to inform Alaska Natives of the potential threat to whatever land title the Natives might have and to show villagers how to file their protests against the state's applications.[55] The rejection of the Native appeals by the BLM Alaska Region office rested on the agency's agreement that aboriginal title was a fanciful notion and that Natives were entitled, if anything, only to the land on which their villages stood. It was the BIA and AAIA advisers who counseled villagers in how to file their appeals over the rejections of the regional BLM officials to the agency's administrative offices in Washington, DC. Historian Donald Mitchell explained that although lead officials in that office did not give much thought to the esoteric problems of Alaska Native land claims, a special assistant in the office, Newton Edwards, had followed the developing conflict quite closely and, finding himself sympathetic to the cause of Indian justice, quietly shelved the appeals without passing them on, since there was no pressure from his supervisors to act on them.[56] This had the effect of slowing the whole process still more. That was when Alaska state officials stopped submitting selection applications and turned to the Department of the Interior and Alaska's new congressional delegation to seek a congressional resolution of the conundrum.

Interior Secretary Stewart Udall had grown up in east-central Arizona, not far from the Fort Apache, San Carlos, Navajo, and Hopi Indian reservations, and also sympathized with the cause of Indian justice. As he came to understand the Alaska situation, he looked for a compromise that would at once honor the promise in the statehood act of land for Alaska's economic development and simultaneously provide land and compensation to honor the unextinguished aboriginal title, past, present, and future. This he considered the just due of Alaska Natives. Udall hoped that oil and gas lease sales on federal land, even before potential transfer to the state, might be helpful to Alaska. Also, oil companies were very interested in obtaining exploration leases on areas of the North Slope. But at the same time, bringing pressure from the other side, Alaska Natives began to manifest a new militancy and organizational capacity. In the early 1960s several new regional Native groups emerged, motivated by the need to respond to the threat of the potential loss of land and their right to compensation for land already lost. They began clearly and forcefully to articulate and defend their rights. Several younger men, representing a new generation, a new awareness, and a new willingness to be visible, provided energetic, intelligent, and courageous leadership. In 1966 the groups and their leaders came together to form the first Alaskawide Native advocacy organization: the Alaska Federation of Natives. This would be the group the state and federal government would need to deal with in addressing the conflict.

As noted, Stewart Udall was also sensitive to the rising new environmental movement. Early in his administration he had organized Interior Department support for the wilderness act that Howard Zahniser and David Brower were shepherding through Congress. The Wilderness Society magazine, *Living Wilderness*, called Udall an outstanding champion of environment.[57] Historian Mitchell wrote that Udall was an environmentalist before the term entered the national lexicon, having introduced, as a congressman from Arizona in 1955, a resolution commemorating the American conservation movement.[58] He was familiar with the Sierra Club and Wilderness Society's fight to save Echo Canyon and with the campaign to establish the Arctic National Wildlife Range. Udall's environmental sensitivity would be important as representatives of the State of Alaska, members of Congress and the Kennedy administration, and AFN and Alaska Native leaders confronted each other in negotiating their way to a settlement of Alaska Native land claims, in which environmental issues would form a central role.

The new state of Alaska had been led through its first eight years by Democrat Governor Egan, a shopkeeper from the small community of Valdez on Prince William Sound; he was a student of American history and an astute politician with an uncanny memory for names and faces. With his administration, particularly his commissioner of natural resources, Egan had pressed the state's view that Native land claims needed to be settled quickly and fairly so state land selection could proceed and the new state could move forward with plans for economic development. He hoped to work cooperatively with federal officials.

In 1966 the energetic and pugnacious Walter J. Hickel replaced Egan as governor. Hickel initially took a less compromising approach toward the issue of Native claims in his relationship with Lyndon Johnson's administration after 1963 and with Secretary Udall, who stayed at Interior. Not long after taking office Hickel filed a suit against Secretary Udall, challenging the legality of the BLM's failure to convey title to the state on the lands it had selected.[59] Various attempts on the part of both the Interior Department and the State of Alaska to find a negotiating framework failed, and little was accomplished, but during the year the new Native leaders became more knowledgeable and gained valuable organizing experience. Recognizing the greater likelihood of progress by working with all parties in the conflict, late in 1967 Hickel appointed a land claims task force that included the board of directors of the new AFN as well as Native members of the Alaska legislature. Not satisfied with the work of the task force, the AFN soon proposed legislation for Congress to settle Native land claims. The proposal included 1,000 acres of federal land for every Alaska Native, a total of about 50 million acres; it also included subsequent issuance to Native village residents of "terminable licenses" to hunt, fish, and gather firewood and otherwise use all other federal land to which Natives asserted aboriginal title.[60] The significance of the latter provision cannot be overstated. It manifested the Natives' traditional, pragmatic use of the land, their necessary harvest of its resources. It also represented the Natives' view of the land's importance to their future, to the maintenance of the Native way of living, both practically and spiritually. It also contained the kernel of potential disagreement with environmentalists regarding the nature of Alaska's wilderness, which environmentalists might view as a pristine entity to be preserved unmanipulated by humans but which Natives might view as their indispensable food locker. The inclusion of the provision for use of federal land for Native subsistence would become a core element in the negotiations over a settlement of Native land claims.

Consistent with the purpose of the generous grant of land to the state in the statehood act, in 1964 the Egan administration had selected, and the BLM had conveyed, without Native protest, the land on the North Slope west of the Arctic National Wildlife Range, between there and National Petroleum Reserve No. 4, "Pet 4."[61] Oil-industry geologists had long indicated their interest in obtaining exploration leases in that area. They also were interested in the lands west of Pet 4, lands still in federal title, on which Udall had announced his intention to sell leases. It was as a consequence of meetings with the new Native leadership, and in response to mounting pressure from the AFN and a new regional Native association representing North Slope villages, that the secretary reconsidered selling the leases. A new Arctic Slope Native group had hired as its attorney William Paul, Sr., the Alaska Native Brotherhood patriarch. Paul filed a claim for all of the land on the North Slope. Seeing the writing on the wall, that is, endless litigation and delay, Udall announced his decision to cancel the lease sale; he would soon extend cancellation of lease sales to all federal land in Alaska.[62]

Because of the state's dire economic circumstances, it is reasonable to assume that there would have been a congressional settlement of Alaska Native land claims before the end of the decade.[63] It was in everyone's best interest to come to some sort of compromise. However much he despised the idea of aboriginal title, Senator Gruening came to accept the prospect of 40 or 50 million acres of Native land in Alaska based on the locations of Native villages and traditional use and occupancy: Alaska's economic future did indeed rest on a resolution of Native claims. Governor Hickel also eventually accepted this figure, and so did the AFN, recognizing that more than that amount of acreage would be difficult to get through Congress. The matter of compensation for extinguishment of Native title to the rest of Alaska was problematical but perhaps not insurmountable. But on the day after Christmas, 1967, everything changed—for Alaska, for Alaska Natives, and for the future.

CHAPTER 4 THE TRANS-ALASKA PIPELINE

Soon after his inauguration as governor in December 1966, Walter Hickel approved the sale of oil exploration leases in the area on the North Slope that the Egan administration had selected for state ownership between the Arctic National Wildlife Range and Petroleum Reserve No. 4, about 2 million acres of land. As was characteristic of Hickel's aggressive approach to policy, it would prove a fateful decision. When, in October 1967, Congress adjourned without taking any action on an Alaska Native land claims bill, Hickel announced that he had ordered the state lands division to undertake a "crash program" to select the remaining statehood land entitlement, at that time 85 million acres. This was a foolish proposition, and little came of it, but it demonstrated Hickel's style of administration and the character of his judgment. It also demonstrated the determination of state leaders to press economic development despite unresolved challenges that might impinge on that development. The following January, just prior to leaving office, Udall signed his public land order withdrawing virtually all Alaska land available, 262 million acres, from selection under the statehood act, a "super land freeze."[1] But by then everyone's attention had turned to Prudhoe Bay.

Historian and former oil scouting service reporter Jack Roderick has described the discovery at Prudhoe Bay. On the day after Christmas 1967, geologists with Atlantic Richfield Oil Company (ARCO) opened a well the company had been drilling on land on the North Slope near Prudhoe Bay, on one of the leases Hickel had authorized, into which they lowered testing tools. There was an immediate blow of natural gas from the well, which, when ignited, flamed for two days before workers could get the tools out of the well. The test showed both gas and oil. It seemed a significant find, but it was necessary to drill a second well into the same formation to determine the extent and richness of the deposit. ARCO began drilling that well in March 1968, and tests soon revealed that the company had drilled into the largest oil deposit ever discovered in North America, a potential 21 billion barrels of oil, an astounding quantity.[2] The discovery was both unexpected and unprecedented.

This was the economic bonanza for Alaska that Gruening and others had long imagined. It would transform the struggling state into a fully modern enterprise, one hardly resembling anything that might be called a frontier for most of its inhabitants. Anchorage would become a high-rise city; a new highway would connect Anchorage and Fairbanks; the state would construct state-of-the-art high schools in every Native village with more than sixteen students; Anchorage and Fairbanks would experience major housing booms; Anchorage would support a repertory theater and would build two convention centers, a sports arena, a three-theater performing arts center, and a new municipal library center. The University of Alaska would expand its existing campuses and establish new ones. All of these and many more new facilities would be funded by tax revenue generated by oil production at Prudhoe Bay and related deposits on Alaska's North Slope. More than ever before, Alaska would adopt and be characterized by the most economically robust material norms of mainstream American culture. This was the vision of what Alaska should be that was entertained by most of its population. Despite the pleas of a minority, little attention was paid to the unique aspects of urban living in a northern climate. Glass office buildings, conventional roofing materials, standard street design, and a host of other replications of American life were imported to the region. Disembarking from an airplane at Anchorage's architecturally pleasing international airport, one found little to distinguish the surroundings from any other major city and airport in the United States. This was the Alaska the residents considered their just deserts for making the sacrifice of living 1,500 air miles from the nearest major transportation hub in the contiguous states. But in 1968 there were still significant challenges in bringing that vision to fruition. And there was a growing segment of Alaska's populace who sought to constrain the replication and keep it away from the unmanipulated vastness of Alaska outside its cities and towns.

The leases being drilled in 1967 constituted only a portion of the state's North Slope land between the Arctic range and Pet 4, and immediately after the confirmation well results were announced, both the state and oil companies organized to get more leases into the hands of the oil industry. In September 1969 the state held the largest oil-lease sale in its history, netting $900 million, three times the size of the 1969 state budget. Alaska governor Keith Miller, who had succeeded to the office when President Nixon had named Walter Hickel secretary of the interior, called the sale "the claiming of Alaska's birthright." It was, he said, "a rendezvous with our dreams."[3] By then the three companies most heavily invested in North Slope development, ARCO, British Petroleum, and Humble Oil Company (now Exxon), had formed the Trans-Alaska Pipeline System (TAPS), an unincorporated entity, to coordinate subsequent development activity.[4] A first task was to determine how best to get the oil to market. In August the tanker SS *Manhattan*, commissioned by Humble Oil, undertook a voyage through the Northwest Passage from east to west. The difficulty of the voyage demonstrated the impracticability of taking the oil out by that route.[5] TAPS settled on the only feasible alternative: an overland pipeline from Prudhoe Bay to Valdez on Prince William Sound. That route would cross federal, state, and Native-claimed land, and in the summer of 1969 TAPS applied for federal permits for the appropriate rights-of-way and for construction.

The Sierra Club, the Wilderness Society, and other conservation organizations finally heeded the admonishment of Alaska environmentalist Celia Hunter that they were slow to understand the significance of Alaska's vast reaches of unmanipulated land, despite their involvement with the campaign for the Arctic range—but only after they realized the threat to Alaska wilderness posed by the Alaska pipeline. Manifesting the maturation of the environmental movement in the 1960s, in addition to their work on the Wilderness Act, national environmental groups had lobbied for a clean air act; fought the supersonic transport aircraft; opposed developing nuclear power; worked for protection of the Florida Everglades and elimination of the proposed Miami jetport; and undertaken a campaign for a new clean water act and, perhaps most important, a national policy act on environmental protection, the latter enacted in 1969.[6] The blowout of an oil rig in the Santa Barbara Channel in California has been credited with generating the support needed for Congress to pass the National Environmental Policy Act (NEPA), but environmental organizations had been working throughout the decade to harness the movement and bring it to bear in effective federal legislation.

Edgar Wayburn, five-time director of the Sierra Club, said in an oral interview in 1992 that it was the pipeline project that awakened the club and other groups to Alaska's place in American environmentalism.[7] At the club's Eleventh Biennial Wilderness Conference held in San Francisco in March 1969, recognizing the seriousness of the threat of construction of an Alaska pipeline to realization of the wilderness idea in the new state, club officers decided to make Alaska the only agenda item, the first time Alaska had been the exclusive or even primary item on a Sierra Club meeting agenda. Several Alaskans spoke at the conference, among them the economist George Rogers and Bob Weeden, president of the Alaska Conservation Society. Their remarks may be taken as the beginning of a four-year battle over authorization of the Alaska pipeline. For advocates in Alaska, the pipeline represented control over their own destiny. When Congress passed the pipeline authorization bill in 1973, Alaska congressman Don Young called the act "the second Alaska statehood act."[8] For opponents, the exploitation of the Prudhoe Bay region and the pipeline project represented the irretrievable loss of the last great wilderness in America, perhaps in the world.

Proponents had more than environmental opposition to contend with. Federal officials still had responsibility for the integrity of most of Alaska land, and though they generally supported development of North Slope oil, from rising environmental consciousness in the country they felt a heavy responsibility to guarantee that that development be carried out with safety and the least impact on the land. Alaskans welcomed the appointment of Governor Hickel as secretary of the interior with great enthusiasm; they expected the appointment to advantage them in terms of protecting the state's land entitlement and clearing the way for pipeline construction.[9] While this proved true to some limited extent, fundamental decisions Hickel might have made soon were taken mostly out of his hands.

The department had established a task force to monitor TAPS's plans and activities on Alaska's federal lands; in May the president expanded the task force into an interdepartmental group and included in its membership both an assistant director of the Wilderness Society and the chairman of TAPS. The task force soon raised questions about TAPS's initial design of a pipeline. Drawing on their experience in the contiguous states, the various oil companies involved on the North Slope proposed burying the line over the entire 800 miles from Prudhoe Bay to Valdez. Federal task-force members quickly rejected this idea. All of the northern portion of the line and other portions intermittently would be underlain by permafrost, permanently frozen ground that the hot pipe would thaw, subjecting it to stress and likely rupture. This sent TAPS back to its drawing boards, and as the year progressed, it became clear both that TAPS as an organization was too unstructured to function effectively and that the industry collectively did not have the information it needed to generate an appropriate design for a pipeline in Alaska's harsh and extraordinary climate.

TAPS's problems were underscored by the Twentieth Alaska Science Conference[10] held at the University of Alaska in fall 1969; like the Sierra Club wilderness conference, it was given over completely to Alaska and oil. Representatives of the American Petroleum Institute addressed the conference, as did the Sierra Club's Edgar Wayburn and also Ted Stevens, Alaska's new US senator.[11] The Alaska advocates called for quick approval by the Interior Department of TAPS's permit requests. They dismissed conservationist concerns about despoliation of Alaska's last great wilderness, the very area Robert Marshall had proposed in 1938 as a permanent American wilderness. Senator Stevens at one point proclaimed that there were "no living organisms on Alaska's North Slope," confirming conservationists' observation that Alaskans were willing to put development ahead of all other considerations.[12]

Through 1969 the battle lines over North Slope development and the Alaska pipeline became clearer and firmer. A major impetus came from a dedicated group of federal land-use agency personnel in Alaska. Congress had been working on the national environmental policy directive for a number of years; Senator Henry Jackson of Washington and Representative John Dingall of Michigan introduced the legislation that would become the National Environmental Policy Act, establishing the Environmental Protection Agency (EPA), early in 1969. Jackson chaired the Senate Interior and Insular Affairs Committee. The relative ease with which the law passed Congress seemed a measure of the national consciousness on environment. President Nixon signed NEPA into law on January 1, 1970.[13] Thus, expressions of concern about Alaska's environment struck a responsive chord in Congress.

Despite the heavy criticism of its design plan, TAPS filed with the Interior Department requests for the permits needed for the right-of-way from Prudhoe Bay to Valdez. Granting the necessary permits would constitute a violation of Secretary Udall's "land freeze." In his confirmation hearings with the Senate, Hickel was forced to commit to leaving the freeze in place until the Interior and Insular Affairs Committee was satisfied that lifting it posed no danger to either the environment or Native claims. In October officers of the major national environmental organizations telegraphed Senator Lee Metcalf of Montana with their concerns about the Alaska project, which the senator had agreed to share with his Senate colleagues. Senator Jackson soon convened hearings on Alaska before his Interior and Insular Affairs Committee, effectively postponing any decision on approving Hickel's request to issue the right-of-way permits. Most of the testimony was highly critical of TAPS, most of it coming from the federal bureaucracy, especially the interagency task force. There was considerable recognition of Alaska's wilderness status and the unique nature of Arctic ecology. But the primary subject of the hearings was TAPS's failure to produce a responsible design for the pipeline. Nonetheless, on Hickel's assurance that he would not issue the permits until the engineering challenges had been adequately addressed, Jackson's committee gave Hickel approval to issue them; the House Interior Committee quickly followed suit. But Jackson advised Hickel to pay close attention to the requirements of NEPA for an impact study regarding the project.

Hickel was taken aback, then, when, in March 1970, three environmental organizations brought suit in the federal district court in Washington, DC, to halt any work on the pipeline. The Wilderness Society, Friends of the Earth, and the Environmental Defense Fund argued that the project violated the requirements of NEPA. Moreover, a few weeks earlier five Yukon River villages near the proposed pipeline right-of-way had also filed a suit, charging a breach of promise by TAPS to hire Native contractors and workers. The Sierra Club had discussed joining the suit, but officers of its Alaska chapter pleaded with it not to. The chapter had been working a bill through the Alaska legislature for the creation of a 500,000-acre state park adjacent to Anchorage, the state's largest city, and its officers feared an action by the Sierra Club would cost them the votes they needed.[14] The club demurred—and perhaps it had good reason to worry. Brock Evans, who would later head the club's Washington, DC, lobbying office, had come up against Alaska's antienvironmentalism on a trip to Southeast Alaska as the club's Northwest representative. He recounted in a later oral interview that he learned of the experience of a nurse who was a new club member. Working at a private clinic, she volunteered her nursing services traveling to remote Native villages. On her return from one such trip, she found a letter from her employer stating, "I understand you've been hanging out with the Sierra Club or some such group like that there. You're fired."[15] As Alaskans gained understanding of the threat environmentalists posed to construction of the pipeline and the economic nirvana they planned on, known members of national conservation organizations often became community pariahs.

The Natives' suit might easily have been disposed of, but the environmental suit threatened to stall and perhaps kill the huge project, as the requirements of NEPA were not clearly articulated and would need careful study and, in the end, judicial judgment. Judge George L. Hart of the federal district court for the District of Columbia soon issued an injunction prohibiting the right-of-way permits and any construction work on the pipeline until such study should be made and he should be satisfied that the requisites of NEPA would be met.

The environmental suit did not arise from a vacuum. In early 1969 a small group of Alaskans concerned about environment organized a new environmental organization, the Alaska Wilderness Council. They included private citizens and a number of Alaska federal land management personnel. The members' principal concern was protecting environmentally significant and sensitive lands from state selection. Because of the state's commitment to economic development, they shared the fear that the state would be a less effective steward of such lands than the federal land agencies.[16] As noted, a number of federal agency personnel already had expressed the same anxiety. Without any authorization, the group undertook a comprehensive survey of Alaska environmental resources, working mostly off record in evenings and on weekends, since no agency had authorization for such work. The group stayed in touch with both the Sierra Club and the Wilderness Society national offices as it crafted a complex map of lands it considered at risk. Early in 1970 one Alaska Wilderness Council member, Dave Hickok, a federal natural resources officer, traveled to Washington, DC, to deliver the map to Secretary of the Interior Rogers C. B. Morton.[17] At the same time, Hickok urged the counsel to the Senate Interior Committee, then working up an Alaska Native claims settlement bill, to include in that bill a provision for a comprehensive review of all public lands in Alaska.[18] William Van Ness, special counsel to the committee, inserted the provision. So by the spring of 1970, when the Wilderness Society and the two newer organizations filed a suit to stop pipeline construction, the national environmental lobby was well aware of the threat to Alaska environmental lands and was becoming knowledgeable about the lands involved.

Alaskan proponents of the pipeline were furious when they learned of Judge Hart's injunction. Within a month the governor, mayors, and leading businessmen had organized a trip of their own to Washington, DC, to lobby the Interior Department and Congress to issue the permits. The injunction, they argued, took Alaska back to prestatehood, to abject powerlessness against the uses of federal power to stifle Alaska's deserved and destined economic development. Alaska leaders seemed unable to understand both the reason for the delay in the project and the judicial process. It was left to Secretary Hickel to try to explain the situation. Having adopted a new, more favorable view of environmental concerns since responding to the Santa Barbara blowout, in a speech at the University of Alaska on Earth Day 1970, he counseled patience on the part of his fellow Alaskans and placed the blame for the environmental suit and the subsequent delay squarely on TAPS, which, he said, had underestimated the formidable challenges of construction in the Arctic. TAPS finally did get the message.[19] In August the seven companies engaged in North Slope investment organized a single new corporate entity to oversee the design of the pipeline and then to operate it, Alyeska Pipeline Service Company.

Remarkably, neither state leaders nor oil industry executives seem to have given much particular thought to the issue of Native land claims. Their focus was on pipeline design and then on Judge Hart's injunction. This was somewhat surprising because the pipeline would have to cross Native-claimed land, and there was no provision for exempting the pipeline project from whatever Native claims might be found valid. But while TAPS had been fumbling with engineering a pipeline, Alaska Native leaders had taken full advantage of Secretary Udall's land freeze to pursue a comprehensive settlement of their land claims. Throughout 1969, 1970, and 1971 they were engaged in intensive negotiation with congressional leaders regarding a comprehensive settlement of those claims, most particularly with Senator Jackson and his Interior and Insular Affairs Committee, where a settlement bill was under concentrated discussion.

As a starting point, Jackson had redirected a presidentially appointed committee formed after the devastating 1964 Alaska earthquake, once most of its work on that disaster was complete, to review Alaska Native conditions and make a recommendation regarding Native claims. The Federal Field Committee for Development Planning in Alaska conducted a comprehensive survey of Alaska Native life and in 1968 proposed the framework for a settlement. In what would prove to be a formative design for a settlement, the committee proposed that Alaska Natives be given legal title to 4.6 million acres of federal land and $100 million in compensation for extinguishment of Native title to the rest of Alaska's land; that Congress establish a statewide corporation managed by non-Natives to administer the land and the money; and that title to land within villages be placed with an incorporated city government established for and by each village.[20] For Natives, there were objectionable elements in the design, most notably the implication that they were unable to manage their own affairs. But the elements could be modified, and they would be. The field committee proposal was a tangible, negotiable place to begin.

The oil companies were not alone in their willingness to ignore Alaska Native land claims; they were joined by the National Park Service. In 1964 an NPS attorney, George Hartzog, who as superintendent of the Jefferson National Expansion Memorial had brought the St. Louis Gateway Arch to near completion, was named NPS director, a job he would hold through 1972. In one of his early initiatives he charged an NPS task force to prepare a comprehensive plan for new national parks in Alaska. "Operation Great Land," issued in early 1965, proposed 76 million acres of new Alaska parkland. Over the next several years nothing was done legislatively to move the plan, and in December 1968, as he was preparing to leave the government, Secretary Udall decided to take a collection of proposals for new conservation withdrawals to Lyndon Johnson to consider as he ended his presidency. Edgar Wayburn, now Sierra Club president, was a good friend of both Hartzog and Udall, and Udall consulted with Wayburn before taking his proposals to the White House. Udall's collection included several of the parks named in "Operation Great Land." As it happened, Johnson did not act on many of Udall's Alaska recommendations, making only a small addition to Katmai National Monument. Historian Donald Mitchell wrote that neither Hartzog nor Udall considered Native land claims in their discussions and proposals, even though Udall was a professed friend of Natives and supporter of the land claims movement, as his "super land freeze" had shown.[21] Udall later noted that he assumed Natives were going to get a "fair shake," and he opined that Hartzog and his team at the NPS were totally focused on their park-expansion mission. This suggests that Alaska Native land claims still were not being taken very seriously by the people plotting Alaska's future.

They should have been. Through 1968, following the formation of the Alaska Federation of Natives and communication among the various Native communities, the organization's leaders settled on a firm position for settlement of their claims. The Natives decided they would not settle for less than 40 million acres of land to be titled to Native entities and a compensatory award for extinguishment of Native title to the remainder of Alaska. Forty million acres amounted to about 500 acres times the 70,000 Alaska Natives at the time, though there was no suggestion that the land would be parceled out to individuals. Rather, both the surface and subsurface estate would be held by a collective entity, though villages would receive a patent to land under and around them, including the surface estate. For a considerable time the compensatory award was set at $500 million and the land at 50 million acres. The source of the money was a sticking point in the negotiations. Some congressmen insisted that it be paid from the revenue coming to the state from development of the Prudhoe Bay oil field, paid over a twenty-year period. Alaska leaders balked at that idea. It would, they argued, defeat the whole concept of statehood. But when it became clear to the Native leadership that Congress would not accept 50 million, they lowered the land demand to 40 million and increased the monetary award to $1 billion, with half to come from the federal treasury and half from state oil revenues. This was vastly more acreage and money than the federal field committee had recommended in its 1968 report. But the report's design was still a workable framework in regard to Native title to acreage and compensatory payment for extinguishment of the remainder, with the award going to a Native entity. When the oil companies and Alaska political leaders realized, sometime in 1969, that they were going to have to settle Native claims before any work could be done on the pipeline, the field committee framework provided a methodology. Even after Native leaders accepted that framework, more than one congressman vowed never to permit millions of acres of land to be titled to Alaska Natives, and many viewed the compensatory award initially as nothing less than ridiculous. But they were arguing about numbers, not the basic structure for a settlement. Moreover, national awareness of the prejudicial history of the nation's treatment of American Indians and Alaska Natives had expanded greatly in the wake of the civil rights revolution, and many members of Congress felt political pressure to settle Native claims on generous terms. Historian Mitchell learned in his investigations that it was Nixon adviser John Ehrlichman who made the decision on the numbers. President Nixon felt that a generous settlement was appropriate and left the details to Ehrlichman, who handled domestic matters with whose details the president did not wish to become involved. When Ehrlichman sent an administration bill to Congress, it included the 44 million acres, the $1 billion, and the provision that the land be titled to twelve regional development corporations headed by Natives.[22]

Edgar Wayburn noted in an oral history interview that when he flew to Washington, DC, in late September 1971 for a Sierra Club board meeting and a wilderness conference, he was met by a highly stressed Stewart Brandborg, executive director of the Wilderness Society. "We've lost everything," Wayburn remembered Brandborg explaining; "ANCSA is going through, and there's no provision for parks or refuges or anything else."[23] Senator Jackson had been working with the various stakeholders in the Alaska claims bill and worried that when the bill became law, there would be chaos in Alaska. Settlement of Native claims would at long last lift Secretary Udall's comprehensive "land freeze," a circumstance Alaska leaders were waiting for with bated breath. So, of course, were the oil companies, for with Native claims delineated, they hoped they could soon begin work on the pipeline. Among others, the federal field committee recognized that new conservation withdrawals were going to be a significant part of Alaska's future. Though since the Prudhoe Bay discovery the national conservation organizations had had Alaska on their radar, they had developed no coordinated or comprehensive policy for environmental protection in the state. Historian Mitchell noted that in July 1970 field committee staffer Arlon Tussing urged in a speech to the Alaska Press Club that before ANCSA was complete, federal conservation withdrawals should be included in it. Otherwise, there was the possibility for significant resistance from the Sierra Club, the Wilderness Society, and other groups that might embarrass both Congress and the State of Alaska.[24] Jackson asked Tussing to work with staff in the Senate office to write a section of the claims bill to include conservation withdrawals. The resulting provision authorized the secretary of the interior to withdraw all unreserved public lands in Alaska from entry, that is, from any use or designation, for five years while he prepared recommendations for inclusion of lands in the national park and national fish and wildlife systems.

This was an extraordinary provision. It was the beginning of what would become the Alaska National Interest Lands Conservation Act of 1980. Its importance to the cause and interest of conservation in America can hardly be overstated. It can be explained only by the rise and force of the modern environmental movement, manifest in the passage of the national environmental policy act in 1969 and the endangered species act in 1973. As explained later, the path to the Alaska lands act would be uneven and hardly inevitable. Yet by mid-1970 it was becoming clearer that there would be no claims settlement and no pipeline without a simultaneous provision for new federal conservation units in Alaska. Through the winter of 1970–1971, representatives of the national conservation organizations met often to prepare collective recommendations for the withdrawals. The Wilderness Society's Brandborg pressed for a provision that would suspend any land conveyances to the State of Alaska until the secretary had made selections for the conservation units. Predictably, Senator Stevens reacted heatedly to the notion of any suspension of Alaska land selections.

Looking ahead to a major battle over congressional approval of a claims settlement with such provisions included, leaders of the Sierra Club, the Wilderness Society, Friends of the Earth, and several other conservation organizations formed a collective lobbying group they called the Alaska Coalition. It comprised young people who had worked in local and regional conservation groups, were members of one or another of the national organizations, and were highly idealistic about protecting the nation's remaining unmanipulated lands. The group would work throughout 1971, 1972, and 1973 on preventing authorization of the Alaska pipeline and would be reconstituted for the battle over the Alaska lands bill at the end of the decade, becoming perhaps the most significant citizen lobbying group in congressional history. In 1970 coalition members persuaded Congressman John Saylor of Pennsylvania to introduce an addition to the Alaska claims bill providing for the development of a comprehensive land-use plan for Alaska and, remarkably, suspension of any land title conveyances, Native or state, until it was completed.

Two parties who wanted the Alaska pipeline built as soon as possible joined Senator Stevens in opposition to any measures that might delay the project. Alaska Natives wanted title to the 40 million acres promised in the proposed legislation so they might begin development of any economic resources, such as timber, hard-rock minerals, or oil and gas. In addition to his expectation of the economic bonanza for the state that the pipeline and development of North Slope oil represented, Stevens supported moving land from federal to Native title both to reduce the federal land-hold in the state and for whatever economic benefit for Natives and for Alaska those lands might hold. With the president weighing in against the environmental addition to the claims bill and members of the Alaska Federation of Natives actively lobbying against it in congressional offices, many congressmen seemed ready to pass the bill without making any provision for new conservation withdrawals. It was that possibility that had brought on Brandborg's consternation, which he shared with Wayburn when the latter arrived in Washington in September. But by then Alaska Coalition members had found a new champion in Congress: Congressman Morris Udall of Arizona, the younger brother of former Interior Secretary Stewart Udall. Udall had promised to introduce language that would preclude the current or future interior secretary from issuing the pipeline construction permits until the land planners had finished their work and the secretary had withdrawn land for parks and refuges. In fact, the environmentalists did not want any pipeline at all and hoped the land-planning exercise might delay the project long enough for it to be killed, one way or another.[25] But because of leadership threats in Congress, Udall had decided against introducing the amendment the coalition wanted. Soon after Wayburn got off his plane in Washington, he and Brandborg and other leaders of the coalition decided to launch an all-out lobbying effort, one unlike anything ever seen from environmental organizations before. One staffer at the Wilderness Society described it as a "full court press."[26] Calling on members in all the coalition groups around the country to write letters, the coalition deluged Congress with mail. At the same time volunteers visited the offices of every member of Congress, leaving lobbying material when they could not speak to the members personally. The coalition maintained a telephone bank in Washington, directing people where to send mail and whom to phone. For coalition member organizations, it was the biggest lobbying effort they'd ever undertaken. For many in Congress, it was the biggest they'd ever experienced.[27]

In the end it appeared to fail, for the version of the claims bill passed by the Senate did not include the delays of Native and state lands the coalition wanted. The Saylor amendment, which provided for a land-planning exercise and no conveyance of title until it was complete, was gone. It appeared that Brandborg's greatest fears were borne out. But the final Alaska Native claims settlement act was not written in the relevant Senate and House committees and passed by each body; it was written in the Senate-House conference committee, which met before and after Thanksgiving 1971. Negotiations there were tense. But the conferees were confronted with two salient political realities. The nation supported a generous settlement of Alaska Native land claims and as well supported some permanent withdrawal of new conservation units in the state. So when the bargaining was done, Alaska Natives received 44 million acres on terms that were workable: all Alaska Natives became eligible to receive 100 shares of stock in one or another of 12 regional economic development corporations and about 200 village corporations; the regional corporations would retain the subsurface rights to all the conveyed land; the regional corporations would received $962.5 million in compensation for extinguishment of title and subsistence harvesting rights to the rest of Alaska; about 50 percent would be distributed to the village corporations in the region; and any one regional corporation would share 70 percent of its profits from oil and gas development on its lands with all the regional corporations. And the act included highly significant conservation provisions: a joint federal-state land-use planning commission would study areas and recommend to the secretary of the interior and to Congress withdrawals for new national parks, refuges, forests, and scenic rivers, a portion of which would be designated as wilderness; within two years the secretary of the interior would reserve 80 million acres of land as study areas to prepare for Congress to make the final designations for the new conservation units; after five study years Congress would act on the secretary's recommendations. This was Section 17 of the act, the 80-million-acre reservation of which would become infamous in Alaska as 17(d)(2).

Very significantly, the act did not include any specific provision for Native subsistence harvest of traditional resources. Assured by the Alaska Coalition that Native subsistence harvesting would be maintained in the new conservation withdrawals, Native leaders and the AFN agreed to support 17(d)(2), trusting that the details of traditional use would be worked out satisfactorily during the study period.[28] Subsistence would prove to be a highly complex and difficult issue. Even though the Alaska Coalition was diligent in honoring its commitment throughout its long lobbying campaign for the lands act, the implementation of the mechanisms for identifying what areas were appropriate for subsistence harvest and what persons should be eligible has been controversial and cumbersome. President Nixon signed the act on December 17, 1971.[29]

Like the Alaska lands act, which would follow in 1980, the Alaska Native Land Claims Settlement Act was unprecedented. Its central ideas were to preserve Alaska Natives' connection with their ancestral lands and to make the compensatory award work in perpetuity for all Natives. The corporations established by the act, chartered under the laws of the State of Alaska, have a fiduciary responsibility to generate profit for their shareholders through the investment of their assets. Those goals have been largely realized, though more fully for some groups of Alaska Natives than others. Of the 211 villages recognized in the act, 178 have formed village corporations; a number of villages have combined in one village corporation. As should have been anticipated, not all corporations found effective investment advisers at the start. Getting the corporations organized and functioning was a huge challenge for many in the Native leadership cadre, as would have been the case for any cohort of leaders suddenly swept into the world of corporate management and responsibility without training and experience. Most did well; some did not. In 1986 Senator Stevens was able to amend the US tax code to allow Alaska Native corporations to sell their net operating losses on the open market, a provision that allowed several failing corporations to reconfigure their finances and effectively start over. The code revision lasted only a few years, but while it did, it saved several Alaska Native corporations. Several of the corporations now are sufficiently robust to pay not only annual but also periodic supplementary dividends to their shareholders. ANCSA prohibited the sale of corporation stock for twenty years; there was anxiety that shareholders would sell their shares, thus vitiating one of the fundamental objectives of the act. In 1987 the act was amended to prohibit the sale of stock unless approved by a majority of the shareholders; to date, no corporation has voted to permit the sale of shares.

Forty years after passage of the act, as financial firms many of the corporations have been highly successful. In 2010 nine of the top ten businesses in Alaska were Alaska Native corporations; five of those were worth more than $1 billion.[30] Alaska Native corporations have become a major economic force within Alaska. A review of corporation portfolios shows that most of their investments are not in Alaska, however. There are not many lucrative investment opportunities in Alaska, and most corporate interest is outside the state.[31] From the beginning of implementation of the act, a major concern has been investment in village life and infrastructure. A frequent complaint is that the regional corporations do little for the villages, and most village corporations do not have the resources to do much. The corporations are in a quandary because their primary responsibility is the generation of shareholder profit, not the social and economic health of the villages. In 1994 Assistant Secretary of the Interior Ada Deer recognized 227 tribal governments in Alaska. Although Congress has recognized the list by including it in the Indian Tribal List Act of 1995, it has not formally confirmed recognition of tribal sovereignty in Alaska.[32] The implicit recognition of Native sovereignty makes the tribal entities eligible for a host of federal grants and programs.

ANCSA afforded Alaska Natives a level of social, political, and economic legitimacy they had not enjoyed previously. Now Alaskans had to deal with

Native entities, governments, and people in a new context, as equal partners, especially in the business world. Neither their ignorance nor their acquiescence could any longer be taken for granted. They rapidly became the largest private landholder in the state,[33] and their investment corporations dwarfed most other private enterprises. Moreover, Congress had recognized that legitimacy with its acknowledgment of the right of Alaska Natives to land and to compensation for land they could no longer call their own. If Alaskans understood anything, they understood property rights.

The conservation lands provisions of ANCSA prohibited the state from continuing its land selections, which had been halted by the "super land freeze" of 1968. And they held out the prospect of large areas the state wanted for economic development being lost for that purpose forever. State leaders were not pleased with that prospect. Neither were Native leaders. As already noted, Natives wanted quick conveyance of their lands authorized under the act. Yet they, too, would have to wait, except for townships on which their villages were located. More important was the absence of explicit provision in the act permitting continued subsistence harvest of traditional resources on lands the Natives had utilized for that purpose from time immemorial, though by mutual consent there were few constraints on such activity. Native leaders worried that the security of their ancestral lands provided in ANCSA would be lost in whatever legislation Congress might finally pass regarding the new conservation units. In particular there was concern over what a wilderness designation for any of the lands might mean. The 1964 Wilderness Act had defined wilderness as land that did not show the permanent imprint of humankind; however, it permitted continuation of uses that predated the act. Without much comment from anyone, subsistence harvesting continued as it normally had after the passage of ANCSA and before ANILCA; remarkably, because of the suspension of Alaska state land selections and the delay in implementing Native selections, as of 1971 most of Alaska was still federal land being managed as it had been throughout the twentieth century.

Many in Alaska did not come to the realization until after Congress passed ANCSA that the pipeline project could not immediately go forward.[34] Judge Hart's injunction halting any activity on the pipeline, issued after his review of the suit filed by the Wilderness Society, Friends of the Earth, and the

Environmental Defense Fund in March 1970, was still in force. But Secretary of the Interior Morton understood the circumstances quite well. Through 1971 an Interior Department working group labored at the US Geological Survey offices in Menlo Park, California, to prepare a final impact statement on the project, a requirement of NEPA. Cooperating with industry engineers, the working group compiled scientific data on all aspects of the pipeline design, most particularly regarding permafrost. In addition, NEPA required a thorough study of alternatives to any proposed environmental impact. When a federal court ruling confirmed that aspect of NEPA, Morton directed a special task force to prepare a statement on a possible line through Canada to the American Midwest rather than the pipeline to Valdez and tankers to Washington state, the task force's initial assumption.

Interior released the final environmental impact statement (EIS) on March 20, 1972, just three months after the passage of ANCSA, raising hopes in Alaska that the long wait would soon be over. The EIS addressed the movement of caribou, permafrost and the relief of heat from the pipe, the large volume of gravel that would be needed for construction, the line's vulnerability to seismic activity, and the fragility of the marine environment through which tankers would travel as they exited Alaska waters, among other issues. Writers of the statement were sensitive to the wilderness values that lay at the heart of environmentalists' opposition to the project. Clearly, they noted, construction of the pipeline and the development of the Prudhoe Bay deposit would "irreversibly and irretrievably" affect Alaska.[35] But writers of the report suggested that the very small amount of land impacted by the pipeline need not detract from the idea of wilderness, which was what they argued was most important to Americans. It was the psychological value of wilderness that was important, they averred.[36] Historian Peter Coates recounted an analogy attributed to Vide Bartlett, the senator's widow, who argued that a single strand of black thread unspooled across a double page of newspaper would represent the impact of the pipeline on Alaska's wilderness.[37]

The three organizations that had filed the lawsuit challenging the Interior Department prepared the environmental community response.[38] The engineering and construction criteria still were flawed, they charged, and, further, were probably unenforceable once work began. In fact, the authors charged, the Interior Department had made itself a pawn of the oil industry, meekly accepting industry representations regarding the integrity and safety of the line. The report argued that claims made by the department and the industry that

Alaskan oil would significantly reduce America's dependence on foreign oil imports were inflated and unrealistic. As evidence, the writers quoted a statement from the secretary of defense, included in the final impact statement, that Alaskan oil would not solve America's oil dependency.[39] Finally, the environmentalists charged that alternatives had not been thoroughly studied and asserted that a route through Canada would get oil to the American Midwest more cheaply and would be environmentally safer because it would not involve jeopardy for Alaska's fragile marine environment. Implicit but easily discerned in the critique was the contention that the Interior Department had made itself the servant of the oil industry's rush to make billions in profit from Alaskan oil, an endeavor the State of Alaska supported because it would tax oil production. The secretary of the interior made no modifications to the impact statement as a result of the environmental review. Morton released the statement in early May.

A far more important response to the impact statement than the environmental critique was that of federal district Judge George Hart. After his own review, in August Judge Hart dissolved his injunction prohibiting any work on the pipeline. He was satisfied. Once the Interior Department issued the appropriate permits, the work could begin but for two issues. But they were issues Hart said the courts could not address. One was the width of the right-of-way. The 1920 Mineral Leasing Act limited the width to 50 feet, inadequate for modern construction equipment; the industry needed twice that. The other was the question of whether or not NEPA applied to the project. Both issues, the judge insisted, would need to be addressed by Congress. For the environmentalists, the strategic litigation phase of the battle was over.

Congress prepared to take up these issues in the spring of 1973, and as it did, Americans began to hear about an energy crisis.[40] It was nothing like the crisis that would develop later in the year, but already in the spring, as part of their lobbying of Congress, oil companies pointed to increases in domestic consumption that necessitated increases in oil imports. Some in Congress discussed prohibiting the export of any Alaskan oil. This idea played well with the environmental groups, which had begun to push for the Canadian alternative to the Alaska pipeline route. In November the Alaska Coalition, following the lead of the Environmental Defense Fund and Friends of the Earth, began actively to lobby for a Canadian line.

In the meantime, Alaskans chafed mightily in the face of more delay in pipeline authorization and state land selection. Joe Vogler, a Fairbanks miner and developer, gathered signatures on a petition calling for the secession of Alaska from the United States. Building on the larger number of signatures collected than he had anticipated, Vogler then founded the Alaska Independence Party, for which he would subsequently be a perennial candidate for various statewide offices.[41] At the same time Senator Mike Gravel founded a lobbying group he called the Alaska Pipeline Education Committee (ALPECO), for which the state legislature appropriated $100,000. The legislature also adopted a resolution proposing to sue the Sierra Club "and all other groups seeking to thwart the orderly development of Alaska."[42] A former president of the University of Alaska denounced the Sierra Club as yet another colonial power retarding Alaska's economic advance.[43] As noted, for these Alaskans, obstruction of the pipeline project seemed to put them back into the prestatehood era, when the federal government, through its jurisdiction in territories, constrained much development in Alaska. Alaskans felt the internal control they had expected from statehood slipping away to organizations and sentiments that were completely alien to their notion of the "last frontier." Most likely did not understand the environmental movement, nor did they grasp the implications of the National Environmental Policy Act for Alaska's development. "Frontier" and "pioneer" were their frames of reference. A majority of Americans would come to understand Alaska as a national treasure for its undeveloped lands and its character as America's "last wilderness." For Alaska's leaders, especially those who appreciated the fragile quality of the Alaska economy, wilderness would always be contradictory to frontier. "Frontier" meant self-sufficiency. The federal government had promised to give Alaska the means to self-sufficiency, the land grant in the statehood act, and Alaska had made good use of it in selecting the potentially oil-rich lands at Prudhoe Bay. Then it had done what the federal government had said the state needed to do: it had leased the land. And the lessees had found oil, the state taxes on which would make Alaska economically independent, Alaskans averred. But now environmentalists, people who did not live in the state and who did not understand the isolation involved in living there, threatened to take away the achievement of statehood and the future of Alaska's coming generations. To this line of thought, wilderness preservation at the expense of a whole people and a way of life made no sense. The two concepts stood in stark opposition to one another, and Alaskans attributed variously ignorance or malevolence to those whose stated objective was to prevent development in the state. *Anchorage Daily Times* editor Robert Atwood would repeatedly express such sentiments, as would officers of the Anchorage Chamber of Commerce and state and municipal officials.

The biggest concern for Senators Stevens and Gravel was compliance with NEPA. By the summer of 1973 the Senate was ready to vote on legislation to authorize construction of the pipeline. Gravel had introduced a provision, as an amendment to the pending bill, declaring that Interior's EIS satisfied EPA requirements. In addition, the bill prohibited further court challenges to the project. It was a gauntlet thrown fully in the path of the environmental lobby and its Alaska vision. Unsurprisingly, the amendment generated a robust national debate. If Congress could waive the requisites of NEPA for such a huge project, did NEPA mean anything at all? Senator Jackson, who had shepherded NEPA through the Senate, opposed the amendment. Environmentalists reacted with a combination of outrage and dismay, stepping up their lobbying of Congress. A large cohort of urban newspapers editorialized against the gutting of NEPA. But it was clear that Congress was supportive of getting the pipeline under way, in part because of concern over oil supplies, a concern the oil companies capitalized on in newspaper and radio advertising.

On July 13 the Senate voted on an amendment to suspend further consideration of pipeline authorization pending a yearlong review of the Canadian alternative, as proposed by Senators Walter Mondale and Birch Bayh. The vote was 29–61 against. The crucial vote on the project came four days later, on the amendment declaring that the pipeline construction plan as approved by the Interior Department satisfied the requisites of NEPA. The vote can be seen as a test of the national strength of conservationist sentiment two years after NEPA's enactment. The environmental lobby had every reason to be confident after its successes with the Wilderness Act and with NEPA. But those acts passed Congress before the looming energy crisis; as always, circumstances in the present were different. No one was certain of the outcome. Senator Stevens later said he had expected the amendment to fail going into the vote. But the outcome was a surprise to him, and to many in the chamber. The amendment passed 49–48. Senator Alan Cranston, Democrat of California, a strong supporter of environmentalism and an outspoken critic of the pipeline, was absent for the vote, and a motion for reconsideration was immediately filed. Cranston arrived for the reconsideration and cast his vote against, creating a 49–49 tie. That threw the outcome to the president of the Senate. Vice President Spiro Agnew, on hand because the vote was expected to be close, voted from the president's chair to approve. For all practical intents and purposes, the Trans-Alaska Pipeline was authorized. The House, debating the companion bill in early August, rejected an amendment that would have deleted from it a section declaring the actions taken by the Interior Secretary in regard to the pipeline to be in compliance with NEPA, 221–198, again a measure of the strength of national conservationist sentiment. When the House vote on the completed bill was taken, it passed 356–60.

Conservationists considered a court challenge to the constitutionality of the provision prohibiting future judicial challenges to the pipeline project. There were few precedents for such precluding of legal challenges, but Senator Stevens, who had crafted the provision, thought it a good gamble. David Brower of Friends of the Earth wanted to undertake the suit, but, he noted later in an oral interview, the other national organizations had lost energy, particularly the Environmental Defense Fund and the Wilderness Society.[44] Attorneys were not sure of winning, and board members worried that there would be too much negative publicity. Edgar Wayburn of the Sierra Club concluded that the forces arrayed against the environmental community, including the American oil companies, were simply too great for the groups to fight successfully. Then events on a different scale took the matter out of the lobbyists' hands. On October 6 Egypt and Syria invaded Israel, beginning the Yom Kippur War. In retaliation for US support of Israel, the Organization of Petroleum Exporting Countries imposed an embargo on oil shipments to the United States, leading to gasoline shortages and voluntary rationing by service stations. It was an energy crisis of a sort not previously experienced, and it both panicked and angered Americans. Following an address by President Nixon to the nation on November 8, the Senate passed the Trans-Alaska Pipeline Authorization Act by a vote of 80–5 the next day.

Congressional approval of pipeline construction was a defeat for environmentalism, particularly as the defeat included the declaration that the construction and operation plan satisfied the requisites of NEPA. The anxiety that the declaration effectively nullified NEPA was widespread in the environmental community.[45] Those who had wanted no pipeline at all had perhaps come close to their goal on July 17 when the Senate had deadlocked 49–49 over Senator Gravel's amendment setting NEPA aside. In the final analysis, the environmental lobby had forced the design of a safer pipeline than TAPS officers had imagined would be possible or necessary at the beginning of the project. And the Alaska Coalition had forced the federal government to begin the work of identifying and putting in place functional protections for America's most valuable and vulnerable environmental lands. Coming as close at it did to stopping the pipeline project, the environmental lobby, organized as a sustained nationwide, grassroots, mostly volunteer campaign for the first time, could take solace from its near victory. There were substantial battles ahead for which the pipeline campaign served as both model and inspiration for environmentalism, and for Alaska.

In violation of the court order prohibiting work on the pipeline project, and without the necessary authorizing permits, the oil companies had already undertaken some preparation work along the proposed right-of-way. Partly that was because they had moved some equipment into position in the winter of 1969–1970, before the court injunction was imposed. Rather than have that equipment sit idle, supervisors had undertaken survey and clearing work more or less on their own recognizance. In 1969 the companies had ordered the actual pipe for the line from a Japanese manufacturer; it was delivered in 1970 and 1971 to the port of Valdez, where it was stacked at the original Valdez town site that had been flooded by the tsunami during the 1964 Alaska earthquake. The stacked pipe became a minor tourist attraction while Alaskans awaited the outcome of the protracted battle over the settlement of Alaska Native land claims and congressional authorization of the pipeline. The popular photo op of the time was of a quizzical-looking someone sitting in one of the 48-inch-diameter, 12-foot pipe sections lying on the ground.

In March 1970 Lewis Lapham, then a contributing editor to *Harper's*, recounted a trip to Alaska that he had made the previous January. His report captured much of Alaskans' attitude toward both Natives and environment. Under the title "Alaska: Politicians and Natives, Money and Oil," Lapham suggested that Alaskan leaders seemed not to appreciate the bitterness of Alaska Natives, who felt they were not being afforded their just due. With a number of politicians and lobbyists, Lapham lamented the apparent bewilderment felt by many at the prospect of the coming oil money being wasted. Governor Keith Miller told Lapham that if the state's position on Native claims—no large land grant and no money from what was due the state from taxation on North Slope production—ended up derailing a congressional settlement, "then that was too bad." "There is a strong instinct in the state against giving the Natives anything," Lapham wrote, and he expected Miller to appeal to that instinct in his upcoming run for election as governor in his own right (Miller had succeeded Hickel after the latter's appointment as secretary of the interior). However widespread such sentiment may have been at the beginning of 1970, it would change as a function of ANCSA and authorization of construction of the pipeline. As noted, the land and money associated with the claims settlement elevated Alaska Natives into a position of economic parity with the rest of Alaska; they could no longer be taken for granted. And start-up of the pipeline eliminated, for the time being, the stress on the state's economy and thus the prospect that the immigrant population would have to desert Alaska. The generation that would come to maturity during the halcyon days of oil production, and taxation, would experience an Alaska in which the equal legitimacy of Alaska Natives would be taken for granted and expressions of any surviving resentment of Natives would be suppressed. Native leaders of the claims struggle became highly respected figures in the broad social and political Alaska community, some of them legends in their own time. The Alaska Federation of Natives' annual convention in October became an important stage in the state's political theater. Occasional public, racially motivated assaults on Natives in the state's larger cities generated community protests and conciliatory actions. A strong Native sovereignty movement became so visible and potent as to make criticism of support for the survival of Native villages vulnerable to charges of racism.

Several people whom Lapham spoke with also seemed not fully to grasp the depth of the environmental movement. One state senator recently returned from a trip to Canada argued that Canadians did not let environmental regulation stop economic development and worried that Canada might build a pipeline before Alaska did and thus "cheat" Alaskans out of the economic boom promised by construction of the line. "All those do-gooders and bug-hunters and bird watchers can mind their own damn business," he remarked. A lobbyist representing the oil industry's advocacy arm, the Alaska Oil and Gas Association, thought that the only reason environment was an issue was because it had become "fashionable." While in Juneau, Lapham attended a hearing before the State House committee on natural resources regarding pollution of fishing waters in Alaska. He heard testimony about effluent from one of the pulp mills on the Tongass National Forest destroying a herring fishery upon which several hundred fishermen depended.[46] Jay Hammond, a hunting guide from the Lake Clark region in western Alaska who would later become Alaska governor, had introduced legislation to prohibit oil drilling in the shallow waters of Bristol Bay, the most prolific and valuable wild salmon fishery in the world. An oil lobbyist whom Lapham spoke to predicted that the bill would never pass. Lapham noted that members of the committee listened politely but manifested no intention of doing anything about the bill. Lapham spoke with the chair of the House rules committee, Clem Tillion, who, repeating the earlier comment Lapham had heard, said he might be able to get Hammond's bill through the House because environmentalism had become "fashionable."

It was remarkable that sensitivity to Alaska's unique conservation values should have become linked with Alaska Native land claims, for despite the work of the Alaska Conservation Society and the Alaska members of the Sierra Club, and despite those few who understood the rise of environmentalism, there was little sympathy in Alaska for the wilderness idea or for preservation of large areas of the state as conservation reserves. As explained, opposition to environmentalism was deeper in Alaska than a reflexive response to the "lockup" of one or another prospect for economic development. The vulnerability Alaskans felt because of the narrow Alaska economy, without the possibility of commercially profitable manufacturing or agriculture, and the remote character of that economy, far removed from sources of supply and markets and without any neighboring economies, had been acute during the period immediately following statehood. The delays in start-up of the pipeline and the possibility of the project being quashed entirely by environmental protest exacerbated that sense of vulnerability and both angered and badly frightened Alaskans. Moreover, the state land-selection process, started in 1959 and halted by Secretary Udall's land freeze, remained stalled after authorization of the pipeline project, as explained earlier. Alaskans felt abused and demeaned. Among Alaskans, Lapham wrote, any mention of the word "ecology" brought "derisive laughter." People did understand the potential for despoliation of the environment in the event of an accident, but, Lapham emphasized, "they want the money." He quoted the prayer with which a chaplain had opened a daily session of the legislature: "We thank Thee, O Lord, for the oil Thou hast given us as a natural resource."

Some people thought in a different frame of reference. Hammond told Lapham that the irony of Alaska was that many in the state were working to make it into a replica of the society they went there to escape. Lapham wrote that Hammond distrusted economic development for its own sake because he saw that only a few people prospered, mostly merchants and those in service industries such as insurance. "No amount of money could justify the destruction that seems to accompany the triumph of American civilization," he told Lapham. But he did not expect his point of view to prevail in the legislature.

A local oil lobbyist expressed a prevailing view of environmentalism, a pervasive fatalism, that Lapham encountered often. Money, the lobbyist said, is the basis of the American dream, and as long as it remained so, people would have to endure the destruction that came with development. If people wanted to retain the environment, they would have to pay for it, with money and by relinquishing such conveniences as automobiles, which consume oil and pollute the air. The American economy runs on oil, the lobbyist averred, and as long as there was oil available, Americans would continue to be profligate with it and careless about development. Identifying what he understood as the core contradiction of the conservation movement, the lobbyist was offended by the hypocrisy of environmentalists criticizing Alaskans for wanting to profit from the development of their oil, even at the expense of environmental integrity. Yet, taking nothing for granted, the lobbyist showed Lapham a film paid for by the oil companies that touted the industry's regard for the North Slope environment, replete with scenes of breaching whales and a species of salmon unknown in the Arctic. The *Anchorage Daily News* denounced the film as deceptive propaganda.[47]

The onset of construction of the pipeline would not relieve the anxiety in Alaska, for the 17(d)(2) provision of ANCSA meant that there would be a new battle for Alaskans: the extent of the new conservation withdrawals Congress was committed to determine and establish. That battle, which would last nearly a decade, would deepen Alaskans' sense of oppression and persecution even as the overheated, temporary economy generated by construction and then operation of the Trans-Alaska Pipeline transformed the state into an incongruous version of modern America.

The Alaska Native Claims Settlement Act of 1971 seemed a dramatic, unparalleled achievement for Alaska's people, Native and non-Native. While empowering Alaska Natives, at the same time it appeared to remove what had often seemed an insurmountable obstacle to construction of an Alaska oil pipeline that would facilitate the development of the giant Prudhoe Bay oil find. Exploitation of the field, it was universally understood, would secure the state's growth and prosperity into a distant future.[1] It was, Alaska's new US senator, Ted Stevens, declared, an economic development act for Alaska.[2] As is often the case, however, the devil was in the details—details that in their euphoria many Alaskans initially did not see or did not understand. When they discovered them, their sense of betrayal was palpable. It was a turning point in the development of Alaska's extreme antistatism.

Alaskans looked on 17(d)(2) of ANCSA with suspicion from the moment the section was added to the act. When they learned of the scope of the federal conservation withdrawals being proposed by the national environmental organizations, non-Natives found their worst fears realized, interpreting the study of over 200 million acres of Alaska for possible withdrawals as a suppression of their independence to generate the economic takeoff promised by statehood. At the same time, despite the Alaska Coalition's assurances, Natives feared loss of the opportunity to roam freely in lands from which they had harvested subsistence resources from time immemorial. But it was Congress, not the environmental lobby, that would write the law. National environmentalists certainly did hope to craft and achieve legislation that would protect Natives and at the same time bar exploitation of resources on millions of acres of Alaska land. Although some federal planners had acknowledged the role of subsistence in sustaining village life, and therefore the necessity of some provision for it in whatever legislation would eventuate from the legislative completion of ANCSA, few seem to have understood the comprehensive range of subsistence harvesting required to sustain the more than 150 roadless villages in rural Alaska, villages with few modern economic opportunities. Nor did many planners and conservationists understand the potential conflict with Native subsistence needs and habits represented by sequestering large acreages of the otherwise unmolested land.

For his part, Senator Stevens set out to prevent the environmentalists from prevailing in their quest to preserve much of the land in Alaska that they considered significant and vulnerable. In that endeavor he was aided by the junior senator, Mike Gravel, elected to replace Ernest Gruening, and by Congressman Don Young, though Young could not do as much in the House, where the environmental lobby had its greatest strength and best congressional friends. Senator Gravel was an opportunist who, in his pursuit of votes and approval in Alaska, refused to cooperate in presenting a united Alaska front in Congress and cost Alaska support it might have had.[3] His antics frustrated Stevens and offended Senator Jackson, who was central to moving Alaska lands legislation.

The agency task force that National Park Service Director George Hartzog had charged in 1964 with developing plans for new parks in Alaska proposed thirty-nine zones across that state that the NPS should evaluate in the 1965 "Operation Great Land" report. Collins wrote much of the report. Hartzog did not immediately publish the recommendations. Among other factors, when he learned about it, Governor Hickel adamantly opposed the idea of new national parks in Alaska. The federal field committee, in its recommendation on a plan for settling Native claims titled *Alaska Natives and the Land*, had also recommended the creation of new Alaska parks, again much to Hickel's irritation. Hartzog made several trips to Alaska in the late 1960s, the first in 1965. Historian Dan Nelson found an account of a dinner held by the Anchorage Chamber of Commerce for Hartzog and Assistant Secretary of the Interior Stanley A. Cain, who accompanied him. The after-dinner speaker was *Anchorage Daily Times* publisher Atwood, the indefatigable booster of Alaska economic development and, as the battle over an Alaska lands act evolved in the 1970s, an increasingly strident and highly vocal, often caustic critic of conservation withdrawals in Alaska. Assistant Secretary Cain left a summary of Atwood's talk and Hartzog's response that is worth quoting in full for its insight into the depth of Alaskans' defensive attitude and states' rights advocacy:

[Atwood] spoke at some length in severe criticism of the Federal agencies operating in Alaska. The burden of his theme was that Washington bureaucrats were shoving good Alaska citizens around. . . . It seemed to me that this tirade embarrassed many people present, for they kept looking at their now empty plates. After objecting to any restrictions on the development and use of natural resources . . . he sat down and the chairman said that closed the evening's program. Someone spoke in his ear after which he got up and asked . . . [Hartzog] if he wished to make any remarks. George spoke briefly and graciously while making it quite clear that the National Park Service intended to fulfill its national responsibilities in Alaska. No direct reference to Mr. Atwood's talk was necessary.[4]

Atwood's self-protective performance at so early a date, before any federal agency had done more than suggest the desirability of planning for conservation withdrawals, reflects well the general Alaskan response, its rhetoric well practiced, manifesting the deeply felt sense of persecution at the hands of federal overseers, a page in the long Alaska tradition. Atwood had edited and published his newspaper in the territorial period, and it is reasonable to assume that he did not use words carelessly, particularly on a formal occasion such as a banquet for visiting dignitaries. His use of the term "shoving good Alaska citizens around" no doubt reflected his own feelings and similar feelings that he wished to elicit from other Alaska leaders.

Not long after Hartzog returned to Washington, DC, he established a regional NPS office in Anchorage. He made trips to Alaska in the summers of 1966 and 1967 to survey areas proposed in Collins's report and in 1968 sought a meeting with Governor Hickel to discuss NPS ideas for new parks. By then Secretary Udall had implemented the first phase of his land freeze by canceling lease sales on federal land and halting conveyances of title to the state. Hickel was not interested in talking with Hartzog, going so far as to refuse to meet with him or any other NPS officials and forbidding his staff to meet with them—such was Alaskan anger and Hickel's own pugnacious style. The NPS was nearly alone in the early 1960s in recognizing the potential conflict between Alaska statehood and Native claims and the protection of Alaska's environmentally significant lands.

Alaska's unique jealousy of its state autonomy intimidated the state's small cohort of conservation-minded residents. When Celia Hunter, Ginny Wood, Bob Weeden, and others established the Alaska Conservation Society in 1962, there was considerable enthusiasm among members that sensitivity to environmental values would attract many Alaskans and help direct public policy. There were also high expectations for liaison with the national conservation organizations. In 1963 Hunter and Wood hosted the Wilderness Society's annual national meeting at their eco-inspired Camp Denali just outside the western boundary of Mt. McKinley National Park, accessible only via the single, unpaved road that ran through the park from the railroad on its eastern boundary. But, as historian Dan Nelson writes, contacts with the national organizations at that time were personal and tenuous.[5] Manifesting their isolation, the Alaskans were constrained by the same provinciality that motivated officials such as Gruening, Hickel, and Egan, namely, an assumption of the right and duty to control Alaska's destiny and the distribution of its lands, independent of any external authority. Nelson quoted Mike McCloskey of the Sierra Club as saying that the Alaskan environmentalists "saw everything in terms of Alaska," failing to understand the broader, national perspective. This was the usual stance of the Alaska Conservation Society.[6] As historian Coates noted, that organization had been founded initially "out of an awareness that in the delicate atmosphere shortly after statehood, any outside efforts from conservationists to influence events in the new state were likely to receive a hostile reception."[7] Throughout its history the ACS hoped to play a mitigating role between Alaska business and political leaders and national environmental groups. Speaking as Alaskans, its members hoped to present a positive view of environmental integrity and protection without the impact of that message being blunted by the charge that it was only the view of outsiders who did not understand Alaska and could not calculate the consequences for the state of arrested economic development. The Sierra Club authorized formation of its Alaska chapter in September 1968. Chapter members pursued the same objective, hoping to lend credibility to the arguments for environmental protection by speaking from an Alaskan point of view. Olaus and Mardy Murie had used this tactic in their campaign for the Arctic wilderness. Even though Olaus gained the endorsement of the Tanana Valley Sportsmen's Association, the Alaska Miners Association and all of the Chambers of Commerce in Alaska opposed creation of the Arctic range.

Section 17(d)(2) of ANCSA authorized the interior secretary to maintain the land freeze for ninety days and over five years to withdraw 80 million acres for study for permanent withdrawal. Ninety days was an almost impossible time frame within which to identify areas for examination in order to construct a logical and defensible withdrawal program. The NPS's "Operation Great Land" study was pressed into service immediately. The Interior Department appointed Theodore Swem of the NPS, who had worked with George Collins on "Operation Great Land," to head an interagency Alaska Planning Group comprising the Park Service; Fish and Wildlife Service; and Bureau of Outdoor Recreation, which had the responsibility for wild and scenic rivers. Occasionally representatives from the Bureau of Land Management and from the US Forest Service (from the Department of Agriculture) attended Alaska Planning Group meetings. Not everyone had the depth of Alaska experience Swem had, but the group was greatly aided by the work of the Alaska Wilderness Council. Unlike at the group's formation, now some of that work was done under official auspices at the behest of visionary supervisors. But much was still completed by people working in their off time, without official sanction.[8] The Alaska Wilderness Council was organized and held together by Mark Ganopole, who had been active in conservation advocacy in Alaska since 1959 and had been one of the founders of the Alaska Conservation Society and the Sierra Club's Alaska chapter. Ganopole's group included people from the Sierra Club Alaska chapter. The group became unofficial advisers to the Alaska Planning Group in Washington; the advice they gave and the maps they generated were central to the proposals the planning group and the conservation organizations made for legislation. The areas most often identified in all the proposals were the Brooks Range west of the Arctic range, the Wrangell and St. Elias Mountains, and the Lake Clark region; there were many others. This work was critical because few people in the federal bureaucracy in Washington, DC, in the national conservation organizations, and particularly in Congress, knew enough about Alaska's wild places to mark out the significant ecosystem boundaries. As the debate evolved with the implementation of the ANCSA environmental provisions, the work of these and a number of Alaska conservationists would become increasingly important.

The language in the ANCSA Section 17 provisions was ambiguous; no one knew for certain whether or not the secretary had the authority to continue the land freeze after ninety days. The national environmentalists hoped so but feared not. The (d)(2) lands were classified as national interest, that is, conservation lands, but there were also (d)(1) lands, classified as public interest, which meant Native selections and state selections. In a confrontational move calculated to capitalize on the ambiguities in the act and to advance aggressive resistance to implementing its provisions, in late January 1972 the Egan administration, predictably taking the position that the post-ANCSA ninety-day freeze did not apply to (d)(1) lands, filed selection requests with the BLM for all the as-yet-unconveyed acreage remaining from the state's entitlement in the statehood act, 77 million acres, to be taken from (d)(1) lands. Many of the selections were in areas the Alaska Planning Group and the Sierra Club had earmarked for (d)(2) withdrawal. State officials said that if their selections were not recognized, they would sue the Interior Department. The battle lines were drawn. Nonetheless, in March 1972 Secretary Morton made a preliminary report on his selections for study areas to be withdrawn within two years of passage of the act. These included 80 million acres for (d)(2) study; he did not approve the state's request for 77 million acres, instead reducing it to 35 million acres; he also set aside 40 million acres for Native regional corporations and additional land for village corporations. The conservation organizations generally approved of these proposed withdrawals, planning to do further work before the nine-month study period would expire in September.

But the state reacted negatively and swiftly. Newspaper editorials again condemned the "lockup" and the trouncing of Alaska's state rights. Senator Gravel complained loudly of the misuse of federal authority. The state's attorney general labeled the secretary's action "a one hundred thirty-five million dollar rip-off" and threatened a lawsuit.[9] Even some conservationists expressed dismay over the seeming disregard of the state's need for land with development potential. Within a month the state assembled its legal team and readied its challenge to the secretary's authority. The state demanded that all of its remaining unfulfilled entitlement, 77 million acres, be conveyed and indicated specifically which were the desired lands. If the secretary refused, the state would go ahead to court. Environmental attorneys doubted the suit would carry, but Secretary Morton seemed chastened by the vigor of the state reaction and over the summer worked with the state to craft a compromise on the issue of its selections, which the court announced in early September. In return for the authorization of immediate selection of 40 million acres that the state wanted on the south flanks of the Brooks Range, a portion of the Alaska range in the vicinity of the Wood-Tikchik region, and land south of Mt. McKinley National Park, the state accepted an out-of-court settlement of its suit.[10] It was the first time the state had been able to prize from the federal government an exception to the stalled land freeze.

Actually, the elements of the settlement had been fashioned by another agency. In an attempt to create an instrument with which a compromise might be forged, section 17(a) of ANCSA included a provision for establishment of a ten-member Joint Federal State Land Use Planning Commission, with half the members to be appointed by the interior secretary, including the governor as cochair, to represent the state; one of the state's members was to be an Alaska Native.[11] The commission was to advise Congress on the various categories of land selection.

During the negotiations over the claims settlement, one of Egan's principal advisers for the state selections was Charles Herbert, who had served as deputy commissioner of natural resources during Egan's first two gubernatorial administrations, 1959–1966. A mining engineer and locater and a steadfast defender of mining interests in the state, Herbert had been largely responsible for ANCSA's provisions for transportation corridors to facilitate access to mineral deposits on the Native lands that would be conveyed as a result of that act. When Egan threatened legal action after Secretary Morton's March announcement of the lands he selected for study, Herbert advised the governor not to settle out of court but to see the case through, advice Egan did not take. Nonetheless, when the state made its appointments to the land-use planning commission, Herbert was Egan's first choice. According to historian Daniel Nelson, Herbert controlled the commission, none of whose state members had land-planning experience and all of whom deferred to him. When they took them up, the commission endorsed Egan's demands.[12] The commission subsequently held hearings in a number of cities outside Alaska but in its final recommendations sided with the state on most points.

At the end of 1973, meeting the deadline set forth in ANCSA, Secretary Morton announced his final study withdrawals, sending a report to leaders in Congress. His recommended withdrawals totaled 83 million acres. Congress would have five years to review the proposed acreage and enact legislation delineating new or extended parks, refuges, forests, and scenic rivers, with some portion of the total to be designated wilderness. Morton recommended much less protection for areas deemed environmentally significant by the conservation organizations than in his preliminary proposals from the year before. There was less parkland and more multiple-use land, and large forest acreage had been added. The National Park Service was the premier conservation agency for environmentalists because its land-use restrictions were much tighter than those of other agencies. Multiple-use lands would permit hunting and mining and recreational use. Sierra Club and Wilderness Society spokespersons were highly critical of the report; they had expected much more land committed to stringent protection than was recommended. But the secretary had probably gone as far as he could. Congress had just passed the Trans-Alaska Pipeline Authorization Act in November, from which battle the conservation lobby was still licking its wounds. The Nixon administration was in considerable disarray, as the Watergate scandal had overtaken its capabilities. In addition, Secretary of Agriculture Earl Butz outranked Morton in the president's cabinet, and Morton had likely been forced to make concessions in order to get the acreage he did.[13] Nonetheless, the secretary's action constituted the first formal recommendation to Congress for implementing Section 17 of ANCSA, the template Congress would work with in crafting federal conservation withdrawals within the state of Alaska that were larger than the size of the state of New Mexico.

The recommendations were no surprise to Alaska's political leaders. They understood that Section 17 provided two years for the secretary to study Alaska lands; they understood that Section 17 provided that 80 million acres of Alaska would be set aside in new national parks, forests, fish and wildlife refuges, and wild and scenic rivers and that some portion of those would be designated wilderness. They had consulted with the secretary on the recommendations made by the conservation organizations. They knew what was coming.[14] But the people of Alaska did not. Few in the general public had likely followed the arcane details and confusing numbers as intermittent news stories on the Interior Department study of Alaska land had appeared over the two years from the passage of ANCSA in December 1971 to Secretary Morton's announcement in December 1973. What had most preoccupied public attention in Alaska had been the injunction prohibiting pipeline construction and the congressional battle over its authorization. The secretary's announcement sparked a storm of negative reaction from Alaska's congressional delegation, which spread rapidly across the state. Senator Stevens was reported to have become "hostile and vituperative" when briefed by an assistant secretary; many of his statements were deemed "irrational."[15] Interviewed in Anchorage, Stevens called the recommendations a betrayal of Alaska's trust in the federal government. Atwood called the report a mockery of Alaska statehood. Chambers of Commerce across the state adopted resolutions condemning the "lockup" of Alaska economic resources.[16] The *Anchorage Daily News* reported that "the state seemed to explode."[17] In retirement, Gruening took to the *New York Times* to ridicule "conservation extremists" who were bent on turning Alaska into a wilderness and zoo, disregarding entirely the interests of the people of Alaska. Countless letters to editors of local newspapers expressed worry about Alaska's future and citizens' jobs.

One editor wondered if Alaska would ever receive its just due from the federal government.[18]

"Lockup" has been a persistent charge leveled at federal land management policies and officials by politicians, journalists, and residents of the western states since the onset of conservation at the turn of the twentieth century. But the factors already noted exacerbate the rancor and anxiety of Alaskans. Alaska's small population—barely over 300,000 in 1974—the narrow, isolated, dependent economy; the long territorial history; the recency of the statehood campaign; and the postponement of selection and conveyance of Alaska's land entitlement all combine to heighten sensitivity in Alaska and to put a keener edge on federal land management issues. Even though Alaska is now fully connected through electronic communication and social media with the nation and the world, the fact of physical separation still exists; it defines self-identity and permeates personal perceptions.[19] These circumstances in combination generate a powerful sense of victimhood among many Alaskans, a sense often mirrored and deepened by the public pronouncements of the state's political elite. Such was the case throughout Congress's deliberations over the Alaska lands bill of 1980.

The Senate Watergate hearings and impeachment debates in the House Judiciary Committee culminating in Richard Nixon's resignation in August 1974 precluded action on Alaska land legislation that year. Nor did 1975 see significant action. When interest finally rekindled in 1976, the key people in Congress were Senator Henry M. Jackson of Washington state, chair of the Energy and Natural Resources Committee (formerly Interior and Insular Affairs), and Congressman Morris Udall, chair of the House Interior Committee. These gentlemen introduced legislation essentially encapsulating Morton's 1973 report; the House bill, H.R. 39, became the framework within which the Alaska lands debate took place. In the meantime, under Sierra Club and Wilderness Society leadership, sustained national interest in protecting America's environment led to the reconstituting of the Alaska Coalition, again staffed mainly by idealistic young people from across the nation willing and able to pursue their convictions through political action. At the height of its advocacy the Alaska Coalition represented nearly 100 national and regional conservation organizations. Ed Wayburn of the Sierra Club led the coalition in fashioning a draft bill representing the perspective of the environmental lobby. Based on the work of the Alaska Wilderness Council, it called for 119 million acres to be preserved with about 70 million to be designated as wilderness.[20] At the same time, Senator Stevens submitted a bill calling for 67 million acres of new withdrawals, with 40 million to be administered by the US Forest Service.[21] The two draft bills represented opposite poles of the Alaska lands battle, the conservation bill providing for nearly twice as much protected land as the Alaska bill and a far greater measure of protection for the land involved.

President Jimmy Carter's election in 1976 seemed auspicious for the conservationists. Carter was much more interested in environmental issues than either Nixon or Ford before him, and he chose as his secretary of the interior Cecil Andrus of Idaho, who had a positive record as governor with successful environmental compromises. At the same time, leaders of the national conservation lobby changed their focus so as to become more effective with Congress. Analyzing the history of the environmental movement since the Wilderness Act, historian James Morton Turner examined this change of focus and tactics as the Alaska Coalition approached H.R. 39. Where before the Alaska Coalition had maintained close and sensitive ties with local and regional conservation organizations and had relied mostly on funding from small donors, it now concentrated on tight organization with the major players, such as the Sierra Club and the Wilderness Society, and on a cadre of veteran, polished lobbyists who knew Washington and Congress and could stay concentrated on a clear, uncontested agenda. They also turned to large donors.[22] Laurence Rockefeller, for example, assembled a group of powerful and effective citizens he called Americans for Alaska who could raise large donations and could be counted on to make phone calls to wavering members of Congress at critical moments. Among Alaska environmentalists, and some smaller regional groups across the nation, this shift in focus seemed an arrogant disregard of local people and their concerns, a disregard felt keenly. For all that, however, the coalition still comprised tens of thousands of common citizens spread across the nation, held together by ever-widening circles of communication and mobilization spreading out from a highly capable professional cadre in Washington, Denver, and San Francisco, the loci of the coalition leadership. Wilderness advocates and the defenders of Alaska in Washington, DC, and around the country, however strong the resentment of the new centralized leadership, were poised and ready to loose their capabilities on Congress in the spring of 1978, for the five years ANCSA had provided for passage of a lands act would run out with the close of the Ninety-Fifth Congress.

Some thought they saw signs of a thawing among Alaska's political leadership. In 1974 moderate Republican Jay Hammond had been elected governor on a platform of "responsible conservation." He was often quoted as saying he believed Alaskans wanted their land neither "locked up" nor "ripped off."[23] In 1977 Hammond introduced an idea into the discussion that he hoped would bring compromise and give Alaska a greater role; he called it comanagement. In exchange for the state accepting a limited amount of protected federal land, 37 million acres in the four conservation systems (parks, forest, fish and wildlife refuges, and wild and scenic rivers), Hammond's fifth system would be 62 million acres of "resource lands" that would be managed by a joint federal-state commission; management would be based on "prime uses," either traditional uses on the land involved or what the commission decided was the best use of the land.[24] Several Alaska Native leaders endorsed the plan, provided that Native groups would have a role in comanagement as well.[25] In the Senate Stevens introduced a separate bill based on Hammond's plan, but it gained few sponsors and no traction.

The plan likely would have assuaged Alaskans' anxiety about "lockup" of the state's lands. But as various analysts contemplated the challenge of maneuvering through Congress, and likely the courts, a compromise of federal sovereignty, the prospect was too daunting for most to imagine, even if there had been a willingness by federal officials to entertain it. For the most part, there wasn't. As it turned out, Hammond was adamant that without comanagement, he would not support any broad-scale restrictions on the use of federal land in Alaska. Perhaps Hammond thought that politically he had no choice. Soon conservationists both in Alaska and Outside realized he would not be in their camp. Historian Nelson quotes Congressman John Seiberling as saying Hammond's uncompromising position reminded him of "the Russian approach: what is ours is ours; what is yours is negotiable."[26]

While Hammond was refining his ideas on comanagement, the Alaska Coalition, capitalizing on Carter's election, brought to fruition the conservation lobby's conception of what an Alaska lands bill should include. Udall introduced it in the House and Lee Metcalfe of Montana in the Senate. It provided for 115 million acres of reserves, including new parks and refuges; 45 million acres would be designated wilderness. The bill included portions of the Tongass and Chugach National Forests, which had been excluded from much of the prior discussion. This was the bill labeled H.R. 39; it would go through a number of permutations before finally becoming law nearly three years later.

The amount of wilderness was its most distinguishing element; no other plan for Alaska had proposed that nearly half of the land set aside would be managed as wilderness. In that regard the plan was both daring and provocative.

The swift and vigorous Alaska reaction was by now predictable and expected. Senator Mike Gravel attacked the presumption of the conservation lobby in its disregard of potential Alaska mining and jobs represented by the limited use permitted by the wilderness designation. The Alaska Chamber of Commerce resolved that Alaskans must resist the second-class citizenship the bill would impose on them. The Alaska legislature voted to allocate $5 million of its fast-flowing petrodollars to a campaign to oppose the bill. Two citizens' groups formed to raise funds and expertise to fight the measure. Citizens for the Management of Alaska Lands represented the mining and timber interests invested in Alaska; member groups included the Teamsters, who had grown wealthy and powerful with cost-plus contracts during pipeline construction; the American Federation of Labor and Congress of Industrial Organizations; and the National Rifle Association. The REAL Alaska Coalition drew from sport hunters and the various guiding organizations; many guide lodges catered to the nation's wealthy elite who came to Alaska in the summer to hunt and fish in the wilderness during the day and enjoy oysters Rockefeller and prime Angus beef for dinner.

Congressman Seiberling would play a critical role in the debate that would develop in 1977 as Udall and Metcalfe worked H.R. 39 through the committee process. Born into a wealthy Akron, Ohio, family, Seiberling had grown up spending his summers in wilderness areas. Committed to wilderness protection and elected to Congress the year after passage of the National Environmental Policy Act, he had led a campaign to prohibit hunting in national parks. In the spring of 1977, when he was taking up H.R. 39 in the House Interior Committee, Udall appointed Seiberling chair of a new subcommittee on Alaska lands that he created. As historian Turner outlined, the Sierra Club and the Alaska Coalition defined Alaska as a national cause. They saw Alaska's wilderness as a national treasure, a valued and fragile possession of the people of the nation, one seriously and immediately endangered. Though they had been slow to become aware of that danger, the battle over the Alaska pipeline had been their epiphany. The danger arose from the two-pronged power Alaska acquired in its statehood act: the authorization to select 104 million acres of land for state title; and the state's commitment to economic development, certain to be destructive of the Alaska wilderness, however necessary it was to the state's economic future. The environmental "crown jewels" in Alaska were not Alaska's; they were the nation's. Udall had captured the concept in the title he gave to H.R. 39: the Alaska National Interest Lands Conservation Act.

With the Alaska Coalition, Seiberling understood that congressional success would depend on embedding in American national consciousness the idea of Alaska as an environmental national treasure. His Alaska lands subcommittee provided him with a mechanism for doing that. In the summer of 1977 he decided to hold hearings on H.R. 39 in five cities spread across the contiguous states as well as the several towns and a number of small villages in Alaska. Many members of Congress at the time did not imagine H.R. 39 was more than a minor matter, a backwater issue when compared with such concerns as national defense and the space program; neither did Seiberling. The subcommittee staff planned for small numbers of people at each of the hearing sites. But the Sierra Club and the Alaska Coalition put their broad network of grassroots organizers to work publicizing the hearings and urging people to testify. The response amazed everyone. The committee heard testimony over seven days in Washington, DC, and a full day each in Chicago, Atlanta, Denver, and Seattle before moving to Alaska for full-day sessions in Anchorage, Fairbanks, Sitka, Juneau, and Ketchikan and twenty days in smaller communities. At every site in the contiguous states enormous crowds turned out: businesspeople; ordinary citizens with an interest in conservation, often with a history of hiking or canoeing or the like; mothers with babies; elementary and secondary school students concerned that their opportunity for future outdoors experience not be lost. In city after city the committee had underestimated the room and time that would be needed. Testimony in the lower states was nearly uniformly supportive of a strong Alaska bill, perhaps as was expected. One of the biggest surprises of the process was the reaction in Alaska. In Anchorage, over the full day of witnesses, fully half were supportive of H.R. 39; in Fairbanks more than half. Seiberling and his fellow committee members took back to Washington the realization that many Alaskans thought environment and economic development could be compatible, or at least that those who did think so were willing to appear in public to say so. The political leadership of the state clearly did not speak for everyone. From the viewpoint of Seiberling, Udall, and the Alaska Coalition, the hearings succeeded beyond anyone's imagining.

Still, there were many in Alaska who strongly opposed the bill. Unsurprisingly, when they realized that people all over the country were taking the measure of Alaska as if it were their own, and as they came to understand what was at stake for them, many Alaskans reacted viscerally with their own sense of possession. It was they, after all, who had separated themselves from their families to move north to the frontier, as many imagined it, who invested their resources and psyches in making a home on the far edge of civilization, enduring the long, dark winters and the high cost of basic goods, communication, and transportation. And, too, they thought that by so doing, they had earned the right to enjoy the unparalleled hunting, fishing, and outdoor recreational opportunities that made Alaska a paradise for many. Most of all, they worried about their businesses and their jobs. Alaska's future depended on development of the state's natural resources. If access to them was to be cut off permanently, what would sustain Alaskans in the future? Responding to the new, national context of the fight, Senator Stevens and Congressman Young employed their own tactics. Stevens charged that those who testified in Alaska in support of H.R. 39 were not true Alaskans. They were Sierra Club plants imported from Outside or fair-weather types who came up to Alaska in the summer for two months and merely called themselves Alaskans. He would repeat the charge throughout the rest of the congressional debate over the bill. For his part, Young complained that all the testimony at the hearings in the lower states had come from Sierra Club professionals, organized and paid, he claimed, by the club and other groups in the Alaska Coalition. He, too, would repeat his charge throughout the campaign.

Udall had worked H.R. 39 through committee challenges and rewrites unscathed. In fact, reflecting the resilience and effectiveness of the Alaska Coalition's nationwide effort, the bill had grown. The final version that came to the House floor in May provided for 124.6 million acres in the four systems, with 65.5 million to be designated wilderness. It was a conservationist's dream and an Alaskan's nightmare. And to the dismay of its opponents, it passed the House handily, 277–31. The vote did not tell the complete story, for nearly a third of the House had not voted, doubtless knowing the outcome and expecting the actual law to be agreed to by compromise in the inevitable conference committee following a vote in the Senate. The strong showing in the House, though, was a strategic advantage for conservation; it would strengthen Udall's leverage in conference.

Senator Mike Gravel, however, had decided that he would not allow an Alaska lands bill to become law on his watch. Because of numerous delays in committee, Senator Jackson was not able to get the bill onto the Senate floor until October. Swift work was needed to complete work on the bill before adjournment, but at that late date there was barely enough time for floor action, let alone a conference committee workup. The only possibility was for the Senate to pass a bill close enough to the one that had passed the House that a conference would not be necessary. But Gravel made it clear that he would filibuster whatever Jackson might bring forward. A last-minute ad hoc conference with Secretary Andrus and Jackson, Udall, and other Senate and House members, including Stevens and Gravel, produced only rancor. Gravel would not allow even an extension of the time limit, a contingency Andrus had planned for. Action was stymied, and Congress adjourned with no Alaska lands act.

Alaskans in Washington and at home breathed sighs of relief. It was unclear what might come next, but for the moment the threat of the economic paralysis in Alaska seemed to have passed. But their reprieve did not last long. Fearing just such a possibility, Chuck Clusen, the Sierra Club's chief public lands lobbyist, who headed the second Alaska Coalition, had met with one of President Carter's chief advisers to urge as a contingency the use of the Antiquities Act, which authorizes executive withdrawals of the public lands. Carter discussed the possibility with Secretary Andrus, who shortly made known his intention to recommend presidential action if Congress failed to agree on a bill. Senator Stevens warned colleagues in the Senate that he expected Antiquities Act withdrawals if the Senate failed to pass a bill, but Senator Gravel pushed ahead with his plans for a filibuster nonetheless.[27] But President Carter's use of the Antiquities Act was not a foregone conclusion. When he learned of the possibility, Governor Hammond approached Secretary Andrus. With the congressional deadline for 17(d)(2) withdrawals expired, the state believed it had the right to continue its selections under the statehood act. If the secretary would promise not to use the act, the state would not select lands that were included in H.R. 39, having already obtained valuable lands it wanted in the out-of-court settlement back in 1973 when Secretary Morton had made his recommendations. Andrus was attracted to the deal. But within weeks, Hammond's commissioner of natural resources filed a request for conveyance of 9 million acres for state title in areas included in H.R. 39 that conservationists considered extremely sensitive. Andrus felt he'd been double-crossed. If he had any reservations about recommending withdrawals under Antiquities, he now set them aside and urged President Carter to move ahead. Carter agreed, and on December 1 Andrus held a news conference to announce Carter's withdrawal of 56 million acres of Alaska as new national monuments. The secretary closed to mineral entry or state selection an additional 40 million acres and, on the recommendation of the secretary of agriculture (the US Forest Service is in the Agriculture Department), withdrew an additional 10 million acres of national forest land. Virtually all of the areas slated for withdrawal in H.R. 39 were now part of the federal management system, most designated as monuments, and were protected from development. At his discretion, the secretary had the authority to make many of the withdrawals permanent until Congress might take action. Congressional action would supersede any executive withdrawal, but no one knew when, or if, Congress might act. Also, there was no precedent for Congress overturning an executive withdrawal of conservation land. Carter and Andrus may have thought of the withdrawals as a tactical maneuver to force Congress to act. But whether or not Congress acted, environmentalists had at least gained extraordinary political leverage and, should Congress remain stalled, significant protection of the "crown jewels."

The Alaska reaction was defiant, aggressive, and sometimes malicious. The Hammond administration went to court to request an injunction to stay the withdrawals. Within two days the court rejected the request, citing the president's authority under the Antiquities Act. The Alaska legislature resolved that the federal action was illegitimate and not binding on Alaska citizens. The president's actions, one publication proclaimed, constituted a "big federal land grab."[28] Atwood used his *Anchorage Daily Times* to encourage civil disobedience, urging Alaskans to ignore the new monument boundaries and the restrictive rules that went with them. The REAL Alaska Coalition organized what it called the "Great Denali Trespass," a snowmachine caravan into areas that had been added to Mt. McKinley National Park.[29] Call-in radio hosts castigated the president and Secretary Andrus, and numerous groups organized citizen marches and printed rebellious bumper stickers. In more than one venue, Carter was burned in effigy. When Andrus proceeded with plans to implement administration of the new monuments, federal land management personnel encountered hostile resistance. When a National Park Service ranger task force arrived in Alaska to manage the new withdrawals, members often found themselves unwelcome and sometimes in danger. Businesses in Bettles and Copper Center refused to serve them. A ranger who sought dental treatment in Anchorage was told to go elsewhere. In Eagle, Alaska, headquarters for a vast wilderness on the upper Yukon River, residents posted signs saying they could not be responsible for the safety of federal employees. Gunshots were fired through the office window of one ranger, and an arsonist torched a private plane that had been hired by two others. Several Forest Service rangers in Haines reported sugar poured into the gas tanks of their trucks.[30] Such incidents, though the irrational acts of angry individuals, reflected the general mood in Alaska, which was sullen, uncooperative, and resentful. There were Alaskans willing to speak out for environmental protection, but when it seemed that economic livelihood might be on the line, self-protection seemed to motivate many more.

In Washington Udall and the Alaska Coalition pushed ahead. Coalition leaders, though, reported that the opposition was much stronger than in previous sessions. The state legislature had allocated an additional $2 million for a national advertising campaign that included full-page ads in metropolitan newspapers across the country explaining the state's position. Groups representing Alaska's construction industry, its banks, and the oil companies invested there funded full-time lobbyists to counter the young staffers of the Alaska Coalition. Coalition leaders sensed that the mood of the country was changing. Conservatives gained seats in both the Senate and House; in California voters approved a property-tax-cap initiative. President Carter had delivered a television address on the national energy crisis. Udall had found considerably more resistance to H.R. 39 in his House Interior Committee and lost a critical vote on moving it to the House floor. Instead the committee sent forward a comprehensive but weaker committee substitute. Nonetheless, on the floor Udall succeeded in resubmitting his own, stronger version, and conservation-friendly members held together to defeat several amendments that would have weakened it again. When the final vote came on May 16, the new H.R. 39 passed the House handily, 268–157, a dramatic victory for conservation and a blow to Alaska's hopes.

That moved the action to the Senate, and there Alaska's Ted Stevens had an antidote he had used before: delay. With the Senate free to pass its own bill, Stevens hoped he could use its rules and procedures to shape much-diminished legislation while at the same time wearing down the opposition. Because the Senate was also busy with energy policy, the Panama Canal Treaty, and other contentious issues, markups of various versions of a bill moved at a glacial pace through committees. At the end of the 1979 session nothing was ready, and everything migrated to 1980. Again Stevens was successful in keeping the pace slow, until July, when a bill finally emerged on the Senate floor. There Gravel took over, using such time-honored tactics as requests for amendments, clarifications, and consultations to keep it from coming to a vote. Finally he simply resorted to filibuster. But there was large support for what many in the body considered a fair level of protection of America's Alaska environment, even if not as much protection as environmentalists desired. The Senate cut off Gravel with a cloture vote of 63–25.

Broad environmental sentiment in the nation was real, not the province of an effete core of impudent snobs who characterized themselves as intellectuals, as Spiro Agnew had said of opponents of the Vietnam War a decade earlier. Congressman Don Young particularly had routinely painted environmentalism as a conspiracy hatched by insensitive idealists funded by a moneyed elite who wanted Alaska as a wilderness playground for themselves and their progeny. Understanding the reality of conservation strength in the country, manifested in the readiness of the Senate to pass a bill, Stevens accepted the inevitable. On August 18 a bill sponsored by Senators Jackson, Mark Hatfield of Oregon, Paul Tsongas of Massachusetts, and William Roth of Delaware came to the Senate floor. It protected 104 million acres of Alaska in the four systems, providing for 56 million of those to be designated wilderness. Knowing it would pass, before the vote Stevens held a press conference in his office that was intended mostly for domestic consumption back in Alaska. He said Alaska had obtained nearly everything it wanted in the bill—everything except hunting in national parks and mining the wildlife refuges. "We will be back for those," he said, "when the American people wake up."[31] He also said ominously that he would not allow the Senate bill to go to conference with the House bill and that he would filibuster any changes anyone proposed. When he returned to the floor, the Senate passed the bill 78–14.

But in the House, Udall found the Senate act unacceptable, as did the Alaska Coalition. The House bill had 119 million acres and more restrictions on the use of those, prohibiting oil drilling in the Arctic Refuge, for example, and permitting less access across reserved land for transportation corridors. Discussions between representatives of the two bodies carried on in desultory fashion until Congress adjourned for the election recess in early October. Everyone wanted to wait to see how the election went.

For the conservationists, it did not go well. The traumatic events of the 1970s, including Watergate, the energy crisis, the decline of industry, the defeat in Vietnam, the Iranian hostage crisis, and rising taxes, had taken a toll on American confidence. Many believed the liberal politics of the 1960s and 1970s had gone too far. The failure of the requisite number of states to ratify the equal rights constitutional amendment, which Congress had passed and sent to the states in 1972, may be taken as representative. Five states that had ratified before the initial 1979 deadline rescinded their approval. Arguments in the campaign against the amendment included family values and maintenance of traditional gender roles; a favorite symbol was American apple pie. Another example is the Tellico dam on the Little Tennessee River and the snail darter fish. Many Americans were incredulous that a tiny fish in an isolated habitat protected by the Endangered Species Act should halt construction of a dam. Ronald Reagan capitalized on what Jimmy Carter had called national "malaise," winning election in November 1980 on a platform of restoring America, implying that it had been damaged by the liberal policies of the 1960s and 1970s. Reagan won 51 percent of the popular vote, Carter 41 percent; Reagan won the electoral vote of forty-five states. More important for conservation and the Alaska lands act, Republicans took control of the Senate from Democrats.

The writing was on the wall. Rather than start over in a conservative-dominated Senate in a country clearly turning right, when Congress reconvened after the election, Udall, having consulted with Alaska Coalition leaders, signaled that he would accept the Senate bill. It passed the House by voice vote on November 12. President Carter signed it into law on December 2, 1980. A decadelong saga had ended; section 17 of ANCSA had been realized.

The Alaska National Interest Lands Conservation Act has been celebrated as one of the three most significant pieces of conservation legislation ever enacted, along with the National Environmental Policy Act of 1969 and the Wilderness Act of 1974. It set aside in new conservation units 104 million acres of Alaska land. It doubled the national wilderness system, adding over 56 million acres. Ninety-nine million acres were put into national parks and national fish and wildlife refuges. It expanded Mt. McKinley National Park and changed its name to Denali National Park;[32] it expanded the Arctic National Wildlife Range and changed its status to wildlife refuge. It used the designation "preserve," less restrictive than "park," for a number of additions. It created the 7-million-acre Gates of the Arctic National Park and Preserve, the more than 8-million-acre Wrangell–St. Elias National Park and Preserve, and the 2.5-million-acre Lake Clark National Park. It created nine new fish and wildlife refuges and expanded many others, including the Alaska Maritime National Wildlife Refuge. It added twenty-five rivers to the national wild and scenic rivers system. It added 3 million acres to the Tongass and Chugach National Forests and designated 5.3 million acres of wilderness in the Tongass. It threw over America's environmental crown jewels a reasonably secure blanket of protection that Alaska conservation advocates had barely dared to imagine when the Alaska Wilderness Council had mapped out its dreams on Mark Ganopole's floor in Anchorage between 1967 and 1972.

ANILCA was a compromise bill, and as Stevens made clear in his office address on the day of its passage, there were also important protections for Alaska's distinct interests.[33] Perhaps most important, subsistence harvest of traditional resources was emphasized as a primary purpose for creation and management of the units; subsistence harvest, however, was limited to rural residents.[34] One and a half million acres of the coastal plain of the Arctic National Wildlife Refuge were set aside as a study area for oil and gas potential. Since creation of the Arctic wildlife range in 1960 and the development of the gigantic Prudhoe Bay oil field after 1967, geologists had determined that the area east of the Canning River likely did contain substantial oil and gas deposits. Congress was free to open the coastal plain for exploration and subsequent development at its discretion, following a comprehensive survey of fish and wildlife resources and seismic testing for oil and gas deposits. The FWS reported to Congress on the results of the survey at the end of 1986. In the Tongass National Forest a boundary was drawn so as to exclude conservation protection of a US Borax mining operation. Also, a number of forested areas were left open for logging. Forty million dollars annually was provided to support timber sales of 4.6 million board feet of timber harvest annually to support the logging industry, sawmills, and two pulp mills at Ketchikan and at Sitka.[35] The designation "preserve" was used for some of the lands administered by the National Park Service, which designation indicated fewer restrictions on use. A transportation corridor was left open across a portion of Gates of the Arctic National Preserve to facilitate mining, and other transportation corridors were guaranteed. National Petroleum Reserve–Alaska (formerly National Petroleum Reserve No. 4) was left intact. Lost in the anticonservationist rhetoric that infused debate over the bill was the fact that the federal government would spend millions of dollars annually to manage its conservation lands in Alaska and that those lands would attract tourist dollars to the state.[36] The new preserves permitted hunting, and mining on preexisting claims. In a highly significant concession, the act prohibited future presidential land withdrawals in Alaska of more than 500 acres without congressional consent. As Stevens noted, the state achieved most of its objectives in the final version of ANILCA.

After his presidency, President Carter often repeated his comment that ANILCA was the legislation passed during his presidency of which he was most proud. From a conservationist perspective it was a stunning victory, one that captured the national aspirations for preservation of Alaska wilderness that had matured during the congressional fight over the act. The protected lands in Alaska stand as a monument to modern American environmentalism. For Alaska, ANILCA is bittersweet. As he left the Senate in 2009 after forty years, Ted Stevens said that ANILCA was the greatest disappointment of his life and that protecting Alaska from conservation was the most important thing he had been unable to do for the state.[37] Most Alaska political leaders have taken their cue from Stevens's statement; for many, ANILCA represents a failure, a quashing of the promise of statehood to open Alaska to major new investment and development. Although it is unclear that this is true, it is an article of faith among countless of Alaska's citizens. Grist for that mill comes from the myriad challenges involved in implementing the complex regulations needed to manage the various areas to which the act applies, some of which are discussed in chapter 7. Historian Turner argued that ANILCA is bittersweet for the environmental movement as well. Although it was an extraordinary accomplishment, at the same time it established precedents for inroads on environmental protection with the allowance for subsistence harvest in protected areas, including the use of motorized vehicles and other exceptions. More substantively, it helped to generate a populist countermovement against environmentalism while at the same time encouraging resource industries to seek their own exceptions on federal land.[38] As will be discussed, this aspect of ANILCA helped to redefine wilderness before the academic community addressed what William Cronon called "the trouble with wilderness": it is peopled.[39] The drafters of the ANILCA law had to confront that fact and allow for it as they worked to throw the mantle of protection over many a rural Alaskan's "food locker."[40]

Yet in Alaska politics and culture, ANILCA is not the default object of complaints about the diminution of state sovereignty and citizen and investor opportunity. That is, instead, what is interpreted as Congress's disregard of the statehood "compact." Alaskans certainly have joined with protestors in the western states in a demand that federal land in those states be turned over to the states, the failure of the Sagebrush Rebellion notwithstanding.[41] But in Alaska that demand has its own unique aspect, as noted earlier. It is related to statehood, and the fact that Alaskans feel still that the federal government betrayed its statehood promises in both ANCSA and ANILCA. As we shall examine, Alaskans were willing to pour state resources into a vain attempt to get people to pay attention to their grievance.

Ernest Gruening while serving as Alaska territorial governor. Gruening helped lead the campaign for Alaska statehood. (Alaska State Library)

Interior Secretary Stewart Udall (far right) with Native leader Emil Notti (center) and Alaska governor Walter Hickel in 1967 as Udall suspended Alaska state land selections authorized in the statehood act. (University of Arizona Library)

Native leader Don Wright, 1971, president of the Alaska Federation of Natives, which led the campaign for a comprehensive settlement of Alaska Native land claims. (Alaska State Library)

Walter Hickel, Alaska governor, 1966–1970. Hickel challenged Interior Secretary Stewart Udall's suspension of Alaska state land selections; later, as Alaska governor, 1990–1994, Hickel unsuccessfully sued the federal government for breach of statehood promises. (Alaska State Library)

Senator Mike Gravel and Governor Jay Hammond greet
President Jimmy Carter, arriving in Anchorage during the
environmental campaign for a strong Alaska lands act. (Alaska
State Library)

US Senator Ted Stevens addressing the Alaska state legislature as Governor Jay
Hammond looks on during Alaska's challenges to congressional legislation on Alaska
lands. (Alaska State Library)

Congressman Morris Udall of Arizona in 1978. Udall led the environmental lobby in the US House, campaigning for a strong Alaska lands act. (Alaska State Library)

Willie Hensley in 1971. Hensley was one of several young Native leaders who led Native advocacy for land claims in Alaska. (Alaska State Library)

Jimmy Carter's interior secretary, Cecil Andrus. He withdrew millions of acres of Alaska land as national monuments when Congress failed to enact an Alaska lands bill in 1978. (Idaho Historical Society)

Alaska US senator Lisa Murkowski. She claimed Alaska sovereignty was violated by President Obama's endorsement of US Fish and Wildlife management policy for the Arctic National Wildlife Refuge. (Office of Senator Lisa Murkowski)

Tongass National Forest, a continuing battleground between Alaskans and others who advocate additional harvesting of timber against other Alaskans and allies who work to extend preservation of the forest. (US Forest Service)

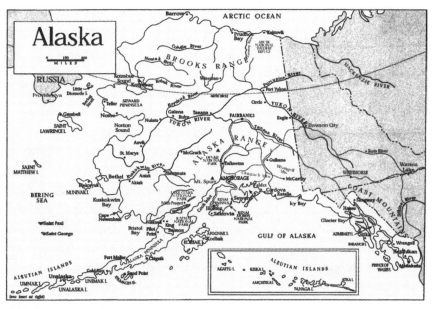

Map of Alaska. (Alaska Geographic Society)

CHAPTER 6 UNFINISHED BUSINESS: SUBSISTENCE AND THE TONGASS

The ardent, populist cadre who staffed the Alaska Coalition in the 1970s was motivated by an abstract conception of wilderness. From their wilderness experiences, most imagined pristine, unpeopled landscapes unmanipulated by human intervention. The numerous compromises necessary to carry the Alaska legislation forward were for most environmentalists a diminution of their idealized notion of nature, whose sublime character inspired awe, reverence, and even fear. Even those more stimulated by ecology and the science of nature held an idea of nature as free of human influence, with natural systems left to their own devices to evolve toward their distinct destinies. They shared this vision of the wild with the tens of thousands of their grassroots supporters who made the phone calls, wrote the letters, distributed the flyers, and testified at the hearings that formed and drove the broad national political base that resulted in ANILCA and other environmental triumphs of the 1970s, including the Wilderness Act and even the National Environmental Policy Act. The environmental historian William Cronon critiqued this wilderness concept in his brilliant 1995 seminal essay, "The Trouble with Wilderness."[1] Although the idea might seem "natural" to those who hold it, it is in fact culturally constructed, a romanticized notion of pristine purity we impose on the natural world that does violence to its reality but transports us from the failures and shortcomings of our own human existence to something we experience or imagine as sublime. As conservation transitioned to environmentalism after World War II, the community of environmental lobbyists set out to isolate and preserve this vision of nature, of wilderness, in actual landscapes. The conservation of the early twentieth century emphasized multiple use; commodification of natural resources, wildlife habitat protection, water management, and recreation were the principal uses, with preservation for those lands that seemed to have no practical benefit. Environmentalism rejected use in favor of preservation, elevating preservation to the primary goal of conservation policy. Howard Zahniser sought to capture and impound nature sublime with the Wilderness Act of 1964 and brought a willing nation with him.[2] The ideal of that act is landscapes absent of and unmanipulated by humans, untainted and uncorrupted by the work of humankind. In the act, Congress offered a legal definition of the vision: "an area where earth and its community of life are untrammeled by man, where man himself is a visitor who does not remain."[3]

But there is no such nature, nor wilderness. Humans have always lived in and utilized nature; it cannot be otherwise. Humans have always drawn their sustenance from earth's resources; to do so they have necessarily manipulated and altered those resources.[4] Still more fundamentally, the human presence in nature is at odds with a conception of nature as pristine and unmanipulated, untrammeled. The concept is false because it is based on that which is not. Moreover, most of those in a position to act on the concept, the vision, are not those who are closest to the nature they envision, those whose livelihood depends on their direct interaction with nature. Cronon emphasized that the greatest beneficiaries of urban-industrial capitalism are often those most anxious and able to escape it, if only momentarily, by decamping to a wilderness retreat where after a day of fly-in fishing or guided hunting they might enjoy not just their oysters Rockefeller and Angus beef but crème brûlée for dessert. Cronon could have been paraphrasing Alaska's Senator Stevens decrying the witnesses at the Seiberling hearings in Anchorage and Fairbanks, who, he charged, were fair-weather sojourners whose lives did not depend on the nature they so revered. The loggers in the Tongass National Forest whose work is classified as among the most dangerous of all occupations have a distinctly different wilderness experience while setting chokers on newly felled, behemoth logs than do those sitting in their camp recliners around prebuilt campfires swapping insights on their stock options. For Cronon and his environmentalist colleagues in the 1990s, the discussion and parsing of the wilderness idea was abstract and theoretical.[5] For Alaskans anxious about the state's economic future and fearing for their jobs and feeding their families, the interaction with nature is direct, daily, intensely human, and very real.

In his essay Cronon lamented the tragedy of indigenous people being forced off their land so that it can be made into the false vision of wilderness embraced by modern environmentalism. "The romantic ideology of wilderness," he wrote, "leaves precisely nowhere for human beings actually to make a living from the land." This is the reality federal managers faced when they approached the complex task of implementing ANILCA in the 1980s, for the Alaska they encountered was a peopled wilderness. Confronting his ambivalence, Cronon expressed his understanding that anything that encourages us to think that we are separate from nature is likely to reinforce environmentally irresponsible behavior; at the same time he acknowledged his belief that we must recognize and honor nonhuman nature as a world we did not create. We must in our experience of nature, he counseled, find the capacity to marry the nonhuman and the human, the sublime and the real. Had academic environmentalists followed the reality of the implementation of ANILCA in the 1980s, they would have witnessed, and been informed by, the intricacies and nuances of just such a marriage, for Alaska's land managers were of necessity quite ahead of the curve in recognizing the falsity of the Wilderness Act.[6]

Interpreting, organizing, and implementing the requisites of ANILCA was a challenge worthy of Solomon. Pursuant to ANILCA, the Interior and Agriculture Departments were called upon to administer thirty-four conservation units in Alaska, in national parks, fish and wildlife refuges, monuments, conservation and recreation areas, national wild and scenic rivers, and the Tongass and Chugach National Forests. Subsistence harvest of traditional resources is a significant aspect of the management regime of these units. Federal administrators must master the difference between managing the 47 million acres of new units that are not wilderness and the 56.7 million acres that are, together with all the exceptions built into ANILCA meant to facilitate development. During the early negotiations leading to passage of the act, leaders of the Alaska Coalition wanted no hunting in wilderness areas at all. It did not take long for them to understand that this position was untenable. It was both logistically and politically impractical. The final House bill, reflecting the environmentalist rejection of inhabited wilderness, included subsistence only for three areas in remote far-northwest Alaska. But the Senate bill that became ANILCA when the House acquiesced following the 1980 election provided that subsistence is a priority use for all of ANILCA lands.

As part of the statehood act, in 1960 management of fish and game was transferred to Alaska state government. This included management on federal lands in Alaska, a policy consistent with that in other states of the Union. But in 1980 ANILCA provided that the state would continue to manage fish and game on federal lands in Alaska only if the state provided a rural preference for subsistence harvest so as to be consistent with the federal law. Knowing there would be resistance to the rural preference, drafters of ANILCA directed that the federal district court in Alaska would hear any claims that the state was not implementing the rural preference provision properly. By the end of the 1970s Alaskans were generally sympathetic to Native lifeways and their pursuit. Moreover, with the passage of ANILCA, state land selections resumed; Native selections pursuant to ANCSA proceeded apace. Virtually all state selections were complete by 1994, though negotiations and court cases involving some parcels would continue for many years afterward.[7]

The foremost federal management principle dealing with people in wilderness Alaska mandates a rural preference for "customary and traditional" subsistence harvest. Just who is rural and who is nonrural is an ongoing discussion.[8] "Customary and traditional" is defined as "a long established, consistent pattern of use, incorporating beliefs and customs which have been transmitted from generation to generation and play an important role in the economy of the community."[9] Anticipating the federal legislation, in 1978 the Alaska legislature adopted the state's first subsistence law. The Alaska Federation of Natives lobbied aggressively for the act. It defined subsistence as "customary and traditional" use and established subsistence as the priority use of fish and wildlife. It created a Division of Subsistence and directed the development of regulations to allow subsistence harvest wherever biological surpluses permitted. But, both reflecting the difficulty of the definition and cognizant of the opposition of non-Native rural and urban residents, it did not explain who was a subsistence user.

Soon after passage of ANILCA, acting on both that act and the state legislature's 1978 subsistence law, the state boards of fish and game promulgated regulations applying a rural preference for subsistence harvesting. The vociferously negative reaction across the state by now seemed habitual. Hunters organized against the regulations and the law on which they were based. Sam McDowell, a Fairbanks outdoorsman, became the primary spokesman for the opposition. He formed a group called Alaskans for Equal Hunting and Fishing, which began a drive to place an initiative on the state general election ballot that sought to prohibit classification by race, sex, or other categories for harvesting fish and game; it would eliminate the rural preference law. "It is an unfair law that treats Alaskans unequally," said one supporter. "I have lived in Alaska since 1949, and I am a friend of the Natives and I neither fish nor hunt. But this is symbolic of how far things have come." McDowell argued that eventually, because of decreasing game stocks, the law would favor

Natives and drive out non-Native hunters.[10] "We are not going to allow these people to whom we gave $1 billion and 44 million acres of land to disenfranchise us," he said.

Natives countered with their own group, Alaskans for Sensible Fish and Game Management. Charles Johnson, president of the Bering Straits Native Corporation, told a reporter, "Natives are quite willing to divide this state racially to achieve their end." Willie Hensley of Unalakleet, then a bank president and later president of AFN and subsequently an oil lobbyist in Washington, DC, said, "What is at issue is a lot more than calories. Nobody is going to stop the Eskimos and Indians from hunting and fishing."[11]

Non-Native spokesmen for the hunters decried the racial rhetoric. It was not a racial issue, they insisted; it was a sovereignty issue. Their sentiment echoed another initiative on the 1982 general election ballot, an expression of the Tundra Rebellion. Ronald Reagan's interior secretary James Watt had encouraged the Sagebrush Rebellion in the western states, the movement to transfer ownership of federal lands in the western states to those states, inspired in part by the closing of homesteading in the Federal Land Policy and Management Act of 1976. Most western states had passed legislation, resolutions, or initiatives calling for those transfers, and in 1982 Alaska voters entertained a similar initiative; the movement in Alaska acquired the name Tundra Rebellion.[12] For Alaskans it was a way of striking back at a federal government they felt had betrayed the promise of a secure economic future for Alaska by postponing state land selection, instead granting acreage to Natives and locking up over 100 million additional acres in conservation.[13] The Tundra Rebellion initiative passed with 73 percent of the vote,[14] whereas the rural preference prohibition failed, 58 to 42 percent. The consensus among postelection commentators was that voters had reacted negatively to the injection of racism into the debate. Nonetheless, antipreference sentiment would grow into an intractable conviction in Alaska.

Immediately after the failed vote on his initiative measure, Sam McDowell filed suit in state court challenging the state's subsistence regulations. In a decision that served as a harbinger of things to come, soon afterward the state supreme court ruled that the state regulations enforcing a rural preference violated the state constitution. In response, the legislature passed a new subsistence law in 1986. It limited subsistence to rural residents and this time defined "rural": areas "where non-commercial customary and traditional use of fish and game is a principal characteristic of the economy." The boards of fish and game were directed to identify resources that were "customary and traditional." Again, McDowell filed suit. In 1989 the Alaska Supreme Court gave McDowell the ultimate victory, ruling that the state's rural preference law violated the "common use" clause of the natural resources article in the state constitution. A rural preference, the court declared, was not common use.[15] The state now was fully out of compliance with ANILCA, and the secretary of the interior warned that if it did not come into compliance, most likely by adopting a constitutional amendment that would allow a rural preference, the federal government would take over management of fish and game resources on federal and adjacent lands and waters in Alaska.[16]

For most Alaskans, subsistence was not a racial issue. Repeated polls showed broad support for a constitutional amendment. But a steadfast minority in the Alaska legislature interpreted it as a state's rights issue and blocked passage of a constitutional referendum. Three successive governors, Steve Cowper (D; 1986–1990), Walter J. Hickel (R; 1990–1994), and Tony Knowles (D; 1994–2002), submitted constitutional amendments and called special sessions of the legislature to deal with the issue, all to no avail. To little surprise, supporters of a rural preference did accuse its opponents of racism. A leader of the sovereignty clique, state senator Dick Bishop of Fairbanks—who was an officer of the Alaska Outdoor Council, which claimed 10,000 members statewide—responded that the charge was "pure nonsense." "We support subsistence hunting for rural Alaskans," he said, "but they should not be discriminated against on the basis of their zip code or the color of their skin."[17] Native leaders formed an Alaska Economic Boycott Committee, which urged a boycott of all Alaska Outdoor Council activities and businesses that supported them. The AFN announced that it would deny its annual fall convention, an economically significant gathering, to Fairbanks, Anchorage, and Juneau until those communities showed support for a constitutional amendment. Answering the challenge, the Anchorage municipal assembly put on the April 2002 primary ballot an advisory referendum urging the legislature to pass an amendment.[18] There were several marches in the city supporting the measure. The vote passed overwhelmingly, but the legislative minority blocking action was unmoved and successful in preventing the two-thirds vote of each house required for an amendment to be sent to voters.[19]

In the meantime, following his success in state court, McDowell sued in federal court to eliminate the rural preference from ANILCA, charging that it contravened the equal protection clause of the US Constitution. But the federal courts rejected the challenge, confirming federal authority under ANILCA.[20] At the same time federal courts upheld a Native claim to ancient fishing rights on navigable waterways in the state. ANILCA provided that the state had jurisdiction over navigable waterways, the federal government over non-navigable ones. In 1964 the state had moved the fishing site of an Athabascan (Ahtna) Indian woman, a grandmother and village matriarch named Katie John, arguing that her site threatened spawning salmon. She sued the state and the US Interior Department for failing to protect her aboriginal right.[21] Losing in lower courts, the state twice appealed to the Ninth Circuit appeals court and lost. The case was remanded, and following the Anchorage advisory vote in 2002, Governor Knowles announced that the state would not appeal again.[22] A Fairbanks state senator called for Knowles's impeachment.[23]

The long state debate over subsistence contributed to the hardening of Alaskan attitudes toward federal authority in Alaska, despite the broad support for a constitutional amendment to confirm a rural preference. Because opposition to the amendment could so easily elicit charges of racism, in a period of the rising legitimacy of Alaska Natives in public consciousness, that charge was generally rejected. Supporting the constitutional amendment was a way of allowing Alaskans to show respect and support for Natives. Not long after the state abandoned the Katie John case, the federal government took over fish and wildlife management on federal and adjacent lands. But the establishment of close cooperation between federal and state managers mitigated the impact, and the issue passed from public debate. Alaska remained out of compliance with federal law, but the public left the complex issues surrounding implementation to the bureaucrats. For most Alaskans, Katie John's victory was their victory, too, and brought what they knew about the complex matter to resolution.

In 1990 federal managers published temporary subsistence and other regulations, making few changes to regulations the state had been enforcing. There soon followed the establishment of a Federal Subsistence Board, which functions as the primary policy body for Alaska, representing the authority of the Departments of Interior and Agriculture. It comprises six members: the chairperson, appointed by the secretaries, and one member each from the US Fish and Wildlife Service, the National Park Service, the Bureau of Land Management, the Bureau of Indian Affairs,[24] and the US Forest Service. Headquartered in Anchorage, the board meets twice annually, once to consider wildlife issues and once to consider fisheries, which were added to the board's responsibility following the success of the Katie John suit. In addition to recognizing subsistence harvest as the highest consumptive use of resources, the board is obligated to protect and perpetuate fish and game populations and to distinguish among subsistence users when stocks of those populations necessitate such distinctions. Subsistence is defined as customary and traditional use, further defined as "a long established, consistent pattern of use, incorporating beliefs and customs which have been transmitted from generation to generation and play an important role in the economy of the community."

The board takes recommendations from ten regional advisory councils made up of rural residents. Meeting twice a year, the councils consider subsistence proposals for fish and wildlife, hear from subsistence users, and make recommendations to the board. The board can reject recommended proposals only if they are not supported by substantial evidence, do not conform to principles of fish and wildlife conservation, or are detrimental to subsistence needs. The regional councils are aided by regional subsistence resource commissions made up of biologists and other technical staff and by subsistence users. The commissions, which had been provided for in ANILCA before the Federal Subsistence Board was established, not only provide technical advice but also establish some continuity among regions. They are the "boots on the ground" people in terms of research knowledge and often find themselves between users and the board, as when, for example, users want to take fish when the science mandates closure of a fishery to perpetuate the resource. Moreover, they sometimes must interpret for users in the regions the inconsistencies that result from the turnover of board and agency personnel as managers circulate into and out of Alaska in various career assignments. In particular, some National Park Service personnel have experienced difficulty in Alaska, where, because of inhabited wilderness, hunting is permitted and motorized vehicles are used, a violation of most park rules in the contiguous states.

Though perhaps the most important ANILCA management challenge in Alaska, subsistence is not the only one. Numerous conflicts have arisen from federal and state perspectives on interpreting how restrictive ANILCA's various requisites should be. The intent of the act may be inferred from its preamble, which restates the sublime and scientific vision Zahniser and others carried into the Wilderness Act a decade and a half earlier: to preserve the "unrivaled scenic and geologic values associated with natural landscapes, to provide for . . . wildlife populations of inestimable value, to preserve . . . unaltered arctic tundra, forest and coastal rain forest ecosystems . . . and to preserve wilderness resource values."[25] But the perspective that obtains at any given moment in time can substantially alter the interpretation of what the statement of intent may mean in practice. One of the critical compromises in the act was a prohibition of any presidential land withdrawals of more than 500 acres without congressional consent. That is both constraining and liberating, for it creates a useful level of stasis, or at least a framework within which everyone has to work. But ANILCA can be remarkably malleable. In their administrative policies, federal managers have sought to limit oil and gas activity, road building, logging, mining, and off-road vehicle use and to prevent private ownership of small parcels in remote and incompatible areas that would result in increased traffic and services that would impinge on the wilderness integrity of the land and waters.[26] Environmental historian Ken Ross has evaluated some of the resulting, persistent clashes that have characterized the differing views of what Congress meant.[27] Naturally, most conflict has arisen from the state's pursuit of economic development opportunities. The act authorizes the president to open any federal conservation units for development in case of emergency; it permits roads, power lines, and pipelines to cross unit land and guarantees rights-of-way to inholdings for state, Native, and private owners; and it allows maintenance of cabins that existed prior to the date of the enactment of the law. Conservationists thought these provisions, which they considered concessions, gave the state adequate and sufficient access.

ANILCA provided for an Alaska Land Use Council intended to establish cooperation between federal and state land managers. Given a ten-year life span, the council included representatives of the heads of federal and state agencies and Native corporations. The federal and state cochairs were high-level officers, and the council had a broad mandate to make recommendations regarding regulations, plans, studies, policies, programs, and more. An active staff did most of the work and came to consensus on many issues, including access regulations, boundary reviews, and wild and scenic rivers guidelines. The council also facilitated understanding of ANILCA exceptions through federal plan review and approval. These exceptions included hunting and trapping in some of the Alaska national parks and the use of planes, helicopters, and motorboats on the preserves. On some refuges Fish and Wildlife allowed timbering, off-road vehicles, and snowmachines. The BLM permits some form of mining on most of its land. As the sunset limit approached, the council became mired in partisan politics that exposed serious disagreements; Congress did reauthorize the body. But federal reserve managers needed an official procedure for assessing subsistence needs and for protecting vulnerable species. In many cases they had to innovate and exercise a high level of individual responsibility. Users were not always happy with their decisions.

The year after ANILCA's passage, the state legislature created a Citizens' Advisory Commission on Federal Areas. It gave voice to Alaskans' specific concerns regarding implementation. Intended to aid the Alaska Land Use Council, it became a sounding board for state citizen complaints and, rather than assuaging those, often exacerbated them. Because of its rancorous effect, the state did not renew its funding after ten years. Right from 1980, however, the state had a powerful ally in Ronald Reagan's interior secretary James Watt. Committed to development and intensely antienvironmentalist, in a somewhat covert attack on environmentalism Watt instructed Interior Department officials to find ways to "open wilderness areas."[28] Under his leadership Interior's highest natural resource priority became maximizing private acquisition of oil, coal, and other minerals on federal land and minimizing protective federal regulations. Watt encountered considerable resistance in Congress, however, and as a consequence sought to implement his policies through executive action and agency budget constraints. As an example, in Alaska he attempted to use an ANILCA provision for boundary adjustments and land exchanges to approve a Native request to establish a base camp with a port and airfield on St. Matthew Island in the Bering Sea to support oil drilling in the Navarin Basin of that sea. A conservation support group, Trustees for Alaska, successfully sued on behalf of the Sierra Club, the Wilderness Society, the Audubon Society, and others to block the project. St. Matthew Island was designated wilderness in ANILCA. In another example, in 1990 the state used its authority over navigable waterways to grant mining permits in Denali National Park, basing its claim on a trip made by rubber raft in water 6 inches deep. But Denali National Park and Mt. McKinley were iconic symbols of America's environmental responsibility, even for most Alaskans, and the public outcry was so significant that the Hickel administration decided to rescind the permits. Also, as will be discussed farther on, the Agriculture Department in the 1980s encouraged timber sales and road building on the Tongass National Forest. Numerous environmental suits challenged the activity. Ted Stevens wrote into ANILCA a specific exception for the US Borax Company to mine in Misty Fjords National Monument, a wilderness area, in the Tongass forest. The mine would have been one of the world's largest, with a discharge pit 2 miles long and 1,800 feet deep. Tailings would have been piped down a valley to an inlet of the ocean. Though the mine was in a "doughnut hole" within the wilderness area, the tailings pipe, and a road and a power line, crossed the wilderness. The Sierra Club requested the Environmental Protection Administration to deny permission for the discharge plan, which the EPA did, based on the Clean Water Act. As the price of molybdenum declined, the company abandoned the project.[29] There were many instances of mining operations successfully operating within wilderness or less-protected areas, facilitated by the exceptions in the act and by use of the navigable waterways doctrine before the decision in the Katie John case. But state and private owners had greater success in retaining inholdings and pursuing construction improvements than they did with mining, mostly because environmental groups used legal defense funds and legal challenges to force the management agencies to tighten implementation and enforcement of their rules and regulations.

James Turner recounted in his study of modern environmentalism the change of focus from legislative to judicial and executive remedies and initiatives in the 1980s and after. That strategy evolved quickly in Alaska as environmentalists were confronted with development activities that they found inconsistent with the spirit of ANILCA. Even before ANILCA, in 1974 Trustees for Alaska, a nonprofit legal defense agency committed to environmental protection, formed to assist on Alaska conservation issues. In 1980 environmental enthusiasts established the Alaska Conservation Foundation, which solicits funds from donors across the nation to support legal work, advocacy, and grassroots conservation organizations. One of the founders was Denny Wilcher, who had worked through the 1960s and 1970s at the Sierra Club with David Brower as the club's in-house fund-raiser.[30]

For the State of Alaska, these actions by the national environmental community represent unreasonable and unwelcome impediments to development that could create Alaskan jobs and capital. Alaska is huge, far larger than twice the size of Texas. Development-minded Alaskans still argue, as they did when protesting hunting regulations in the territorial period, that the small impact that economically desirable projects will have on the whole should justify their undertakings. So state resentment smolders when federal land managers seem to favor an environmental interpretation of the act. For example, agencies have used the authority for wilderness and other "studies" to begin to formulate proposals for additional withdrawals that might be taken to Congress. The Park Service used a definition of "traditional" to ban the use of snowmachines within the original boundaries of Denali Park. "Traditional" has been an issue, also, in matters of access, including roads and trails. In a highly politicized and dramatic episode, the Park Service, arguing the wilderness character of the land, forbade access to an inholding being used by an extended family of homesteaders in Wrangell–St. Elias Park and Preserve.[31] As one analyst noted, the federal agencies pursue a "closed until open" policy with regard to access while the state pursues an "open until closed" policy. On wilderness land, the two contenders differ on such things as the use of chainsaws, tent platforms, fish ladders, and off-road vehicles.[32] These and other complexities often provide grist for the resentment many Alaskans reflexively feel whenever confronted with federal authority.

In 2007 Fairbanks state representative Pete Kelly secured passage of a bill to revive the Citizens' Advisory Commission on Federal Areas. Although the ostensible purpose for reconstituting the commission was cooperation with ANILCA agencies, the mission statement belies a cooperative approach: "The commission is responsible for identifying and reducing negative impacts on Alaska and its citizens from federal actions on any of the 239 million acres of federal land in the state, and shall consider research and hold hearings on the consistency with federal law and congressional intent on management, operation, planning, development and additions to federal management areas in the state."

Under the gubernatorial administrations of Sarah Palin (2006–2008) and Sean Parnell (2008–2014), Alaskans' resentment of federal actions in the state seemed to grow and to be manifest in numerous challenges to agency and executive department constraints. As political rhetoric seemed to escalate, in August 2013 the citizens' advisory commission held a "federal overreach" summit in Anchorage. Its objectives were to "examine the legal promises made to Alaska at statehood by the federal government for accessing, managing and developing our lands and resources"; to "document specific examples of how the federal government has failed to honor those promises"; and to "develop achievable state and Congressional policy initiatives and redouble efforts to reverse federal actions that infringe on Alaska's sovereign right to manage and access its land, water and wildlife resources and maintain the Alaskan lifestyle."[33] Commission officials called the meeting a major success, citing 175 presentations and discussions on a wide variety of subjects. Yet no discernible direct action proceeded from the meeting, which seemed to some a harkening back to the failed Tundra Rebellion of the 1980s.

For many Alaskans, federal ownership and management of state land is an unjust and intolerable affront to the state's right to control its destiny. The reference to federal promises at statehood and to infringement on the state's sovereignty originating in the statehood act is also now a venerated Alaska tradition, an example of a deep bitterness still harbored by unreconstructed pioneers.

Few conservation battles have so fully manifested the clash between environmental protection and economic development as the Tongass National Forest in Southeast Alaska. The forest covers 17 million of the 18-million-acre, 300-mile-long Alexander Archipelago lying along the Pacific Northwest coast, the Alaska Panhandle, an area somewhat larger than the state of West Virginia. The original forest was set aside by President Theodore Roosevelt in 1905 and 1908. From soon after World War I the Forest Service worked to establish investment that would use the forest, following the early-twentieth-century canon that, as for all resources, the highest and best use of a forest is to use it, to commodify the resource. Though some early conservation leaders wanted preservation of some areas of the Tongass, it was not until after World War II and Congress's passage of the Tongass Timber Sales Act of 1947 that preservation advocates began to challenge the utilitarian, utilization doctrine there. When they did, they found that the Forest Service was unsympathetic to the wilderness idea and to preservationist and recreational values and was in the main not open to discussion of them. For their part, Alaska political leaders viewed advocates of preservation as blinded by their idealism to Alaskans' need for development that would sustain settlement and ensure their children's futures. In their clashes with environmentalists, Alaska's leaders had powerful allies in the Forest Service and the timber industry, the latter of whose investors were eager to take the risks involved in harvesting the forest and proved themselves ready to play unfairly and illegally to maximize the profitability of their ventures.

The silviculture of the early twentieth century, developed in such citadels of forest science as the Yale School of Forestry,[34] played a significant role in how the Tongass would be classified. The forest is home to the largest tracts of old-growth timber in North America, trees that have attained great age, often over 500 years, without substantial disturbance. They exhibit unique ecological characteristics, including diverse species of differing heights that provide habitat for wildlife, multilayered canopies and canopy gaps, and a forest floor with organic coverings of forest debris. Such forests provide ideal living conditions for a wide variety of species of animal and plant life. For environmentalists, they are ancient treasures to be honored and preserved for future generations. But for forest scientists of the old school, old-growth trees represented nothing optimum because they are "overripe," taking up space that could be occupied by second-growth stands that would be sufficiently mature for harvest in seventy-five years. Old-growth stands should be clear-cut, they believed, to create proper conditions for a new, monocultural forest that would comprise 25 percent more trees that would be easier to harvest because all would be virtually alike in character. For the silviculturalists, old-growth forests were dead forests. But the timber and pulp industries were highly covetous of the old-growth forests because the large trees contained easily obtainable board feet of potential profit.

The silvicultural view of the Tongass forest had no greater devotee and advocate than B. Frank Heintzleman. Heintzleman went to work for the US Forest Service soon after earning a graduate degree at the Yale School of Forestry in 1910. After a few years in the Pacific Northwest, he was transferred to Alaska at the beginning of World War I. He would spend the rest of his life in Alaska, with the exception of three years, 1934–1937. He was assistant regional forester, 1918–1934; then regional forester, 1937–1953; then territorial governor of Alaska, 1953–1957, and on the University of Alaska Board of Regents and adviser to the Alaska Rail and Highway Commission until his death in 1965. He was throughout his career dedicated to the economic development of Alaska. Unlike other apologists for Alaska economic development, he is virtually unknown in the state today.

Heintzleman had only one view of a forest. He articulated it clearly in a 1950 address to the National Academy of Sciences Alaska Science Conference: "As is readily apparent to the many persons who sail along the Inland Passage of the Alaska coast, these rugged national forest lands are primarily valuable for timber growing." Small tracts might be available for "homesteads, residence tracts, summer homes, town sites, resorts, industrial sites, fur farms and water power development. Mining claims can be filed, roads and trails constructed." The reason for government ownership of the forest, he stated, is "for the sustained production of forest crops."[35] He believed his role was to use the government's resources to facilitate private industrial development. Profitable private development, he held, would establish economic sustainability for an Alaska population. This would be the US Forest Service vision of the Tongass Forest for virtually all of the twentieth century, and for most of Alaska's leadership for the same period.

Heintzleman understood that lumber from Alaska, however good its quality, could not successfully compete with product from British Columbia and the Pacific Northwest because of the distance from markets. Where Alaska could be competitive, he reasoned, was with wood pulp for paper and other products. But his first attempts failed. Investors undertook five projects before 1927; all were unsuccessful, though one operated briefly at Speel River. After World War II, however, when the nation experienced a newsprint shortage, investors had incentive to try again.[36] As discussed in chapter 3, Native land claims were a potential problem that Congress solved with the 1947 Tongass Timber Sales Act. That act authorized the Forest Service to enter into fifty-year contracts with logging companies so as to guarantee an uninterrupted supply for the pulp investors. Justifying what was essentially a subsidy by the high costs associated with investment in Alaska, Congress provided that proceeds of the timber sales would be held in escrow until the courts sorted out Alaska Native land clams—money for the Natives if they prevailed, for the Forest Service if they did not. Consistent with Forest Service silviculture, the logging plans for the mills included tens of thousands of acres of clear-cutting, much of it of old-growth timber.

Heintzleman could get only the two pulp mills established on the Tongass forest; the one at Ketchikan opened in 1954 and the one at Sitka in 1959, the latter Japanese-owned.[37] Throughout the negotiations in Congress and with the pulp and logging companies, Territorial Governor Gruening and Congressional Delegate Bartlett were steadfast Heintzleman allies.[38] Part of their motivation stemmed from a provision in the timber sales act that 25 percent of timber sale revenue would go to the territory and, later, state.[39] For the pulp mills, the fifty-year contracts included a requirement for bilateral agreement on any alteration of the terms, securing the companies from the possibility of the Forest Service or the government suddenly cutting their supply. The 60,000 people that Heintzleman thought five mills could support was equal to the total population of Alaska in 1940. It was an ambitious, and overly optimistic, dream for Alaska, one that beguiled Gruening and Bartlett, and most other Alaskans who knew of it.

After statehood, and after Congress's passage of the Wilderness Act, in 1965 the Forest Service negotiated a third fifty-year contract with St. Regis Paper Company. Nineteen sixty-five was not 1947, and conservationists raised concerns about the ecological impact of clear-cutting as well as other issues. St. Regis encountered financing problems, and three years later the Forest Service gave the same contract to US Plywood–Champion Papers. But by then environmental sentiment ran high in the United States, and NEPA was enacted the following year. When the company announced plans to construct a $100 million pulp plant near Juneau, the Sierra Club, along with the Sitka Conservation Society and other locals, sued to stop the project. In 1960 Congress had passed the Multiple Use–Sustained Yield Act, directed toward forcing the Forest Service to honor other use-policy obligations along with commodification. The Sierra Club suit charged that in managing the Tongass, the Forest Service was violating the 1960 act. The timber sales to support the new pulp mill were planned for Admiralty Island. Admiralty Island was iconic wilderness, though not legally designated so until 1978. It was famous for its scenic exceptionality and as home to an extensive, and famous, population of brown bears.[40] Conservationists had petitioned for its protection numerous times, always unsuccessfully. Without official protection, it was subject to Forest Service harvest policies, and the service planned clear-cut sales for nearly the entire island for the US Plywood contract, projecting that sufficient new-growth timber would mature to harvest size in 100 years. The suit was significant for all Forest Service lands in Alaska, for the multiple-use mandate opened an avenue for protection of some areas. The Sierra Club argued that clear-cutting most of Admiralty Island amounted to single, not multiple, use.

In the end, US Plywood gave up the contract, but not because the court agreed with the Sierra Club argument. Ed Wayburn, president of the Sierra Club in the 1960s, had become enamored of Alaska's environmental sublimity and was especially charmed by Admiralty Island. Through an independent investigation he learned that in fact, in order to satisfy the quantity of timber specified in the contract, US Plywood would have to clear-cut the island every fifty years. The Forest Service calculations were off by half. With that information, the case was remanded, and the company threw in the towel. The importance of the episode was its revelation of the subservience of the Forest Service to the doctrine of commodification of the resource to foster Alaska's economic development.

For environmentalists seeking to preserve old-growth forest in the Tongass and to save its scenic grandeur for future generations, litigation seemed the most promising strategy. The Sierra Club sued in 1972 to require environmental impact statements for every proposed timber sale; the Forest Service wanted a single EIS for the whole forest. Several local conservation groups sued to prevent timber sales too close to small communities, to prevent roads being built into communities that did not want road connections, and to prevent clearcutting. The Forest Service made some accommodations on its own and was forced into others as a result of court actions. But by the end of the 1970s wilderness advocates had lost hope that much of the Tongass would be protected.

As described in chapter 5, the debates over authorizing the Alaska pipeline and over the Alaska lands act were intense in Alaska as citizens watched and waited while their land selections were on hold and people far away and not always very knowledgeable about conditions in the state debated Alaska's fate. Nerves were raw. People known to be favorable to conservation measures were sometimes unwelcome in their communities. Alaskans who were committed to an exclusive development viewpoint sometimes socially shunned environmental activists, and those who held an environmentalist perspective sometimes had to suppress knowledge of their organizational affiliations in order to keep their jobs and their community relations. However, local residents found themselves allied with environmentalists in some communities where logging operations had negative impacts. In 1985 local protest in Juneau stopped the Forest Service from building a logging road through a popular recreation area near the city. At Tenakee Springs, residents sued the Forest Service in 1986 to prevent a road near the community. The court agreed with the demand for an individual environmental impact assessment and eventually prevented construction.

As the 1970s drew to a close, both Alaskans concerned for their economic future and the national environmental community expressed great hopes for the pending Alaska lands act. As it turned out, Alaska development fared better than the conservationists. The act prohibited logging and most other kinds of development on 5.4 million acres in the forest, including most of Admiralty Island. Most of that would become designated wilderness. But to guarantee a continued supply of timber to the pulp mills, and to several sawmills in Southeast Alaska, Senator Stevens was successful in writing into the legislation the mandate for the harvest of 4.5 billion board feet of timber every decade. The federal treasury would provide $40 million annually, tied neither to the congressional budget process nor to timber sales, to facilitate the mandate with surveys, road construction, and whatever else might be necessary. Four hundred fifty million board feet was about the amount of timber harvested from the forest annually at that time; 275 of the 450 million annual harvest was dedicated to the pulp industry. The future of pulp on the Tongass Forest seemed secure.

Alaskans saw ANILCA's favorable positioning of the logging and pulp industries in Alaska as a fair balance with the environmental withdrawals and as their just deserts. The annual appropriation, Stevens argued, was "the cost of taking the wilderness areas out of the harvest cycle." The vice president of the Alaska Loggers Association asked why taxpayers shouldn't pay for timber sales. Other industries received federal subsidies—general farming and tobacco, for example. The intent of the subsidy was "to keep jobs in the American economy." If people wanted the subsidy eliminated, then the wilderness reservations should go with it.[41] Critics called the harvest target "mining the forest," for the rate of cut was so great as to violate the sustained yield principle; the forest couldn't recover within any reasonable time frame. Only about 10 percent of the old-growth portions of the forest were protected.

The Forest Service was not the only object of environmentalist criticism. ANCSA granted Alaska Natives about 600,000 acres of forestland in the Tongass. The regional corporation, SEALASKA, implemented a financial strategy based on liquidating its timber allotment to raise cash for investments and to pay dividends to shareholders. Unencumbered by federal or state environmental regulations, SEALASKA and its member village corporations pushed contractors to harvest quickly and carelessly. Harvesters high-graded (taking only the best trees, cutting poorer stock out of the way and leaving it to rot) and clear-cut up to stream banks and on steep hillsides, causing landslides that destroyed salmon streams and damaged wildlife habitat; they simply ignored the idea of sustained yield.[42] The Southeast Alaska Conservation Council (SEACC) publicized the devastation, but the corporation protested that in order to generate the revenue it needed to pay annual shareholder dividends, it had no choice but to utilize one of its few assets.

Agitation by environmentalists over the failure of ANILCA to protect much of the Tongass began almost as soon as the act became law. Logging-company operations and actions of the pulp mills, the negative publicity generated by Native corporation exploitation, the Forest Service resistance to accountability, and the machinations of Alaska's congressional delegation all played into the environmentalists' hands. The pulp mills pumped toxic effluent into the waters around their plants. The companies fired whistle-blowers and falsified their records. Investigations by the EPA uncovered numerous violations, and the companies paid fines more than once for violating the Clean Water Act. When the EPA threatened to put one of the mills on the pollution Superfund list, the congressional delegation fought the listing. When the EPA persisted in its investigations, Senator Frank Murkowski, who had replaced Mike Gravel in 1980, threatened to cut off the agency's funding. When an independent logging firm sued the two pulp mills for collusion and antitrust violations resulting from their driving down the price paid for logs, the public learned of the companies' secret agreements not to bid against one another and the use of false bidders at timber sale auctions.[43]

ANILCA required the Forest Service to report to Congress on timber harvesting in the Tongass Forest at five-year intervals. Conservation organizations took advantage of the requirement to call for public hearings. Ken Ross analyzed the environmental campaign to revise the forest provisions of the act, as did former Portland Oregonian reporter Kathie Durbin.[44] The SEACC arranged a national tour coinciding with the hearings to raise national consciousness, then staffed a Washington, DC, office to lobby Congress. The National Taxpayers Union signed on because receipts from timber sales came nowhere near the cost of holding the sales and funding the roads required by the leases; there was no incentive for the Forest Service to be accountable with the guarantee of the $40 million annual subsidy.

Environmentalists' publicity focused on the peril to old growth in the Tongass, the last such appreciable stands on the continent. In a remarkable turnabout, even the Alaska Department of Fish and Game joined the crusade. Scientific work had demonstrated the need for varied species of trees for a healthy forest. Studies showed that forest-floor debris was necessary for a healthy ecosystem and that Sitka black-tailed deer needed it for cover and forage. Wolves also needed undergrowth for protection and denning. Once again the Sierra Club published effective full-color magazine and coffee-table-book spreads glorifying the forest and its wild denizens for broad public consumption. Both *Reader's Digest* and the *New York Times* weighed in with lengthy articles on the inefficiency of the Forest Service bureaucracy and on the practice of the logging and mill companies firing employees critical of their operations, as well as the magnificence of the forest as a national environmental asset. As noted in this book's introduction, 500-year-old old-growth trees were being sold for an unconscionably low price.[45]

Again, Alaska's congressional delegation fought for Alaska jobs and the state's economic future. When a reform bill was introduced, Murkowski managed to hold it out of debate several times. Congressman Young attacked environmentalists as careless and insensitive to the dependence of Southeast Alaska wage earners on logging and pulp-mill jobs. The mayors of Sitka and Ketchikan testified that their communities could not survive economically without the employment provided by the pulp mills in their towns.

Two developments spelled trouble for opponents of reform. Much of the log production that did not go to the pulp mills went to the Asian market. But in the 1980s that market began to collapse. Steel and plastics began to replace construction lumber on a broad scale. In addition, the timber industry became far more global as rising national economies inserted themselves into the global supply. At the same time the Asian market for Alaska wood pulp began to atrophy. The Alaska mills had always been at a disadvantage because of their distance from markets, and as those markets shifted increasingly from the rayon- and other wood-based materials produced in the mills to polyester and other synthetic materials, Alaska's share of the market declined precipitously. The other problem was political. On March 24, 1989, an over-tasked crew drove the oil tanker *Exxon Valdez* onto Bligh Reef in Prince William Sound, spilling between 11,000,000 and 30,000,000 gallons of crude oil into the waters and onto the beaches of some of the most pristine and sublime wilderness landscape in North America.[46] Coming as it did in the midst of a national publicity campaign about the vulnerability of Alaska's natural grandeur and exposés on the character of its management, the oil-spill disaster played directly into the hands of critics of the Forest Service in the Tongass. Comparisons were inevitable, and those orchestrating the national campaign made the most of their opportunity.

The culmination came in November 1990 when Congress passed the Tongass Timber Reform Act. It eliminated the 4.5 billion per decade board feet cut mandated by ANILCA; it replaced the annual $40 million subsidy for timber sales and related activities with funding tied to market realities; it modified the fifty-year contracts to prohibit high-grading and other wasteful harvest methods; and it required 100-foot forest buffers on salmon streams and tributaries. It also protected over 1 million new acres in the Tongass from logging, nearly a third of that in new designated wilderness. The law provided for periodic land-use plans to be prepared by the Forest Service after review by stakeholders, which included conservation groups. For environmentalists, it was a major improvement over ANILCA. At the same time it demonstrated the sustainability of the national sentiment favoring conservation in Alaska and in other parts of the nation. And it confirmed the lobbying capacity of the national conservation organizations.

The limitations on harvesting methods and the loss of a million acres of potentially harvestable forest were unwelcome for those focused only, or mainly, on Alaska's economic prospects, but they were not devastating. In the 1980s tourism had grown exponentially in Southeast Alaska, with several companies expanding or initiating summer cruise-ship visits with port calls at Ketchikan, Wrangell, Sitka, and Juneau. When surveyed by the Alaska tourism authority, visitors indicated their desire to see wilderness and wildlife. The Forest Service began to place forest rangers on Alaska ferry vessels plying Southeast waters and constructed or upgraded tourist facilities across the region. Logging continued, both through Forest Service timber sales and Native corporation harvesting of Native land. But, in a development that might have been more traumatic than it was, within three years the Alaska Pulp Company closed its mill in Sitka.[47] The closure eliminated 400 Sitka jobs and the property tax paid on the mill property.

To ease the impact, Alaska's congressional delegation secured passage of a transition fund to help the town weather the closure. Laments were profuse, but Sitka's mayor, who headed a transition team that focused on enhancing tourism and diversifying the local economy, commented that in the long run, he thought, Sitka would be better off without the mill, its pollution, and the bad publicity. Three years later the Ketchikan mill closed. Owner Louisiana Pacific Corporation had employed 500 people in Ketchikan. Again, the delegation generated a transition fund and a settlement that kept a company sawmill in operation for two additional years. Congress terminated the fifty-year contracts on a technicality, namely, that the companies were not honoring their harvest obligations.[48] But that was cover for two aspects of reality. The first was the market, already discussed. Second was the EPA, which directed that the mills comply with the requirements of the Clean Water Act. The companies said they could not afford the mitigation and remediation measures the EPA wanted, which were substantial, particularly in Sitka, where pollution of the waters around the mill was devastating.

The economic impact on both communities was not as severe as expected.[49] The transition funds bought time, and fishing and tourism took up the slack more quickly than townspeople had anticipated. The rancor directed toward environmentalists was strong but short-lived as the transition money and good planning finessed recovery. Wisely, conservation operatives did not engage in demonstrations of triumph. And in many ways they continued their efforts as they had before the closures. In the meantime, management of the Forest Service evolved. Although the commitment to industrialization of the forests remained a favored priority, appreciation of the aesthetic and ecological value of forest landscapes gained favor with many in the service. In 1990 retired and active USFS personnel in the Willamette National Forest in Oregon started a reform effort, founding Forest Service Employees for Environmental Ethics (FSEEE), dedicated to defending the national forests from industrialization.[50] "Together," the organization mission statement proclaims, "we must work toward an ecologically and economically sustainable future." Many Forest Service personnel in Alaska became members, protected by a new generation of legal safeguards for dissident federal workers. FSEEE echoed the lament of a retired USFS planner from Angoon who said that during his twenty years with the service he had advocated an enlightened land ethic and had trusted the Forest Service and tried to instill trust in others. Upon leaving the service, he said, he wanted "to publicly apologize to those people. . . . I convinced them that the Tongass Plan would mean multiple use on the national forest."[51]

Nationally, all three branches of the federal government were drawn into the evolution of the Forest Service. In 2001, after three years of study driven by considerable debate between logging and mining interests and national conservation organizations, the Forest Service adopted the Roadless Area Conservation Rule. The government held over 600 public hearings on the rule and received 1.6 million comments, a record for an executive order. President Clinton issued the rule before leaving office. The rule protects about 30 percent of the national forests from new road construction on the grounds that roadless areas, like wilderness, preserve habitat for threatened and endangered species and sensitive plant and animal species. Spur roads on public land inevitably lead to feeder roads that open more areas to utilization. Upon taking office that year, President George W. Bush modified the rule, permitting state governments to designate the national public lands they wished to remain roadless, a policy later overturned in federal court. Over the next decade various states either challenged the roadless rule judicially or asked the administration to order its implementation in their states. In 2006 and again in 2009 federal circuit courts affirmed most of the original roadless rule. In Congress a number of lawmakers introduced bills providing for a national roadless policy. Cost savings was an issue for Congress; in the first decade of the twenty-first century the Forest Service spent $30 million on road construction for timber sales that netted $2 million.

The Tongass forest was included in the original roadless rule, which did not affect existing roads but prohibited new construction. But in 2003, responding to Alaska's long-serving congressional delegation,[52] the Bush administration exempted the Tongass. The State of Alaska brought suit to permanently exempt both the Tongass and Chugach National Forest from the rule. Late in the year the administration agreed to an out-of-court settlement protecting some Tongass areas from road construction but temporarily exempting most of the Tongass from the rule. Unsure of the meaning of "temporary," for five years the Forest Service did not sell timber leases in areas of the forest that might be included in the roadless rule. But in July 2009 President Obama's secretary of agriculture, Tom Vilsack, approved a lease sale in a roadless area on the Tongass. In 2011 Judge John Sedwick of the Alaska federal District Court vacated the Tongass exemption and reinstated the original roadless rule for the forest. In 2014 the Ninth Circuit Court reversed Judge Sedwick but upon petition agreed to rehear the case.

There was considerable confusion about the roadless rule in the Tongass, partly because its application is complicated and also because communities, logging groups, and local conservation organizations regularly traded accusations about it. The rule contains an exception for funding roads to connect communities, so such roads would not be prevented where they were desired. The rule did not prohibit harvest for personal use. Nor did it prohibit power-line construction, most of which is done by helicopter because that method is much cheaper than road access. The rule did not inhibit hydroelectric development. And it superseded most applications of both ANILCA and the Tongass Timber Reform Act. The anxiety of resource developers was understandable; for the various court cases, the judgments—which some-times seemed contradictory to one another—generated misunderstanding and often bewilderment.[53]

For most of the fifteen years since proclamation of the roadless rule, most of the 5.8 million acres that would be included in it have not been opened to timber sales, pending finality in the litigation. In 2013 the District of Columbia District Court, the court that hears appeals in land cases, ended the State of Alaska's challenge to the rule, saying it had exceeded the statute of limitations. But the rehearing of Judge Sedwick's decision was still pending.

Many in Southeast Alaska seemed to come to understand the devastation caused by clear-cutting and by the destruction of the old-growth groves. They also witnessed the rise of tourism and its role in the local economies, as did economic analysts for the state.[54] For the Forest Service, understanding its relationship with other agencies and with the state and the public meant giving up the old silviculture commitment to commodification at any cost and changing the focus of Frank Heintzleman's vision of an economy based on an unremitting harvest of whatever trees could be reached. It meant also leaving behind the Forest Service's notion of itself as a primary driver of Alaska's economic development. Many Alaskans likely did not appreciate the degree to which evolution to an ecologically informed vision of the Tongass National Forest better represented the independence they hoped statehood would bring than did dependence on logging and pulp production.

The preceding chapters have sought to explain Alaska's exaggerated antistatism and to show how it is directed at federal environmental legislation and regulation. The most unique component of resistance to federal power in the state is a deeply held conviction that Congress and the executive-branch agencies operating in the state have violated promises made in the Alaska Statehood Act of 1958. That conviction is exacerbated by the memory of the long delay imposed by Congress, the president, and the Departments of Interior and Agriculture on the state's selection of 104 million acres of resource-rich land to be used to generate revenue to support the costs of state government. State leaders argue that the statehood act constitutes a binding compact between Alaska and the federal government that cannot be changed by either party without the expressed consent of the other. To understand the claim that Alaska's sovereignty has been trampled by the federal government, it is useful to examine the legal elements on which the state makes its argument.

In 1977 James G. Watt founded the Mountain States Legal Foundation in Denver. A libertarian public interest law firm dedicated to "the right to own and use property, limited and ethical government, individual liberty and the free enterprise system," the foundation took the lead in the 1980s in challenging federal environmental laws and regulations across the American west. Watt went on to serve as Ronald Reagan's secretary of the interior, where he encouraged curtailment of environmental regulations and supported oil and gas development on federal public lands and logging in the national forests. He believed that local and state governments are constitutionally responsible for regulating land use, not the federal government.[1] As secretary, Watt made several trips to Alaska, first during the Sagebrush Rebellion and again during litigation over timber harvesting on the Tongass Forest.[2] Before his appointment as secretary, when working as a lobbyist for the natural resources committee of the US Chamber of Commerce, he spent five days helping to prepare Alaska governor Walter Hickel for his Senate confirmation hearing as Richard Nixon's secretary of the interior appointee.[3]

At Mountain States, Watt's brand of legal confrontation with environmentalism and his commitment to the cause of divestiture of federal title to land in the western states seemed tailor-made for Alaska. A number of attorneys in the state were attracted to the kind of legal representation the foundation provided. One, Cheri Jacobus, was one of the attorneys who took on the case Sam McDowell brought against the state over the rural preference subsistence law that the legislature passed in 1978.[4] She won that case, which put the state out of compliance with ANILCA and led eventually to the federal government taking over the management of fish and wildlife on federal and adjacent lands and waters in the state.[5] She would later serve as an Alaska assistant attorney general. With others, Jacobus helped Alaska leaders craft their arguments about the statehood compact.

In 1990 Commonwealth North, a public service nonprofit in Anchorage that provides a forum for visiting speakers and forms study groups on critical issues facing the state, produced a report on statehood promises. Commonwealth North was founded in 1979 by former Alaska governors William Egan and Walter Hickel. In 1990 the organization undertook an extensive study of Alaska's relationship with the federal government. Members of the study team included Governor Hickel, a former Alaska attorney general, a superior court judge, several attorneys, a Native corporation director, Dave Hickok from the former Alaska Wilderness Council, *Anchorage Daily Times* publisher and editor Robert Atwood, and several others. The group published its findings and conclusions as a small book titled *Going Up in Flames: The Promises and Pledges of Alaska Statehood under Attack*.[6] The book laid out many of the arguments that would be used as a basis for a major lawsuit that the state would bring under Hickel's second gubernatorial administration (1990–1994) against the federal government for breach of the Alaska statehood compact. The publicity arm of the governor's office produced a video on the same theme that was distributed to all the state's school districts.

Compact theory holds that the federal union was created by the states and that states, therefore, have the final determination over the limits of federal authority. It relies heavily on the Tenth Amendment to the US Constitution, which provides that powers not delegated to the United States are reserved to the several states or to the people. Opponents of the theory argue that the union was created by the people when their elected delegates approved the Declaration of Independence and point to the opening words of the

Constitution: "We the people." The US Supreme Court has rejected the compact theory. Opponents of it often cite the assertion of Justice Joseph Story in his 1833 *Commentaries on the Constitution of the United States* that the union, created by the people, not the states, is the supreme law of the land, not a compact.[7] This has been the majority constitutional position throughout the nation's history. It was Lincoln's argument in the Gettysburg Address.[8]

In a brief foreword to the Commonwealth North book, Thomas Trotter, then president of a small private college in Anchorage, Alaska Pacific University, laid out the context for the study, the contention of Alaska's exceptionality: "The intent of this book is to alert Alaskans and others interested in the future of federal-state relationships to understand the special circumstances that led to Alaska statehood . . . [and] the special legal tradition . . . [that] poses special consideration for Alaska."[9] This is the premise on which Alaska's case against the federal government rests: that the statehood act created a special relationship between Alaska and the federal government, privileging the state with a special compact that allows it to veto actions the federal government takes in regard to lands in Alaska, should it choose, by not agreeing to them. What gives Alaskans who subscribe to this notion, a majority of the political leadership, confidence in their conviction is the use of the word "compact" in the relevant section of the statehood act: "As a compact with the United States said state and its people do agree and declare that they forever disclaim all right and title to any lands or other property not granted or confirmed to the state or its political subdivisions by or under the authority of this act the right or title to which is held by the United States or is subject to disposition by the United States." The section goes on to preserve from Alaska any lands that may be subject to Native right or title.[10] This is the only instance of the use of the word "compact" in the statehood act. Proponents of the notion of an Alaska special legal tradition argue that the use of the word in that one article applies to the whole act and means that the statehood act is analogous to a binding contract between Alaska and the federal government. They argue that the notion of a binding contract that cannot be altered unilaterally is reinforced by a plebiscite mandated by Congress in the statehood act in which voters in Alaska were asked if they approved of the act. The state presented three propositions at a special election in Alaska on August 26, 1958; first, "Shall Alaska immediately be admitted into the Union as a State?" Second, "The boundaries of the State of Alaska shall be as prescribed in the Act of Congress approved July 7, 1958 and all claims of this State to any areas of land or sea outside the boundaries so prescribed are hereby irrevocably relinquished to the United States." And third, "All provisions of the Act of Congress approved July 7, 1958 reserving rights or powers to the United States, as well as those prescribing the terms or conditions of the grants of lands or other property therein made to the State of Alaska, are consented to fully by said State and its people." The results were overwhelmingly in favor of all three propositions, 40,452 to 8,010, 40,421 to 7,776, and 40,739 to 7,500, respectively.[11] Compact proponents assert that the positive vote constitutes Alaska's agreement to a contract and that President Eisenhower's official proclamation of Alaska statehood, which included the "whereas" clause "I find and announce that the people of Alaska have duly adopted the propositions required to be submitted to them by the act of July 7, 1958, and have duly elected the officers required to be elected by that act," constitutes the United States' corresponding agreement to the contract.[12] As seen later in this chapter, the courts have not agreed with that conceptualization of the Alaska statehood act. It is somewhat ironic that the portions of the statehood act that compact theorists rely on most heavily are those in which the state and its people agree to forfeit forever any claim to federal lands in Alaska.

The charge of violation of the compact rests on the reasoning behind the extraordinary grant of land to Alaska in the statehood act, 104 million acres. Only the state of Texas has more land under state title, and that is because Texas was an independent nation before entering the American union.[13] Congress made clear that the land grant was to nurture Alaska's economic development. Section 6(a) of the statehood act begins "For the purposes of furthering the development of and expansion of communities, the State of Alaska is hereby granted and shall be entitled to select . . ." Congressional testimony on the statehood bill shows that the state was expected to select mineral-rich lands with the goal of generating revenue from leasing the land. In Section 6(i) the state is prohibited from alienating any minerals on the land, that is, selling them or giving them away in grants. If it does so, such lands revert to the ownership of the federal government. Section 6(i) mandates that the state must lease its mineral lands.[14] The thrust of the compact theorists' argument is that the federal government reneged on its commitment to the state's economic development first by interrupting and postponing the state's land selection process and then by denying the state the opportunity of selecting potentially mineral-rich land by granting 44 million acres to Alaska Natives in ANCSA and later by restricting the use of an additional 104 million acres in ANILCA.[15] Many Alaskans view the exceptions in ANILCA that provide some access and some development as compensation for barring economic development on the rest. Their sense of betrayal is intensified when they are prohibited access and utilization that they believe was promised in ANILCA, particularly the coastal plain of the Arctic refuge. They view as duplicity any congressional support for conservationist efforts to ban development on ANILCA lands and efforts to bring still more land under conservation protection, which many Alaskans view as attacks on the state and the future of its citizens.

Alaska shares with other states the broader context of the compact theory of federalism. Proponents usually cite the 1785 Land Ordinance and the 1787 Northwest Ordinance, which include the phrases "articles of compact" that are to be "forever unalterable unless by common consent." Courts have held that the ordinances do not apply to lands not included within the boundaries covered by the ordinances. Proponents often cite several court cases drawn from public land law history in which the notion of compact is used, most recently a case from Wyoming in which the court held that it found no modification of the principle that a compact between the United States and Wyoming is unalterable and obligatory. Again, the courts have found that a law applicable to Wyoming is not necessarily applicable to other states. Generally, the US Supreme Court has ruled that Congress is not bound into the future by its legislation unless it states in the legislation clearly that intends to be so bound.[16] The Commonwealth North report noted the ordinances and the judicial history.[17]

The Commonwealth North report returned repeatedly, however, to the notion of Alaska's exceptionality. "Alaska, of all states," the authors claimed, "is particularly vulnerable to federal encroachments on state authority."[18] Echoing the thrust of the later stages of the Alaska Coalition campaign for ANILCA, the authors noted that "few Californians think they own Nevada," or "few Ohioans believe they own New York," but "virtually all Americans claim ownership of Alaska." That provides the rationale, they averred, for the paternalistic view Congress had taken of the state, choosing "to become intimately involved in nearly every decision affecting Alaska and its resources." Aside from the hyperbole of the statement, it ignores the fact that Americans do in fact own 60 percent of Alaska's lands and can be judged to have the proprietary right to manage it in the interests of the American people. Alaskans assert, though, that Congress must manage its Alaska lands only in such a way as is agreeable to the people or the state. Unlike most states, the Commonwealth North report continued, Alaska has not one governor but many. The many are the various conservation unit managers who establish policy for the lands under their jurisdiction: the many parks, refuges, wild and scenic river corridors, and forests and the undesignated lands managed by the Bureau of Land Management.[19] Each of the federal areas, the report maintained, has a unique management plan that results in regulations that may be different from those that obtain on other units, making allowable uses different from unit to unit. At least one exception to that would seem to be the functioning of the Federal Subsistence Board, which strives for as much consistency as possible among the ten regional advisory councils, within the constraints imposed by local technical data. Still, if one traps for furs in a wildlife refuge, any visitors to one's operation might need approval from the refuge manager. If one owned an operational gold mine before ANILCA in an area absorbed by the Park Service, the mine might be shut down even though compliant with environmental regulations. Owners of inholdings in conservation units might have to conform their use of them to the unit manager's restrictions. The inconveniences and dislocations felt by Alaskans were and are myriad and threatening. The report's authors complained that the Alaska Land Use Council established by ANILCA to develop cooperation between federal and state land management failed completely, unlike other analysts who have suggested that it functioned usefully for most of its ten years. "As a result of political manipulations on both sides," the authors wrote, "the Governor of Alaska left the table. . . . State and federal positions on issues became polarized. Recommendations to the president and the governor were reduced to split opinions. . . . Little consensus was developed and almost no action was taken."[20] The statement takes no account of the aggressive posture of the state in the late 1980s, when, encouraged by Interior Secretary Watt, the state challenged not just the rural preference for subsistence harvesting and the Forest Service commitment to industrialization of the Tongass Forest but other ANILCA implementations as well.

Alaskans' nerves had been rubbed raw during the battle over ANILCA in the late 1970s, and much ANILCA implementation in the early 1980s kept them frayed. Then, in 1985 and 1986, the state faced financial shock as oil prices fell, state revenue shrank by 30 percent, jobs evaporated, financial institutions collapsed, and tens of thousands of people left the state. Just as oil prices began to recover and some equilibrium was restored, the 1989 Exxon

Valdez debacle jolted Alaskans yet again. *Exxon Valdez* left many feeling particularly vulnerable because in the struggle against federal environmental administration in the state, the oil industry had been viewed as an ally, pushing back with Alaskans against both federal power and environmental proprietorship.[21] It is little wonder that Alaskans felt attacked and abused.

Soon after taking office for his second gubernatorial term in December 1990, Walter Hickel determined to address head-on the matter of federal betrayal in abrogating the statehood compact. One development that contributed to his decision was a change in the federal government's allocation of funds due the state from mineral lease royalty collected on federal lands. From just before statehood, the government had passed to the state 90 percent of those funds, using the remaining 10 percent to defray the administrative costs involved in processing the leases. But beginning in 1990, the government instead began to deduct the administrative costs from the 90 percent. Ostensibly, nothing in the law prevented the government from changing its assignment of costs.[22] But in a remarkable action, in 1993 Alaska filed a suit in the US Court of Federal Claims charging the federal government with violating the statehood compact.[23] The suit charged that in the statehood act the government, knowing that Alaska would rely on revenue sharing (the 90 percent of federal mineral lease revenue) to pay for state government, promised to develop federal lands in Alaska. But the federal government had not done that. Most particularly, it had failed to develop the coastal plain of the Arctic refuge. As required by ANILCA, the Interior Department had conducted a six-year study of the oil and gas potential of the refuge, and in 1987 Secretary Donald Hodel had recommended that Congress allow oil drilling.[24] To date Congress has not been able to do so. In addition, the federal government had titled 44 million acres of Alaska land to twelve Native economic development corporations in ANCSA, eliminating the possibility of collecting federal mineral lease revenue on those acres, and in 1980 had taken another 104 million acres out of circulation in ANILCA, where it was unlikely to sanction mineral leasing. There would be no revenue sharing for Alaska on any of those lands. In failing to fulfill its promise, the state charged, the federal government violated the statehood act, a solemn compact between two parties, Alaska and the federal government, that cannot be altered unilaterally.[25] The state asked for $29 billion in compensation plus the amount of the administrative costs taken from the revenue share the state had received from the time that the government changed its method of allocation. In most respects the suit mirrored the arguments made in Commonwealth North's *Going Up in Flames*.

It was a daring and breathtaking action. It was one thing to debate compact theory in a law library or at a miners' association meeting, but to enter a formal lawsuit based on the idea, and to claim damages of $29 billion, was more than bold. Politically, the lawsuit's significance is to demonstrate the depth and tenacity of Alaska's resentment of federal presence and power in the state. Hickel styled himself a champion of that resentment, but there has been hardly any Alaska political figure in the years since statehood who has not. The ideology aside, there was an audacious irony in asking the federal government for such a vast sum of money given that Alaska receives the highest per capita federal expenditures annually of all the states. The irony is exacerbated by the fact that Alaska has neither a state income tax nor sales tax. Moreover, by constitutional provision, 25 percent of state oil tax revenue is deposited in a publicly owned investment, the Alaska Permanent Fund, a portion of the earnings of which are distributed per capita to all Alaska residents annually.[26]

Both houses of the 1994 Alaska legislature adopted resolutions supporting the suit, in the Senate 17–2, in the House 36–3. The state's attorney general expressed the great hope many Alaskans had for the suit: "We anticipate that we will achieve a resolution of the statehood promises."[27] Indicating the gravity the state attached to the suit, the attorney general contracted with one of the nation's most prestigious and expensive law firms, Heller Ehrman, White and McAuliffe, to pursue the suit.[28]

In rejecting the state's contentions, the government, represented by the Environmental and Natural Resources Division of the Justice Department, contested the reality of a statehood compact. Congress's one use of the word "compact" in Section 4 of the statehood act, the Justice Department argued, referred only to the land grant to the state, if to anything at all, not to any other part of the act, and not to the act as a whole. Not only was the statehood act not a binding contract, government attorneys said, repeating the long-settled tradition that Congress is not bound into the future unless it says expressly it intends to be, but the statehood act did not in any way mandate that the government was obligated to sell leases for mineral development.

Due to several motions for summary judgment and a number of responses and cross-motions and further responses, Judge Erik Bruggink of the court did not render a finding until 1996. When he did, his conclusions were not the definitive ones the plaintiff and the defendant were looking for. Somewhat in the state's favor, he did not say whether the Alaska statehood act was a compact or not. He said that statehood acts are sui generis; in some respects they have the character of a contract, which would indeed bind both parties and prohibit unilateral action, and in other respects they have the character of normal legislation, which would not bind Congress into the future.[29] To the state's consternation, however, he agreed with the government that in the Alaska Statehood Act, the word "compact" referred only to the grant of 104 million acres to the state. The cases the state cited to demonstrate the compact theory of federalism, he found, also referred only to Congress's land grants to the individual states, not to the statehood acts in their entirety.[30]

He rejected the state's claim that revenue sharing was a necessary component of the state's financial viability, an easy finding in the heyday of the state's independent tax revenue from oil production at Prudhoe Bay. In sum, the findings were far more a victory for the federal government than for the state. The state appealed the decision to the US Court of Appeals for the Federal Circuit, but to no avail. That court said simply, "Judge Bruggink's decision is thoroughly supported with cited and quoted authority and record evidence. Nothing more needs to be said."[31] The state petitioned the US Supreme Court, but the writ was denied.[32] The state's investment in its failed quest to demonstrate a statehood compact cost its citizens hundreds of thousands of dollars.

The Supreme Court's refusal to take up the case means there is yet no finality on the question of whether the Alaska statehood act is a compact with the federal government that cannot be altered unilaterally. But the state's failure to prevail with its best arguments presented by some of the country's best lawyers casts doubt on the validity of those arguments—doubt that might have tempered the intensity of the protestations about federal governance on federal lands in the state. And the fact that the government prevailed in much of its counterargument to the state's assertions might confirm the legitimate permanence of the federal environmental definitions and management of its Alaska lands. But there has been little diminution in the frequency or volume of Alaskans' protestations in the decades since Judge Bruggink's findings. Using the same arguments that appeared in Going Up in Flames and in the state's filing in Alaska v. United States, state leaders continue to charge that the federal government has broken its promises made in the statehood act and that its actions constitute a violation of law and a betrayal of trust.[33] Yet in recent years the federal government has sold enough leases on its land in Alaska to cover the state of Delaware. But 99 percent of those lands sit idle, waiting for energy companies to decide to develop them.[34] Bob Bartlett warned delegates about this eventuality in an address to Alaska's constitutional convention in 1956.[35] In *Going Up in Flames* Commonwealth North counseled that if Alaska were to succeed in remaining economically self-sufficient and contribute to the nation with its abundant natural resources, "it must learn to stand firm for its rights in such a manner that it wins the respect and support of the American people as a whole."[36] Hickel perhaps showed what the authors meant by this. Immediately after Judge Bruggink announced his decision, Hickel proclaimed that Alaska should fight on, that "a promise is a promise."[37]

Clearly the state's frustration is great. The complaint against the federal government is directed at the Arctic Refuge specifically and at virtually all environmental restrictions generally. Little is directed at Native corporations as a function of the 44 million acres titled to them in 1971. Criticism of Natives in Alaska is heavily politically circumscribed by sensitivity to perceived racism and because the corporations, their veneration of the land notwithstanding, have pursued development where the economic returns merit it. Environmentalism is the target because it necessarily involves land and because most of the federal land in Alaska is now in conservation units that afford some level of restriction on development activity. Yet the statehood grant of land to Alaska far outstrips any other statehood grant of land in congressional history. Political leaders' claims of betrayal are false in at least one regard: the state has received title to nearly all the land promised in the statehood act. Moreover, much of the land has mineral potential, and important parcels that have minerals were exempted from ANILCA so they would be available for state title. Nonetheless, as described later in this chapter, environmental concerns have led to potential prohibitions on some parcels, most notably the Bristol Bay watershed.

Alaskans are sensitive to environmental and other protection of their own land. They use state land and waters at a higher rate than the residents of other states, unsurprisingly as little of Alaska's land is developed and opportunities for outdoor experiences are what draws many people north. The state has designated 3.3 million acres in 123 units as state park land. Of the 5.4 million annual visitors to the parks, two-thirds are state residents. One of the largest state parks in the nation, at half a million acres, lies adjacent to the city of Anchorage, affording convenient access to all levels of outdoor experience. The state parks department says Alaskans participate in wilderness recreation at twice the national average. When the term "Alaskan lifestyle" is used by locals, it generally means some level of active engagement in outdoor recreational activity. Sport fishing is immensely popular, with salmon the primary object. Hunting is less popular, but there are many world-class hunting opportunities available on state land.

The state Department of Environmental Conservation (DEC) focuses on environmental quality, particularly of food and water. It regulates and monitors air and water quality, sets standards for and directs hazardous spill response and contamination, and manages safeguards for environmental health. The department was deeply involved in the aftermath of the grounding of the Exxon Valdez. The DEC also enforces regulations for cruise ships operating within the 3-mile limit of state waters and the inland waterways of Southeast Alaska, the Alexander Archipelago. It also oversees a village safe-water program. Many of Alaska's small, isolated Native villages do not have reliable safe-water systems or acceptable waste and wastewater disposal systems. The DEC provides financial and technical assistance for the design and construction of adequate systems for these communities. State environmental sensitivity is manifest also in an Alaska Oil and Gas Conservation Commission, which governs responsible conservation practices relating to drilling, pumping, transporting, and storing oil and gas. The department has imposed serious penalties for environmental despoliation of Alaska land and waters.

As with any public bureaucracy, the issues of dealing with environmental protection and quality and public health on Alaska state lands and waters are a function of funding, scope, and politics. And as for all other environmental issues in Alaska, economic reality establishes the context. Concern for the environment, whether as scenic landscape or in regard to quality and public health, is not the problem for Alaskans. It is a fair generalization to say that Alaskans love their environment. But a problem arises when environmental protection comes into conflict with and threatens in any way to curtail, constrain, or inhibit economic development, for Alaska's economic past, present, and future is limited to and dependent on the commodification of its natural resources.[38] Three salient projects will help to illustrate this.

Lands directly across upper Cook Inlet from Anchorage in South-Central Alaska are rich in subbituminous coal with low sulfur content, highly desirable for coal-burning operations where there is a concern with reducing sulfur dioxide emissions, an agent in producing acid rain. PacRim Coal, a company owned by Richard Bass and William Herbert Hunt of Dallas, Texas, proposes to strip-mine in a 20,000-acre lease it holds in the area; it acquired the lease in 1987 from previous holders. Proven reserves measure 770 million tons. The company projects three mining units; it hopes to mine 12 million tons annually from the first unit over a twenty-five-year period. In time the development could spread over 30 square miles. The coal will not be used in Alaska; only about 10 percent of Alaska's energy use is supplied by coal. Chuitna coal is intended for the global market. The company plans various support facilities, including housing; a mine road; an airstrip; and 12 miles of covered conveyor that will carry the mined coal to a port on Cook Inlet that the investors will build, which will include a 2-mile causeway to carry the coal from the shore to ships. The first mine site is 2 miles from the Chuitna River, a watercourse rich in salmon and salmon habitat. Several of the river's tributary creeks run through the area PacRim proposes to mine. The company plans to remove 13.7 miles of one of the streams from bank to bank, 350 feet deep. Five thousand acres are slated for development in the first twenty-five years of the project, with the potential for expanding the operation over not just this coal-rich province but also others like it in the area. PacRim estimates that operating the first mine will create 350 or more high-paying jobs, with an additional 300 or more needed during the construction period. The state anticipates approximately $350 million in lease royalties over the first twenty-five years of development. As it did before the exploitation of the Prudhoe Bay oil field, the state legislature may impose a specific corporate income tax. Alaska law requires restoration of the land after completion, but one expert testifying before a state Senate committee said everyone should understand that full restoration is not possible following the level of disturbance being planned.[39]

Many Anchorageites cast a willing eye toward the project, which in 2015 had not yet been fully permitted. In the early 1980s the state issued exploration and feasibility permits required under the Alaska Surface Coal Mining and Reclamation Act. The leaseholders completed an environmental impact statement, as required by federal law (NEPA). However, the world downturn in oil prices affected energy company viability, and no development work was undertaken then. In 2006 the company and the state agreed that new permits were required, and the company is preparing its applications. In the meantime, the Environmental Protection Administration transferred its oversight of the project to the Army Corps of Engineers, which has asked for a supplemental EIS. The various federal and state permit requirements take place in a significant environmental context: there is no Alaska state law that prohibits plowing up a salmon stream, and it has never been done under state auspices. Critics of the project worry that allowing this development to go forward will establish a highly destructive precedent, not just for Alaska but also elsewhere. They have suggested that if this project goes forward as planned, no salmon stream in Alaska, or perhaps anywhere else, will be safe. Alaska coal mining law provides for citizens to petition to have salmon streams on which people are dependent for harvest classified as "unsuitable for surface mining." In January 2010 the conservation group Cook Inlet Keeper petitioned for such a classification for the Chuitna and its tributaries. In August 2011 the state Department of Natural Resources (DNR) denied the petition. An Alaska superior court judge directed the department to undertake a second review. In the meantime, the PacRim website informs readers that beneficial changes to its project design for Chuitna have resulted in a 74 percent reduction in infrastructure footprint and a 72 percent reduction in affected wetlands. Toxic solids and waters will be collected in four settling ponds and effluent piped to Cook Inlet. Several conservation groups have been successful at raising community consciousness of the Chuitna project, which until the latest permit applications seemed not to have generated much interest. Numerous voices have been raised in protest, in letters to newspapers and blogs on news servers. At the same time, both the state and Anchorage Chamber of Commerce web pages link to the PacRim website.

Chuitna is similar to other contests between environmental regulation and economic development in Alaska, but it differs in three aspects. First, the absence of specific legislation that would prohibit the deliberate destruction of salmon habitat for industrialization places responsibility for approval of the project with the state bureaucracy, specifically the state Department of Natural Resources, which has been an ally in development of the state's resources, a circumstance that favors proponents of the project. The Corps of Engineers must approve the supplemental EIS and can request such alterations to the development plan as it deems appropriate. Second, the product of the project will not benefit Alaska directly, for all of the coal will be shipped to the global market. The state will benefit only secondarily, in jobs and in revenue from taxes and royalties. A second state approval of the permits necessary for the project would be consistent with the long tradition in Alaska of approving any economic development project regardless of the environmental consequences. Third, the precedent established by preapproval of habitat destruction could have significant implications for future industrial resource development. In the early 1960s oil industry executives wanted the state to select land between NPR-A and the Arctic refuge for state title because they anticipated that the state's oil and gas leasing and development regimes, should oil and gas be found in that land, would be more favorable to the industry than would the federal regimes.[40] Many Alaskans in 2015 were hoping for a similar favorability regarding Chuitna coal.

One hundred fifty miles farther southwest from Anchorage than Chuitna lies the genesis of one of the most significant challenges to environmental regulation since passage of the National Environmental Policy Act in 1969, the outcome of which could confirm or change the nation's environmental policies and politics. The Pebble prospect is a more than 250-square-mile low-grade copper, gold, and molybdenum deposit, perhaps the largest in the world, measured either by the amount of contained metal or the amount of ore. Parts lie near enough to the surface to be strip-mined; other parts would entail underground operations; it is over 5,000 feet deep. Experts estimate the deposit contains $300 to $500 billion worth of recoverable metals. Its scope is nearly impossible to imagine; it rivals the largest mined deposits ever known. If developed with current technology, gross annual value of the product would be above $2 billion.

Investigators for the Canadian mining firm Cominco first identified the prospect from coloration visible with air reconnaissance. In 1987 they obtained exploratory drilling permits from the State of Alaska and carried out seismic and drilling examination through 1992. The estimate then was a 500-million-ton deposit; a second drill campaign, permitted by the state and begun in 1997, doubled the estimate.[41] A deposit of that magnitude would require significant funding, and soon afterward another Canadian firm, Northern Dynasty of Vancouver, acquired the rights, and two of the world's largest mining companies, Rio Tinto and Anglo-American, along with Mitsubishi of Japan, joined with Northern Dynasty to form the Pebble Limited Partnership, tasked with developing the project.

The Pebble prospect lies about 50 roadless air miles west of Cook Inlet under a pristine, shallow valley in a wetland of ponds and lakes amid low hills between two large lakes, Clark and Iliamna. The valley is the beginning of drainage for two water bodies, one flowing into the Kvichak River, which empties into Bristol Bay far to the west and south, the other a creek that empties into the Nushagak River, which empties into Bristol Bay to the south and west. Bristol Bay is the richest and most prolific wild salmon fishery on the planet, producing upward of 40 million fish and $500 million and the equivalent of 5,000 full-time jobs annually. Hundreds of commercial fishing vessels harvest in Bristol Bay for all five species of salmon every year.[42] The Kvichak River is the world's most abundant red-salmon river. There are about a dozen Alaska Native villages in the area and several larger Native towns on Bristol Bay. About 7,500 Natives live in the vicinity or downriver from the prospect. The Natives rely on salmon and other subsistence resources and follow a subsistence-based lifestyle.

The Pebble Limited Partnership has not promulgated a specific development plan for the project, though general descriptions accompanying the applications for permits for drilling and water use provide a broad picture. The initial development would consist of an enormous open pit several thousand feet deep and 2 to 3 miles wide. The rock removed, most of which would be waste, would be stored in two artificial containment lakes behind earth embankments, the largest of which would be 740 feet high and 4.3 miles long. Hundreds of miles of new road bridged over scores of salmon streams will be needed, along with power lines and pipelines to carry fuel, and rock slurries. It is likely a submarine cable will be necessary to carry power from the Kenai Peninsula to the east. The partnership estimates 1,000 operating jobs and twice that for construction. Potentially the state would reap substantial tax revenue, though new taxes would need to be legislated. Northern Dynasty has applied for additional water-rights permits from the state.

The state and Anchorage Chambers of Commerce support the development of Pebble, as does the nongovernment Resources Development Council, and the Alaska Miners Association and most of the state's political leaders. Statewide polls have produced conflicting results regarding support of or opposition to the project. In 2008 voters rejected an initiative that would have prohibited development of the mine, 43 percent to 57 percent. Then-governor Sarah Palin opposed the measure and is given credit by some for generating the negative vote. However, in 2014 voters adopted a measure that directs that the Alaska legislature authorize or disapprove the project rather than the state bureaucracy, 66 percent to 34 percent. The measure requires that the project be deemed not harmful to salmon if approved. The Bristol Bay Native Corporation, which opposes Pebble development, supported the measure. But a minority of Natives in the region support the mine, arguing that the region is impoverished and the jobs development would create could lift the region's people economically, psychologically, and even spiritually.

The proposed Pebble prospect has generated a vigorous controversy in Alaska that has animated the public for nearly a decade. Television, print media, and bulk-mail material have inundated voters and citizens, funded by both local and Outside conservation and resource development nongovernmental organizations. Antidevelopment funders include the Moore Foundation of Intel founder Gordon Moore, electronics billionaire William Hewitt, and the private foundation of the jewelry company Tiffany's, all interested in conservation.[43] The primary issue is potential harm to the Bristol Bay salmon fishery. The fundamental debate is whether the risk involved in a project of Pebble's size and character at the headwaters of the world's most valuable fishery is acceptable. Critics argue that mining operations threaten salmon waters both in the area of the mine and downstream because of an inevitable failure to fully contain toxic discharge.[44] Pebble counters that the mine will be operated safely with no discharge and that Northern Dynasty has a "no net loss" environmental policy.[45] Even if the mine were operated without damage to the fishery, reclamation will be highly costly and incomplete, critics say, and most abandoned mines with containment basins leach toxins into the water table.[46]

The state Department of Natural Resources has since statehood produced regional management plans for various areas of state land. In 1984 the DNR produced its first Bristol Bay Area Plan (BBAP), covering about 12 million acres; the Pebble prospect lies within the BBAP. The department at that time classified the land as habitat, which would prohibit mining. But in 2005 the DNR changed the plan, classifying portions of the area as suitable for mining. The Bristol Bay Native Association sued, forcing the DNR to rewrite the plan and reclassify some land in the vicinity of Pebble as habitat. At the same time a report on the seismic characteristics of the area concluded that too little is known about fault lines and fractures in the area to estimate its earthquake risk.[47]

But Pebble's significance for the future of environmentalism is not a function of a classic debate between the risk of environmental damage measured against the benefits of development. Pebble is threatened by the agency Alaskans love to hate: the Environmental Protection Agency. In 2010 a coalition of Natives, Alaska conservation groups, and Alaska commercial fishers petitioned the EPA to conduct a preliminary review of the ecological impact of a mine such as Pebble.[48] The group could not ask the agency to examine Pebble's actual development plan because, despite having been requested by the state and by Alaska's Senator Lisa Murkowski to produce one, the partnership has yet to do so. A section of the Clean Water Act allows the EPA to block the Corps of Engineers from issuing required permits for environmental impacts on water bodies,[49] in essence, a veto on a project such as Pebble even before the submission of a development plan and application for the appropriate permits. After a three-year study of the region and what was known of Pebble's plans, including hundreds of interviews with the principals on both sides of the issue and hours of public testimony, EPA released a preliminary draft watershed assessment. The report indicated that a mine development such as Pebble's would have a highly negative impact on the region.[50] Administrator Gina McCarthy acknowledged that the EPA had rarely used the authority granted it by the Clean Water Act—in fact only thirteen times in the agency's history—and on only one of those occasions had it actually halted a project, a small agricultural development. But, calling the watershed an ecological treasure, she said that the danger posed by proposed exploitation of the area mandated extraordinary measures.

The swift and angry predictable protest in Alaska followed, relying on the familiar arguments that have characterized Alaskans' view of their prerogatives. For Alaska's Governor Sean Parnell, it was an "egregious" and "unprecedented" action. The EPA had decided that it, not Alaskans, knew what is best for Alaska's future. Congressman Don Young called it a "power grab" and accused the agency of having been corrupted by politics. Senator Murkowski said it further detracted from investors' willingness to bring capital and jobs to Alaska. The state attorney general wrote to the EPA's Region 10 chief Dennis McLerran that the agency's action had cast a cloud over any development in Bristol Bay and over Alaska's economic future. But rhetoric was not the only response. Several months after the draft was released Anglo-American vacated the Pebble partnership.[51] The company's chief executive officer said that the directors want to focus on lower-risk projects. "It is unlikely that this project will go forward to construction and operation," he told an interviewer. Then, in April 2014, Rio Tinto decided to abandon the project, leaving the

Pebble Limited Partnership. The corporation gave its shares in the company to two Alaska charities.[52] Northern Dynasty was the only investor left. Unlike Anglo-American and Rio Tinto, two of the largest mining conglomerates in the world, Northern Dynasty is not an operating company. It is an exploration and development company whose mission is to organize projects and bring them to the permitting stage. The company vowed to stay with Pebble and search for new investors. Rio Tinto said it still considered Alaska an attractive prospect, but it needed to turn its attention elsewhere. Senator Murkowski praised Rio Tinto for its charitable disposition of its shares but repeated that Alaska needed reliability from federal regulators for its economic future.

But that was not the end of the Pebble story. In May 2014 Pebble Limited Partnership filed a lawsuit against the EPA, challenging the agency's authority to block planned development prior to the submission of a comprehensive detailed plan and applications for water-use permits.[53] The State of Alaska later joined the suit. In September a judge with the federal Alaska District Court dismissed the suit, saying it was premature until the EPA issued a final report actually blocking the project. Pebble immediately filed a second suit, alleging that the EPA had collaborated with nongovernment scientists and conservation organizations in a preplanned design to prohibit development of the Pebble prospect. Such collusion would be a violation of the Federal Advisory Committee Act of 1972, which obligates nongovernment citizens and committees who consult with federal agencies to provide relevant and objective information transparent to the public. Pebble charged that Trout Unlimited, the Natural Resources Defense Council, and the Bristol Bay Native Corporation had all colluded with the EPA as early as 2008, two years before the agency's formal investigation began. Pebble based its allegations on materials obtained through a Freedom of Information Act request for EPA records relating to the assessment review. A month later the partnership filed a third suit asking for further documents relating to the assessment, contending that important, relevant materials turned over to Pebble by the EPA did not include known, relevant documents. Pebble claimed the Wilderness Society, the Nature Conservancy, the National Wildlife Federation, and the Alaska Conservation Foundation were among organizations that had provided the EPA with information that directed its assessment.

In October Pebble and the State of Alaska asked for an order to stop the EPA review, and in November the judge issued a preliminary injunction against the EPA, requiring the agency to halt all work on the Bristol Bay watershed assessment until he has ruled on the suits relating to documentation. Though the injunction was temporary, it was a ruling to be cheered by everyone in the resource development community in Alaska and around the country, one spokesman proclaimed, because a successful EPA veto of Pebble would chill resource investment around the nation.[54] The EPA asked for clarification on the scope of the injunction, and the judge responded that the agency "is barred from any activity whatsoever to advance its work on the Pebble issue."[55]

There is much at stake in the judicial review of the EPA's potential veto of the Pebble project. Leaders in Alaska and prodevelopment organizations around the country are correct that should the EPA prevail, resource development investors will need a set of guidelines that will allow them to make prudent decisions on where to undertake commodification projects. By the same token, the cause of environmental preservation will be strengthened considerably. The judge is likely to make a very specific legal determination, based on what is required by the Federal Advisory Committee Act and what is not. But his decision will raise a much deeper question: What balance do the American people want between the resource commodification on which they depend for the material norm of American culture, on the one hand, and, on the other, the preservation of pristine wilderness that exists more in the imagination than in the reality of inhabited wilderness?

Nearly 900 miles west of Anchorage, near the tip of the Alaska Peninsula, which separates the Bering Sea from the Pacific Ocean's Gulf of Alaska, lies the Izembek National Wildlife Refuge, at 300,000 acres the smallest FWS refuge in Alaska. On the north shore of the refuge, on the Bering Sea coast, is Izembek Lagoon, 30 miles long and 5 miles wide, containing one of the world's largest concentrations of eelgrass. It is separated by a narrow strip of land from Moffet Lagoon; the lagoons are on the migratory-bird Pacific flyway. Millions of migratory waterfowl and shorebirds feed on the refuge during their annual movement between breeding and fattening grounds. Over 200 species of wildlife visit the site, which hosts 9 fish species. It is a wildlife wonder, recognized by the Ramsar Convention, a nongovernmental consortium of 133 nations committed to the protection of wetlands. Izembek was the first American wildlife refuge to be so listed. About 130,000 Pacific brant geese, 90 percent of their population, use the refuge, as do half of the world's emperor geese, about 62,000; so do 50,000 Taverner's Canada geese, 300,000 ducks, and 80,000 shorebirds. About 50,000 Steller's eiders feed on the refuge in winter. The refuge was established in 1960, and most of it was designated wilderness in ANILCA in 1980.

On the south shore of the refuge is Cold Bay; on that bay, near but outside the refuge boundary, sits a community of the same name with fewer than 100 people. In addition to some refuge personnel who are housed there, most residents service an airfield and weather station. The airfield is the fifth-largest in Alaska, with two paved runways, 10,000 and 6,000 feet, built during World War II for the Aleutian campaign. An army base there was headquarters for the Eleventh Air Force; several thousand American servicemen were stationed there. The base served as well as a transfer point for 149 ships and watercraft given to the Soviet Union during the war; 15,000 Soviet naval personnel were trained there. Today the airfield operates as an emergency runway on the trans-Pacific route and to service Alaska Peninsula and eastern Aleutian communities. Near the entrance to the Cold Bay water body sits King Cove, a community of nearly 1,000 people, half of whom are Aleut. King Cove is the location of one of the largest seafood-processing plants in Alaska, owned by Peter Pan Seafoods. The cannery processes salmon and crab and also pollack, cod, and black cod, bottom-dwelling fish taken mostly in the Bering Sea by trawlers. The town is economically dependent on the cannery, which employs about 500 people year-round, many of them Filipino. The weather in the region is often severe, and the town is served by a small airstrip; in bad weather small planes are often grounded. There is no direct road connection between King Cove and Cold Bay, 44 miles distant by land. The Izembek refuge, a national wilderness area, lies between the two communities.

Since creation of the refuge there has been agitation to construct a road connection between King Cove and Cold Bay to facilitate medical evacuation to the all-weather airfield. With the designation of much of the refuge as wilderness, that project has become problematical. If built, the road would pass for 9 miles along the narrow isthmus between the two lagoons and Cold Bay; its total length within the refuge would be 17 miles. But the Fish and Wildlife Service has consistently rejected the notion of a road through the bird sanctuary. The isthmus is too vulnerable, officials say, and the birds too valuable.[56] Responding to King Cove residents' pleas, the state has offered the FWS 43,000 acres of state land and the Native corporation 13,300 acres in exchange for 206 acres of Izembek and 1,600 acres of a refuge on Kodiak Island. The FWS has said no; the 206 acres of Izembek are critical to the birds on the Pacific flyway. In 1997 Senator Stevens secured a $37 million congressional grant to purchase for King Cove a sophisticated $9 million hovercraft that can transport people to Cold Bay and to fund an extensive upgrade of medical facilities in King Cove. Although the craft has been used, the townspeople in King Cove say its use is too difficult, it cannot be used in the most severe weather, and they do not have the funds to pay for its upkeep.[57]

In 2009 Interior Secretary Ken Salazar ordered a comprehensive environmental impact assessment of the Izembek road question. After four years of review his successor, Sally Jewell, announced in December 2013 that the Interior Department would not approve the road proposal.[58] She acknowledged the serious concerns of the people of King Cove and said the department would continue to work with them to find alternative solutions to meet their needs. The review noted that when the hovercraft was in service from 2007 to 2010, "it completed every requested medical evacuation," contrary to the claim that it was unserviceable at times.

Negative reaction to the report was shrill. Alaska's Governor Parnell called the decision "unconscionable," saying that just in the week before Jewell's announcement several medical evacuations had shown the critical need for the road. Senator Murkowski said it put birds before people. Congressman Young vowed to introduce legislation to force the proposed land swap. The administrator of the Native village corporation charged that the secretary's trust responsibility to the Native people was "meaningless."[59] The state decided to sue the Interior Department, asking the court to mandate construction of the road based on the RS2477 provision of ANILCA, which allows continued use of historical roads and trails. In September 2015 a federal judge found that Secretary Jewell did not violate the law in refusing to approve a road through the Izembek refuge.[60] Some critics of the road charged that the seafood-processing plant wanted the road to facilitate shipment of its products, but the manager of the plant said it had no such plans, though he would not rule it out as a future possibility.[61] The national group Defenders of Wildlife reported that a broad coalition of Alaska and national conservation organizations delivered to the FWS comments from 50,000 Alaska residents opposing the road.[62]

For the FWS, the primary concerns are disturbance of the habitat for the wildlife using the protected habitat and the inevitability of the road being an opening wedge in transforming the refuge. For conservationists, the principal concern is that allowing road construction in a designated wilderness violates the concept and congressional definition of wilderness, in effect, de-designating a wilderness area, for which there is no precedent.[63] Because the isthmus is narrow and the habitat highly critical for the species that use it, Izembek may be one of the intractable situations where coexistence is not possible, where people do indeed need to yield to birds and find an alternative solution.

Chuitna coal, the Pebble prospect, and the Izembek road exemplify the essence of environmental conflict in Alaska. Alaska leaders, whatever their politics or sensitivity to nature, have little choice but to maximize any opportunity for economic development in a state with no alternatives to utilization of its natural resources. That is why a majority support such development at Chuitna, the product of which has little to do with Alaska but instead is destined for a global market. The *crise de coeur* of the statehood movement was that Outside investors were exploiting the territory and indirectly its people by removing or destroying a resource without any compensatory benefit for Alaskans. Statehood would put Alaskans in control of such resources and allow them to prevent such exploitation, and instead compel recompense. State supporters of Chuitna coal development seem to find acceptable the extraction of a nonrenewable, finite resource with very little benefit to the state. In the Pebble prospect, Alaskans find themselves in a true dilemma that few can relish: whether to participate in some way in the billions of dollars of profit to be realized from perhaps the largest copper and gold mine in the world or to deny that development so as not to risk the largest and one of the most lucrative fisheries in the world. To support development in such a circumstance seems to many an ideological commitment that defies a reasonable assessment of the odds. Yet for many Alaskans, the power of the federal government to stop a project of such magnitude is unacceptable because, since it is on state land, it should be the state's decision to make. They see in such an exercise of federal power a trammeling not of nature but of the sovereign right and dignity of state government. For the courts to allow such federal action to go forward seems to these Alaskans the abnegation of the Tenth Amendment, shredding the US Constitution and American federalism. At Izembek Lagoon, in placing birds above the deepest concerns of the local people, life and death, the Interior Department and the Fish and Wildlife Service are but following the mandate of a broader constituency, the people of the nation, who in the Wilderness Act and ANILCA made clear their intention to protect their wildlife and its critical habitat at pretty much all costs. At least 50,000 Alaskans, and probably more, seem comfortable enough with that judgment to endorse it by signing their names to public information messages, an endorsement that to others seems unreasonable and even inhumane. These examples of environmental conflict show Alaska to be a beleaguered battleground, one few might wish to fight on. It also manifests the tragic nature of settlement in Alaska, whose residents enjoy America's most extensive and celebrated natural environment but whose continued residence depends on some level of despoliation of that very environment. At the same time Chuitna, Pebble, and Izembek are surrogate battles, stand-ins for a national discussion about the definition and implications of wilderness and sustainability, a debate most citizens seem loath to undertake or remain blissfully unaware of. But it's a discussion that cannot be postponed indefinitely.

Alaska is the most antistatist of the American states. A fierce strain of anti-statism runs throughout the American west, but in Alaska it becomes virulent. It is manifest in a reflexive resistance to virtually any exercise of federal power in transportation, communication, education, health, and safety but most particularly in regard to land and environmental regulation. That is because Alaska's economy is uniquely remote and isolated and dependent on natural resource development, and because the population is small and mostly urban, and Alaska's people demand the material norm of American culture. Alaskans must depend on their land for their economic livelihood; economies of scale defeat profitable commercial manufacturing or agriculture. Understanding Alaska's distinctive circumstances, in the 1958 statehood act Congress provided the most generous grant of land to come under state title in the history of westward expansion, an area larger than California yet only 28 percent of Alaska's total acreage. The state was to select potentially mineralized land where possible because Congress anticipated that the revenue to fund state government would come from mineral leasing. So central was the land grant to Congress's notion of Alaska's economic sustainability that it forbade the state to alienate the land; the state could lease it but not patent it. Congress also committed 90 percent of federal mineral lease revenue collected on its land in Alaska to the state to further guarantee the state's economic viability.

But barely had the state begun to select its entitled land, gaining title to a small percentage of the entitlement, when the federal government in its executive, legislative, and judicial capacities halted the selection process, first on orders from the secretary of the interior, then Congress itself, and finally the federal judiciary. The government was responding to a fundamental shift in two spheres of American culture of which it was an institutional representative. First, the civil rights movement's redefinition of equal rights generated a new sensitivity to the aboriginal land claims of Alaska's Native people. Empowered by new knowledge and aided by sympathetic individuals and the Bureau of Indian Affairs, Natives organized to protest state land selection of areas they regarded as their own. In 1971 Congress passed the Alaska Native Claims Settlement Act, reserving to Alaska Natives 44 million acres of Alaska land in regions associated with their traditional use of it. Though initially skeptical of extensive Native land claims, most Alaskans grew to accept and support Congress's conferring some of Alaska's lands on Natives. At the same time, the suspension of Alaska's land selection while Congress and the Native leadership sorted out the Natives' claims produced considerable discomfiture among many Alaskans. Their anxiety was somewhat assuaged by the discovery of America's largest oil field on already titled state land at Prudhoe Bay in 1968. Prudhoe Bay seemed the economic bonanza for Alaska that Congress and Alaskans had anticipated at the time of statehood.

The second cultural shift to affect Alaska was the rise of modern environmentalism, which developed simultaneously with the evolution of the civil rights movement. Based first on an idealized conceptualization of nature, with an attendant regard for wildlife, and subsequently also on a concern with pollution, health, and safety, national conservation organizations raised the nation's environmental consciousness. Manifesting the nation's changed sensitivities, Congress passed the Wilderness Act in 1964, moving to protect large areas of undeveloped land from permanent human imprint. Then, in 1969, Congress created the Environmental Protection Agency to monitor and manage environmental impacts on the public lands. The Endangered Species Act followed in 1973. Remote and not contiguous with the rest of the continental states, Alaska was settled late and thus contains the greatest expanses of land in America that do not show permanent human imprint. As conservationists across the country came to appreciate the apparent pristine character of Alaska's wild lands, they organized a national campaign to place Alaska's wild lands in the national consciousness. Alaska segued in American perception from America's "last frontier" to America's "last wilderness." Alaska, the environmentalists said, held America's "environmental crown jewels." Congress responded by planning legislation to preserve a large portion of those lands under federal ownership and permanent environmental protection. While that legislation was pending, from 1971 to 1980, Congress continued the suspension of Alaska's selection of the lands the statehood act entitled it to own. In the meantime, the great Prudhoe Bay oil discovery in 1968 seemed to assure Alaskans the economic prosperity they hoped statehood would bring. But national environmentalists, noting that the planned trans-Alaska hot-oil pipeline would traverse some important Alaska wilderness land, organized to prohibit its construction. Demonstrating the strength of America's new environmental consciousness, they nearly succeeded. In a classic contest between environmental protection and economic development, Congress passed the Trans-Alaska Pipeline Authorization Act in 1973 only by appending to the authorization a declaration that the design of the project satisfied the requirements of the National Environmental Policy Act, the legislation that had created the Environmental Protection Agency just a few years before. Conservationists worried that setting aside NEPA for the Alaska pipeline would vitiate the long-term effectiveness of the act. At the same time, to Alaskans' unease with the withdrawal of Native lands from the acreage from which the state might select its desired land and the discomfiture Alaskans felt over suspension of the selection process, now was added the fear and fury they felt over the national conservation community threatening to take away their major prospect for economic salvation. Nor was their ordeal yet complete.

Maintaining the suspension, Congress set about to craft its own selection of Alaska land to be protected in new national parks, fish and wildlife refuges, national forests, and wild and scenic rivers, some portions of which would be formally designated wilderness. That process turned into an epic, highly contentious debate over two different visualizations of Alaska lands. Environmentalists imagined vast stretches of sublime, often breathtakingly beautiful and scientifically significant natural landscapes set aside to awe and inspire the current generation of Americans and to be preserved into the future for uncounted succeeding generations. Some Alaskans shared their view. Most others and a host of Americans committed to development imagined vast known and unknown mineral, forest, and water resources in Alaska put to work to fuel the national economy; to create jobs and material prosperity for millions; and to sustain Alaskans into a rich, energized, hopeful future of responsible consumption and citizenship. Not unsympathetic to environmental values, Alaskans projected perhaps 60 million acres of their state protected in the new federal reserves, much of it classified for multiple uses. They sought to enlighten conservationists that the land had always been used, that much of what they called pristine was in fact inhabited by Native and non-Native rural Alaskans who harvested its subsistence resources to sustain their way of life, and that throwing an impermeable blanket of preservation over the land was unrealistic and selfish. For their part, conservationists projected perhaps 160 million acres of newly protected land, much of it designated formally as wilderness and all of it restricted to one degree or another from the scar of the bulldozer, the blast of dynamite, the noisy throbbing of helicopter blades, and the crack of the hunter's rifle. They sought to enlighten developers that their persistent encroachment on mostly untrammeled landscapes cannot go on forever, that it is unsustainable in the long run because someday there will be no unmolested landscapes left. They sought to convey their reverence for the wonder and beauty of animal species in their natural habitat, unaffected by human influences and available in perpetuity to study and to marvel over. Spokespersons for these two visualizations often talked past one another, each unable to understand the other's commitment and dedication and often inclined to suspect or attribute nefarious motives to the other.

In the meantime, Alaskans had to watch while people who for the most part knew the state only through an occasional visit and could not be fully knowledgeable about it deliberated the terms of Alaska's future. The national environmental community proved organized, competent, and highly effective at communicating its point of view and amassing political pressure. As it became more ascendant, Alaskans' fear and fury grew accordingly. Not only did they worry over their future, but many grew frustrated and exasperated in their perplexity over Congress's failure to honor the promises they believed it had made to guarantee Alaska's economic future with its statehood grant of usable land.

Many felt betrayed and grasped at the remote compact theory of federalism to try to bend federal power to their will. Though they eventually failed in that endeavor, Alaska's congressional delegation had some success in limiting and rationalizing the scope and content of environmentalists' vision of Alaska. But Alaskans had to accept the force of a national will informed by that vision and ready willingly to embrace it.

The environmental lobby's strength came from the Alaska Coalition, a nationwide, grassroots network of tens of thousands of volunteers organized on a state and regional level who made phone calls; wrote letters and public opinion messages; hosted community meetings, often with film and slides from wilderness trips in the field; and testified at public hearings. Established national, regional, and local conservation societies led by the Sierra Club and the Wilderness Society funded a small corps of paid professionals in Washington, DC, who pursued a sophisticated lobbying strategy and meticulously executed tactics. Meanwhile, the national offices produced lavishly illustrated books, monthly bulletins, and timely newsletters that promoted the aesthetic and abstract values of the Alaska lands environmentalists wanted to protect from development. At the same time bulletins tracked virtually every commodification initiative by the mining, oil and gas, and timber industries as well as documenting pollution and wilderness despoliation. These were tactics first developed in the campaign to establish an Arctic wilderness, the first iteration of the Arctic National Wildlife Refuge, and honed during the battle over authorization of the Trans-Alaska Pipeline. The environmentalist dream of Alaska was sweepingly broad and comprehensive. It was not fully realized.

What curtailed the national environmental community's ambition for Alaska was partly a flawed understanding of the nature of nature but far more a seismic shift in national politics. Ronald Reagan captured the presidency in 1980 and Republicans the US Senate in the beginning of a conservative turn in attitudes toward and faith in government. In pursuing its design for Alaska, the environmental lobby in Congress settled for what the opposition led by Senator Ted Stevens would give them, and President Carter signed the Alaska lands bill as one of his last major actions before leaving office. For the cause of environmentalism, ANILCA was an immense achievement. It brought federal protection to vast areas of Alaska that, though for the most part not in fact pristine, did not show much human imprint and could be appreciated for their scenic and scientific value as in situ nature. The final version added over 100 million acres of new conservation lands and doubled the acreage in the national wilderness system. Wherever possible and relevant, the withdrawals were based on scientific identification of natural ecosystems. The act recognized and provided for the utilization of wild lands in Alaska by both Native peoples, who had used them from time immemorial, and rural non-Natives with a subsistence harvest tradition. It also facilitated development potential within protected lands in many places where prospects for development were known to exist. In this last result ANILCA may represent a new vision of sustainability.

Finally, with ANILCA passed, the state was able to resume selection of its entitled lands. That process was virtually complete by 1994, but the animosity lives on. Neither the selections for Natives in ANCSA nor the reserves in ANILCA denied the state much land that it might have taken for its own. But indignation at having to wait nearly a decade and a half to complete the process, and the inability of resource development advocates in Congress to force open the Arctic Refuge for oil drilling, fueled the perception that the federal government had failed to honor its promise to support Alaska's economic independence by conveying or making accessible for development Alaska's mineral lands. A constant target of antistatism complaints is the Arctic Refuge, the coastal plain of which may be rich in oil deposits and which most Alaskans hope will be the next economic bonanza for the state.

It is the failure of Congress to open the Arctic National Wildlife Refuge that most galls Alaskans. The peak of production at Prudhoe Bay was reached in 1989–1990. Because of the nature of oil deposits and the technology of extracting oil, as the amount of oil in the deposit decreases, it becomes more difficult to get it out. The industry has developed remarkable new technologies to coax the oil out, including injecting large amounts of seawater and reinjecting the natural gas that occurs with oil deposits. These have substantially increased the total recovery on Alaska's North Slope. But the fields must eventually become nonproducers. From the peak of production from 1989 to 2015, throughput in the Alaska pipeline has decreased from 2 million barrels a day to 300,000. Estimates of how long oil can be economically produced vary from ten to thirty-five years, with many uncertain variables. Faced with the demise of Alaska's economic bonanza, state boosters look to the Arctic refuge, adjacent to the Prudhoe Bay deposit and now estimated by the US Geological Survey to contain between 4 billion and 11 billion barrels of oil.[1] As the refuge is federal land, some percentage of the lease revenue would come to Alaska, most likely 50 percent. And exploration and production of coastal plain oil, should it prove economically feasible to develop, would mean jobs for Alaska. The revenue for Alaska would be far less than that generated by Prudhoe Bay development, but with few other prospects on the horizon, Alaskans look to the refuge as the next economic savior.

They blame national environmentalists for the long postponement of state land selections and especially for Congress's failure to open the refuge coastal plain. Opening the refuge to drilling is a constant political mantra in Alaska, one in which the oil industry readily participates. And as environmentalism is seen as the villain, any environmental initiative in Alaska becomes the object of political attack.

It is in the oil industry's interest to open the refuge to development, and the industry has been a steadfast ally of the insistence by Alaska politicians that Congress has reneged on its promises to facilitate Alaska's economic growth by finally declaring the coastal plain an economic development area. But as the assertion of broken promises, and therefore recompense owed, is a false history, persisting in it opens the protesters to the charge that they're being manipulated by the industry. Critics argue that many of Alaska's better-known political figures have willingly made themselves industry pawns.[2] They complain that campaign contributions by the oil industry in Alaska drive much of the political rhetoric related to the refuge and play a significant role in producing state legislation. Between 2004 and 2010 the Public Integrity Section of the US Justice Department, along with the Internal Revenue Service and the Federal Bureau of Investigation, conducted a widespread investigation of the Alaska Legislature and Senator Ted Stevens and Congressman Don Young, which resulted in indictments of six members of the Alaska Legislature for corruption and indictment of Senator Stevens for violating government ethics laws. Two executives of the VECO Corporation, an oil field services contractor, pled guilty to charges of bribery and conspiracy. They were filmed in a Juneau hotel, by a hidden FBI camera, offering bribes to sitting legislators.[3] Five of the legislators were convicted. Investigators disclosed no findings regarding possible connection between oil industry executives and the VECO Corporation, but the concert of interest was clear. The bribery convictions were related to oil-tax legislation pending before the Alaska Legislature. Senator Stevens was convicted shortly before his reelection bid in November 2008; he lost the election.

In a larger context the continued misrepresentation of the history of Alaska's relationship with the federal government and the prejudicial use of the notion of an inviolable statehood compact have substantial negative consequences. They complicate negotiations with federal officials over implementing ANILCA, inevitably putting them on the defensive. More critically, they put the Alaska public at risk of being manipulated for political advantage. An objective judgment on the future of the refuge coastal plain, and its implications for Alaska, is colored by the persistent distortion of the federal government's role. As Jeannette Paddock Nichols advised decades ago, a false history of Alaska reinforces misunderstanding, generates misguided initiatives, and serves neither truth nor the state's citizens.

ANILCA, then, did not end environmental conflict in Alaska; far from it. Scrapping began immediately over utilization of the Tongass National Forest, with conservationists protesting the subsidization of what seemed an excessive, mandated harvest that cost taxpayers tens of millions of dollars annually when the market for timber production had fallen significantly. The result was new legislation for the forest that more realistically drove toward a balance between protection and consumption.

Alaska has challenged a wide variety of federal environmental agency actions in Alaska in the decades since ANILCA became law. Cook Inlet hosts a distinct species of beluga whale. The National Marine Fisheries Service (NMFS) has monitored the population for several decades and in 1998 found that although at one time the number may have been 1,300, surveys have shown a significant decline; in 2012 the NMFS found only 312. The cause of the decline is unknown, but ship strikes, industrial activity, and noise pollution are suspected. In 2008 the NMFS listed the whales as endangered as defined by the Endangered Species Act. In 2011 it classified several areas in the inlet as critical habitat for the whales, a designation that restricts activities that require a federal permit, such as construction and operation of oil rigs, port construction and dredging, and EPA-monitored discharges. The NMFS exempted the port of Anchorage from the designation. In June 2010 the state filed a federal lawsuit challenging the endangered species listing. A year later a federal judge upheld the designation, dismissing the state's suit.

In another case, in 1991 the state issued permits for strip-mining of coal on state land adjacent to a suburban area east of Anchorage within a half-mile of numerous homes in a secluded, forested landscape. In addition to strip-mining, the developer's plans call for a coal-washing plant, a rock crusher, and loaded coal trucks making trips at night from the mine to a nearby port. A coalition of local environmental groups, supported by Trustees of Alaska and the Sierra Club, have challenged the project repeatedly, to no avail, both the state and the federal Office of Surface Mining Reclamation and Enforcement maintaining the validity of the state's permits.[4] The federal office has the responsibility to monitor mining operations for a balance between production and protection of the environment.[5]

In far northwest Alaska near the Chukchi Sea coast lies the world's largest zinc deposit; it's on land owned, since ANCSA, by the Northwest Alaska Native Association (NANA), the regional corporation. A surface deposit, it was discovered in the mid-1950s by a pilot who noticed stains in the free-flowing creeks in the area. In 1982 NANA went into partnership with Comino Mining (now Teck Resources) to develop the prospect. By the agreement, NANA receives a 50 percent royalty on production, which is projected to last until at least 2031, if not longer. The local government, the Northwest Arctic

Borough, taxes the mine's production. By the terms of ANCSA, the Native corporation shares 70 percent of its profit on the project with the other eleven Native regional development corporations. The mine employs about 450 people, over half of whom are Alaska Natives. The Northwest Arctic Borough covers an area about the size of Indiana. There are eleven villages in the borough, which has a population of about 7,000; no roads connect the villages. The two villages closest to the mine, Noatak and Kivalina, each with about 400 residents, are 60 and 50 miles away, respectively. The ore concentrate must be transported by truck 55 miles from the mine to a port on the Chukchi Sea.

The State of Alaska permitted the mine and funded the road to the port. Since production began there have been issues with acid drainage and "fugitive dust" from the operation. Water used in the mining, 1.35 billion gallons annually, is captured in tailings ponds and treated before being released into the streams. The zinc- and lead-laden dust blows from the strip-mining and from the trucks transporting the concentrate. Teck has paid several multimillion-dollar fines resulting from the pollution. The EPA has asked for a pipeline that would carry toxic slurry to the sea, but Teck has not yet complied, perhaps finding payment of annual fines cheaper than the pipeline cost. The village of Kivalina has filed suit over the fugitive dust. For Native Alaskans, the mine is a devil's bargain: living with the pollution is the price for the jobs created, the benefits for the Native shareholders, both in NANA and the other corporations, and the production tax, which have funded needed improvements and infrastructure in the villages. If it can be satisfactorily brought under control, all parties to the mine development may enjoy its benefits.[6]

Few issues engage more environmental thinking about Alaska in recent years than global climate change. The Arctic is warming at twice the rate of the rest of the planet. Arctic sea ice is retreating northward and becoming soft on its surface. The disappearance of sea ice increases warming, for white ice and snow reflect 90 percent of the sun's radiation back into space, whereas dark water absorbs it. On land in Alaska, permafrost is melting, causing undulations and instability and releasing methane into the atmosphere. The ocean is warming, contributing to more severe winter storms. Several Alaska villages on bluffs above the seacoast have been undercut by severe storms, and state and village leaders are searching for funds that will allow the villages to be moved.[7] The state has established an executive advisory group, the Alaska Sub-cabinet on Climate Change, to advise the governor and other executive offices. Trustees of Alaska and other environmental groups have advised villages on legal actions that might mandate support for relocations, generally without success. Addressing and mitigating the effects of climate change in Alaska will require cooperation between federal and state government, Native leaders and local governments, and environmental organizations that can encourage and support scientific study and counsel communities on options available to them. On a broader scale, pressing issues include acidification of the oceans, toxic waste, deforestation, and the future of the Arctic. Analysts anticipate significant traffic through an ice-free corridor suitable for cargo ships in the Northwest Passage by 2030. Already a few ships annually ply the route. The Arctic Council, a voluntary assemblage of Arctic nations, recently adopted a binding protocol for search and rescue that eight governments have signed. The breadth of climate change has brought a new urgency to address environmental challenges cooperatively. Accordingly, President Obama traveled to Alaska in September 2015 to address an international meeting of scientists on climate change and the Arctic.

These and other contentions keep environmental conflict alive and ever present in Alaska. The state's congressional delegation and most of its political leadership apparently have concluded that the strategy most likely to advance resource development in Alaska is to stay on the attack against what is labeled "federal overreach." In his first address to the Alaska Legislature in March 2015, the state's newest US senator, Dan Sullivan, devoted most of his talk to areas where Alaskans need to resist and assail exercises of federal power in the state. The still closed refuge was the first instance he cited. It seems a strategy that risks ridicule, given the persistence of the national will to maintain the level of protection of Alaska's federal lands manifest in Congress's failure to open the coastal plain and to rescind other aspects of ANILCA. The state's leadership might do better to focus on the development of alternative energy and on the potential benefits of drilling in the Chukchi and Beaufort Seas, which President Obama endorsed. In March 2015 the National Petroleum Council, which advises the US energy secretary, urged that the United States focus its future oil development on the Arctic Ocean, thought to hold up to 35 billion barrels of undiscovered oil deposits.[8] But environmental organizations actively protest Arctic offshore drilling because they consider the risk to the environment there too great. Shell Oil secured leases in the Beaufort Sea and undertook a drilling program in 2012. It was fraught with significant problems, including the grounding of a sophisticated drilling rig while under tow.[9] In 2015 the company abandoned the program.

The Alaska congressional delegation charged that federal regulations were the reason for Shell's decision, a claim not supported by the evidence.[10] Alaska's North Slope holds 35 trillion cubic feet of known natural gas reserves, which the state has been attempting to develop for decades. This, too, might be a better policy for Alaska than lamenting the continued closure of the refuge. The state has worked for years to generate investment in a natural gas pipeline from the North Slope to tidewater, where it could be liquefied and shipped, but market conditions have discouraged investment in the project.[11]

Perhaps the state's Independent governor, Bill Walker, elected in 2014, understands the futility of Alaska's persistent antistatism. In a cost-saving measure after he took office, he proposed eliminating two programs: the Public Access and Defense Unit in the Department of Natural Resources, said to save $1.5 million annually, and two attorneys in the Department of Law and an outside contractor whose responsibilities were to handle conflict between the state and federal governments over implementing the Endangered Species Act. They cost a lot, the governor said, and had limited effectiveness.[12]

In his comprehensive study of the US environmental movement since 1964, James Morton Turner argued that since the legislative attainments of the 1960s and 1970s, the movement has evolved toward pragmatism, toward searching for compromises that protect environmental values while recognizing the human element in nature. He asserted that even in their halcyon days of legislative success, "wilderness advocates knew that even the nation's wildest lands often include remnants of old dams and mines, abandoned homesteads, and the scars of overgrazing."[13] Not all analysts are in agreement, seeing in Zahniser, Brower, Wayburn, and others the idealization of wilderness that Cronon addressed in his seminal essay in 1995.[14] Be that as it may, the pragmatism since the earlier period has kept wilderness advocates at the negotiating table, engaging with ranchers, hunters, Native Americans, industry, off-road vehicle drivers, and others.[15] The Wilderness Act, Turner argued, initiated political engagement among environmental activists and Congress and between activists and resource developers. Wilderness, he suggested, means "engaging citizens—both for and against wild lands protections—in a sustained discussion toward the common interest, a third wave of environmentalism."[16]

For environmentalists, particularly wilderness advocates, perhaps the most difficult challenge of pragmatism will be, as suggested by historian Timothy LeCain, learning to see humans and their technologies as entirely natural and inextricable parts of nature.[17] Any environmental ethic must begin with a firm grasp of the connection between the material norm of modern culture and the origins of the products of that norm. All of them entail some manipulation of nature, and more manipulations are involved in their processing, packaging, transportation, marketing, distribution, and the disposal of the waste left behind. Sustainability and balance are the common interest both Turner and LeCain spoke of. The pragmatic negotiations of third-wave environmentalism are aimed at discovering and implementing that balance. For Alaskans, the most difficult challenge is to leave behind the obsession with failed promises; to accept the legitimacy of the American people retaining ownership and management of the land the nation acquired from Russia a century and a half ago; and to embrace and nurture the potential of the land over which they have control, that area larger than California. It would also be helpful to future relations if they could recognize the federal government for the friend and helpmate it has been to Alaska since its acquisition. At the conclusion of a history of the Kennecott Copper Corporation, which developed highly lucrative deposits in Alaska, in Utah, and in Chile, Alaska mining historian Charles Hawley suggested that the huge surface mine at Bingham, Utah, with its symmetry of terraces and deep-earth exposure and interconnecting roadways has a beguiling aesthetic quality.[18] It is at one and the same time a gash on the landscape and a human-made work of intriguing beauty. Visitors to the state want to see the five great national parks, Canyonlands, Capitol Reef, Arches, Zion, and Bryce, but they also want to see the Bingham Canyon mine. Humans working the earth are symbolic of a true view of nature, one that accepts that humans and nature have always been inextricably intertwined. It cannot be otherwise.

The majority leader in the House of Representatives of the Twenty-Ninth Alaska Legislature introduced the following bill on February 18, 2015.

DOCUMENT

An Act relating to the sovereignty of the state and the state's right to a credit or setoff for amounts or injuries inequitably or unlawfully caused or claimed by the federal government; requiring the United States to lift certain land orders and federal withdrawals; relating to the transfer of public land or interests in public land from the federal government to the state and to the disposal of that land or any interest in land; and providing for an effective date.

SPONSOR'S STATEMENT

Although there are a number of state and federal constitutional issues regarding the provisions contained within the bill, this bill was introduced since the 35-year deadline from the time Alaska was admitted into the union as provided within the Statehood Act is long past. I believe there is a breach of good faith since the state is still entitled to and awaiting the transfer of the remaining 5.5 million acres. Thus far the state has received patent to 99.5 million acres.

Rep. Mike Chenault, Majority Leader

A minority member of the House subsequently requested from the Legislative Affairs Agency an opinion on the constitutionality of the bill.

DOCUMENT

LEGISLATIVE AFFAIRS AGENCY STATE OF ALASKA
State Capitol Juneau, Alaska 99801-1 182 Deliveries to: 129 6th St., Rm. 329
FROM: Aipheus Bullard Legislative Counsel
LEGAL SERVICES

MEMORANDUM: February 18, 2015
SUBJECT: Constitutionality of a state law requiring the federal government to transfer certain lands to the state
(FIB 115; Work Order No. 29-LS0587\A)
TO: Representative Andy Josephson, Attn: Johnathan Church

You asked about the constitutionality of the bill described above. The bill is unconstitutional.

The state disclaimed all right and title in property belonging to the United States at the time the state achieved statehood. Article XII, sec. 12, Constitution of the State of Alaska substantially incorporates sec. 4 of the Alaska Statehood Act.[1] Article XII, sec. 12 reads as follows:

Disclaimer and Agreement. *The State of Alaska and its people forever disclaim all right and title in or to any property belonging to the United States or subject to its disposition, and not granted or confirmed to the State or its political subdivisions, by or under the act admitting Alaska to the Union.* The State and its people further disclaim all right or title in or to any property, including fishing rights, the right or title to which may be held by or for any Indian, Eskimo, or Aleut, or community thereof, as that right or title is defined in the act of admission. *The State and its people agree that, unless otherwise provided by Congress, the property, as described in this section, shall remain subject to the absolute disposition of the United States.* They further agree that no taxes will be imposed upon any such property, until otherwise provided by the Congress. This tax exemption shall not apply to property held by individuals in fee without restrictions on alienation. [Emphasis added.]

Even if the state had the power to order the federal government to transfer federal public land to the state, the order could not be based on any interest in that land retained by the state after achieving statehood. That interest was disclaimed at statehood. Where ownership or a right-of-way is in dispute, the appropriate remedy would be to pursue a quiet title action. See, for example, *Alaska v. United States*,[2] where the state filed action against the federal government to resolve the state's interest in submerged land in Glacier Bay and parts of Southeast Alaska.

The bill is similar to AS 38.05.500.38.05.505, the codified provisions of an initiative passed in 1982[3] that purports to gain control of federal land in the state on the following findings in AS 38.05.500:

Sec. 38.05.500. Electorate determinations. The people of the State of Alaska determine that:

the intent of the framers of the Constitution of the United States was to guarantee to each of the states sovereignty over all matters within its boundaries except for those powers specifically granted to the United States as agent to the states;

the attempted imposition upon the State of Alaska by the Congress of the United States of a requirement in the Statehood Act that the State of Alaska and its people "disclaim all right and title to any land or other property not granted or confirmed to the state or its political subdivisions by or under the authority of this Act, the right or title to which is held by the United States or is subject to disposition by the United States," as a condition or precedent to acceptance of Alaska into the Union, was an act beyond the power of the Congress of the United States and is thus void;

the purported right of ownership and control of the public land in the State of Alaska by the United States is without foundation and violates the clear intent of the Constitution of the United States; and

the exercise of that dominion and control of the public land in the State of Alaska by the United States works a severe, continuous and debilitating hardship upon the people of the State of Alaska.

The provisions in AS 38.05.500–38.05.505 have never been implemented. In 1983 the attorney general advised the commissioner of natural resources that the initiative, popularly known as the "Tundra Rebellion," was unconstitutional under art. XII, secs. 12 and 13, Constitution of the State of Alaska.[4] The commissioner followed the advice in the opinion, and the state has not implemented the provisions enacted by initiative.[5]

If you have any questions, please do not hesitate to contact me.

ALB: lem

15-102.lem

Ignoring the opinion from its own attorney, on April 6, 2015, the Alaska House of Representatives passed the bill, HB 115, by a vote of 27-11. In the Senate the bill was referred to the Natural Resources Committee, where it died upon conclusion of the legislative session.[6] Perhaps an observation from Ecclesiastes is apt:

That which has been is that which will be. And that which has been done is that which will be done. So there is nothing new under the sun. Is there anything of which one might say, "See this, it is new?" Already it has existed for ages which were before us. There is no remembrance of earlier things; And also of the later things which will occur, There will be for them no remembrance Among those who will come later.[7]

NOTES

PROLOGUE

1. US Department of the Interior, press release, "Obama Administration Moves to Protect Arctic National Wildlife Refuge," January 25, 2015; Juliet Eilperin, "Obama Administration to Propose New Wilderness Protections in Arctic Refuge—Alaska Republicans Declare War," *Washington Post*, January 26, 2015.

2. Senator Lisa Murkowski, public appearance, January 25, 2015, https://www .youtube.com/watch?v=1dzCJExt_jM&feature=youtu.be; Eilperin, "Obama Administration to Propose New Wilderness Protections in Arctic Refuge."

3. Alaska Governor's Office, press release, "Obama, Jewell Attacking Alaska's Future," January 25, 2015, http://gov.alaska.gov/Walker/press-room/full-press-release .html?pr=7063; Richard Mauer, Alex DeMarban, and Nathaniel Herz, "Obama Plans to Block Development in Arctic Refuge; Alaska Leaders Irate," *Alaska Dispatch News*, January 25, 2015.

4. Associated Press, "Alaska Senator: Make NYC's Central Park a Wilderness Area," February 2, 2015, http://www.nytimes.com/aponline/2015/02/02/us/ap-us -central-park-wilderness-area.html?_r=0.

INTRODUCTION

1. "Let Us End American Colonialism," keynote speech at the Alaska Constitutional Convention, November 9, 1955, http://xroads.virginia.edu/fficap/bartlett/colonial .html.

2. Morgan Sherwood, *Big Game in Alaska: A History of Wildlife and People* (New Haven, CT: Yale University Press, 1981), 1–3, 18–21.

3. Stewart Udall, *The Quiet Crisis* (New York: Holt, Rinehart, and Winston, 1963), 22.

4. Though I tried to remain mindful of Samuel P. Hays's distinction between conservation, focused on production, and environmentalism, focused on consumption, the two terms are often used interchangeably here except where the distinction is relevant; Samuel P. Hays, *Beauty, Health and Permanence: Environmental Politics in the United States, 1955–1985* (New York: Cambridge University Press, 1987).

5. Linnie Marsh, *John of the Mountains: The Unpublished Journals of John Muir* (Madison: University of Wisconsin Press, 1938), 313; Wallace Stegner, "Wilderness Letter," in *Marking the Sparrow's Fall: The Making of the American West*, ed. Page Stegner (New York: Henry Holt, 1998).

6. "There is just one hope for repulsing the tyrannical ambition of tyrannical civilization to conquer every inch of the whole earth. That hope is the organization of spirited people who will fight for the freedom and preservation of the wilderness." Roderick Nash, *Wilderness and the American Mind* (New Haven, CT: Yale University Press, 1967), 200.

7. James Morton Turner, *The Promise of Wilderness: American Environmental Politics since 1964* (Seattle: University of Washington Press, 2012), 107.

8. On August 30, 2015, on the eve of a three-day visit to Alaska, President Obama by executive order changed the name of Mt. McKinley to Denali.

9. The name "Gates of the Arctic" was coined by Marshall for two mountain peaks, Frigid Crags and Boreal Mountain, on opposite sides of the North Koyukuk River in the southern Brooks Range.

10. Robert Marshall, "The Problem of Wilderness," *Scientific Monthly* 2 (February 1930): 32.

11. US Congress, Senate, Committee on Interstate and Foreign Commerce, Subcommittee on Merchant Marine and Fisheries, Hearings, S. 1899, A Bill to Authorize the Establishment of the Arctic Wildlife Range and for other Purposes, 86th Cong., 1st Sess., Part 1, 3.

12. Peter A. Coates, *The Trans-Alaska Pipeline Controversy: Technology, Conservation and the Frontier* (Bethlehem, PA: Lehigh University Press, 1991), 202.

13. US Secretary of Commerce Maurice Stans to Deputy Undersecretary of the Interior Jack O. Horton, *Trans-Alaska Pipeline Final Environmental Impact Statement*, Vol. 6, A-63-8, April 16, 1971.

14. Nash, *Wilderness and the American Mind*, 299.

15. Timothy Egan, "Tongass Old Growth Tress at Risk," *New York Times*, August 22, 1989.

CHAPTER 1. ANTISTATISM IN ALASKA

1. Francine Keilor, "Alaska's Senator Murkowski Says War Declared against Alaska," *Christian Science Monitor*, January 27, 2015.

2. R. McGregor Cawley, *Federal Land, Western Anger: The Sagebrush Rebellion and Environmental Politics* (Lawrence: University Press of Kansas, 1993); Brian Allen Drake, *Loving Nature, Fearing the State: Environmentalism and Antigovernment Politics before Reagan* (Seattle: University of Washington Press, 2013); Christopher Ketcham, "The Great Republican Land Heist: Cliven Bundy and the Politicians Who Are Plundering the West," *Harper's* 1987 (February 2015), 23–31.

3. Daniel A. Farber, "Completing the Work of the Frames: Lincoln's Constitutional Legacy," *Journal of the Abraham Lincoln Association* 27 (Winter 2006): 1–12; Harry V. Jaffa, *A New Birth of Freedom* (Lanham, MD: Rowman & Littlefield, 2000).

4. Governor Bill Walker, "Walker to Obama: ANWR Wilderness Call Violates Statehood Compact and ANILCA," *Alaska Dispatch News*, January 31, 2015; John Coghill and Chad Hutchinson, "Haycox Wrong on ANWR and Alaska's Rights as a State," *Alaska Dispatch News*, February 11, 2015.

5. Alaska Department of Law, 1969 Op. Att'y Gen. No. 2 (March 28).

6. *Alaska v. U.S.*, 35 F. Cl. (1996); Ivan L. Ascott, "Comments: The Alaska Statehood Act Does Not Guarantee Alaska Ninety Percent of the Revenue from Mineral Leases on Federal Land in Alaska," *Seattle University Law Review* 27 (2004): 999–1034.

7. The ideal of the statehood compact is examined in detail in chapter 7.

8. Walter J. Hickel, "Decisions Made in 1959 Should Stand Forever," *Anchorage Daily News*, June 29, 1996, B6.

9. Alaska Constitution, Article VII, Section 1.

10. Alaska Statehood Act, Section 6(a) begins "For the purposes of furthering the development of and expansion of communities, the State of Alaska is hereby granted," Public Law 85-508, 72 Stat. 339, July 7 1958. One hundred four million acres is greater than the entire state of California, which is over 101 million acres; Alaska comprises 375 million total acres of land.

11. U.S. Congress, House, 80th Cong., 1st Sess., Subcommittee on Territorial and Insular Possessions of Public Lands, Report on H.R. 206, A Bill to Provide for the Admission of Alaska (1947); 85th Cong., 2nd Sess., Senate Report 1163 (1958); 104 Cong. Record 12 (1958).

12. Ascott, "Comments," 1012.

13. Ibid.

14. See Michael Kammen, "The Problem of American Exceptionalism: A Reconsideration," *American Quarterly* 45, no. 1 (March 1993): 1–43, an extended essay on the case for and against the existence and persistence of an American exceptionalism.

15. William J. Novak, "Myth of the 'Weak' American State," *American Historical Review* 113 (June 2008): 756; Louis Hartz, *The Liberal Tradition in America: An Interpretation of American Political Thought since the Revolution* (New York: Harcourt Brace, 1955).

16. Sean Wilentz, *The Rise of American Democracy: Jefferson to Lincoln* (New York: W. W. Norton, 2005); "Against Exceptionalism: Class Consciousness and the American Labor Movement, 1790–1920," *International Labor and Working Class History* 26 (Fall 1984): 1–24.

17. Novak, "Myth of the 'Weak' American State," 754, 758; see, for example, Max M. Edling, *A Revolution in Favor of Government: Origins of the U.S. Constitution and the Making of the American State* (New York: Oxford University Press, 2003); Richard White, *"It's Your Misfortune and None of My Own": A New History of the American West* (Norman: University of Oklahoma Press, 1991); Sidney M. Milkis, *The President and the Parties: The Transformation of the American Party System since the New Deal* (New York: Oxford University Press, 1993).

18. Hannah Arendt, *On Revolution* (New York: Viking Press, 1963). On the dependence of American western development on the federal government, see White, *"It's Your Misfortune and None of My Own,"* 57, 61–178, but also Karen R. Merrill, "In Search of the 'Federal Presence' in the American West," *Western Historical Quarterly* 30 (Winter 1999): 459.

19. David Lowery and William D. Berry, "The Growth of Government in the United States: An Empirical Assessment of Competing Explanations," *American Journal of Political Science* 27, no. 4 (November 1983): 665–694; Jerry Mitchell and Richard Feiock, "A Comparative Analysis of Government Growth in the 50 American States," *State and Local Government Review* 20, no. 2 (Spring 1988): 51–58; Harry N. Scheiber, "Federalism and Legal Process: Historical and Contemporary Analysis of the American System," *Law and Society Review* 14, no. 3 (Spring 1980): 663–722; Ballard C. Campbell, "Federalism, State Action, and 'Critical Episodes' in the Growth of American Government," *Social Science History* 16, no. 4 (1992): 561–577.

20. Kammen, "The Problem of American Exceptionalism"; Seymour Martin Lipset, *American Exceptionalism: A Double-Edged Sword* (New York: W. W. Norton, 1997). See also Michael Lind, "The American Creed: Does It Matter? Should It Change?" *Foreign Affairs* (March/April 1996): 665–694.

21. See, for example, Bruce Walker, "Running against Washington," *American Thinker*, August 9, 2014.

22. Jeannette P. Nichols, "Alaska's Search for a Usable Past," *Pacific Northwest Quarterly* 59 (April 1968): 57–67.

23. See, for example, Walter R. Borneman, *Alaska: Saga of a Bold Land* (New York: Perennial, 2003); Claus-M. Naske, *Alaska: A History of the 49th State* (Norman: University of Oklahoma Press, 1994); William R. Hunt, *Alaska: A Bicentennial History* (New York: W. W. Norton, 1976); Ernest Gruening, *The State of Alaska* (New York: Random House, 1954).

24. Stephen Haycox, *Alaska: An American Colony* (Seattle: University of Washington Press, 2002); Stephen Haycox, *Frigid Embrace: Politics, Economy and Environment in Alaska* (Corvallis: Oregon State University Press, 2002); Roxanne Williss, *Alaska's Place in the West: From the Last Frontier to the Last Great Wilderness* (Lawrence: University Press of Kansas, 2010); Susan Kollin, *Nature's State: Imagining Alaska as the Last Frontier* (Chapel Hill: University of North Carolina Press, 2001); Kathryn Morse, *The Nature of Gold: An Environmental History of the Klondike Gold Rush* (Seattle: University of Washington Press, 2010).

25. Melody Webb, *The Last Frontier: A History of the Yukon Basin of Canada and Alaska* (Albuquerque: University of New Mexico Press, 1985); see a review of Webb's book by Kenneth Coates in *BC Studies* 74 (Summer 1987): 42–44. See also Gruening, *The State of Alaska*; and Nichols, "Alaska's Search for a Usable Past," 57–67.

26. Nichols, "Alaska's Search for a Usable Past," 63.

27. Paul Wallace Gates, *History of Public Land Law Policy Development* (Washington, DC: Wm. W. Gaunt & Sons, 1967). Gates is considered the foremost authority on the history of federal land policy. Malcolm J. Rohrbough, *The Land Office Business: The Settlement and Administration of American Public Lands, 1789–1837* (New York: Oxford University Press, 1968); Roy M. Robbins, *Our Landed Heritage: The Public Domain, 1776–1936* (Princeton, NJ: Princeton University Press, 1942).

28. Two major exceptions were Texas, which was an independent country before its acquisition by the United States in 1845 and entered the Union directly as a state, and California, which came in as a state nearly immediately after its acquisition through US victory in the Mexican War in 1848.

29. Mark Stein, *How the States Got Their Shapes* (New York: Smithsonian Books/Collins, 2008).

30. Morgan Sherwood, *Exploration of Alaska, 1865–1900* (New Haven, CT: Yale University Press, 1965), 1–4.

31. Ted C. Hinckley, *The Americanization of Alaska, 1867–1896* (Palo Alto, CA: Pacific Books, 1972); Haycox, *Alaska.*

32. The 1910 census showed also 30,000 Natives.

33. Haycox, *Frigid Embrace*, 20.

34. Gruening, *The State of Alaska*, 307.

35. Author's interview with Robert Atwood, publisher, *Anchorage Daily Times*, January 21, 1992, Anchorage Pioneers Oral History Project, Series 2, University of Alaska Anchorage Archives and Special Collections; Stephen Haycox, "Mining the Federal Government: The War and the All-American City," in *Alaska at War 1941–45: The Forgotten War Remembered*, ed. Fern Chandonnet (Fairbanks: University of Alaska Press, 2007), 203–210.

36. Author's interview with Lucy McDannel Whitehead, January 22, 1992, Anchorage Pioneers Oral History Project.

37. Gerald E. Bowkett, *Reaching for a Star: The Final Campaign for Alaska Statehood* (Kirkland, WA: Epicenter Press, 2009); Claus M. Naske, *49 at Last: The Fight for Alaska Statehood* (Kirkland, WA: Epicenter Press, 2009).

38. Claus-M. Naske, *Ernest Gruening: Alaska's Greatest Governor* (Fairbanks: University of Alaska Press, 2004).

39. Gruening, *The State of Alaska*. See also Peter A. Coates, *The Trans-Alaska Pipeline Controversy: Technology, Politics and the Frontier* (Bethlehem, PA: Lehigh University Press, 1991), 209; John Albertus Hellenthal, *The Alaskan Melodrama* (New York: Liveright Press, 1936); Jeannette Paddock Nichols, *Alaska: A History of Its Administration, Exploitation and Industrial Development during Its First Half Century of Rule by the United States* (Cleveland, OH: Arthur H. Clark Publishing, 1924).

40. Ernest Gruening, *Many Battles: The Autobiography of Ernest Gruening* (New York: Liveright Publishers, 1973), 397.

41. Claus-M. Naske, *History of Alaska Statehood* (Lanham, MD: University Press of America, 1985).

42. Ernest Gruening, "Let Us End American Colonialism," keynote speech at Alaska Constitutional Convention, November 9, 1955.

43. See Haycox, *Alaska*; Haycox, *Frigid Embrace*.

44. Richard A. Cooley, *Politics and Conservation: The Decline of the Alaska Salmon* (New York: Harper and Row, 1963); J. A. Crutchfield and G. Pontecorvo, *Pacific Salmon Fishery: A Study of Irrational Conservation* (Baltimore, MD: Johns Hopkins University Press, 1963); David F. Arnold, *Fishermen's Frontier: People and Salmon in Southeast Alaska* (Seattle: University of Washington Press, 2011).

45. Steve Colt, *Salmon Fish Traps in Alaska: An Economic History Perspective*, ISER Working Paper (Anchorage: University of Alaska Institute for Economic and Social Research, 2000), http://www.alaskool.org/projects/traditionalife/fishtrap/fishtrap.htm.

46. John H. Clark, Andrew McGregor, Robert D. Mecum, Paul Krasnowski, and Amy M. Carroll, *The Commercial Salmon Fishery in Alaska*, Alaska Fishery Research Bulletin 12 (Juneau: Alaska Department of Fish and Game, 2006), http://www.adfg.alaska.gov/static/home/library/PDFs/afrb/clarv12n1.pdf.

47. Alaskans use the term "Outside" to denote the contiguous states.

48. James Mackovjak, *Alaska Salmon Traps* (Gustavus, AK: Cross Sound Publications, 2013), vii: "The use of traps to catch salmon [was] the gut issue that energized the fight for statehood, the ultimate symbol of the absentee cannery owners."

49. Gruening, *Let Us End American Colonialism*; Gruening, *The State of Alaska*, 260; Gerald McBeath, *The Alaska State Constitution* (New York: Oxford University Press, 2011), 20; Carmel Finley, *All the Fish in the Sea: Maximum Sustained Yield and the Failure of Fisheries Management* (Chicago: University of Chicago Press, 2011), 23.

50. George Rogers, *The Future of Alaska: Economic Consequences of Statehood* (Baltimore, MD: Johns Hopkins University Press, 1962), 129.

51. Naske, *49 at Last*.

52. Since the 1920 Mineral Leasing Act, the federal government had been contributing 37.5 percent of revenue collected from mineral leases (coal, oil, and natural gas are classified as minerals) sold on federal land in various states to help defray the economic and social impacts of development. In the statehood act, to assist Alaska in paying the expenses of state government, Congress provided that the federal government should contribute 90 percent of such revenue to Alaska.

53. Terrence Cole, *Blinded by Riches: The Permanent Funding Problem and the Prudhoe Bay Effect* (Anchorage: Institute of Social and Economic Research, University of Alaska, Anchorage, 2004), 84.

54. Rogers, *The Future of Alaska*, 194; Cole, *Blinded by Riches*, 73.

55. George W. Rogers, *Alaska in Transition: The Southeast Region* (Baltimore, MD: Johns Hopkins University Press, 1960), 299.

56. Cole, *Blinded by Riches*, 74–75.

57. Quoted in ibid., 87.

58. Morgan Sherwood, *Big Game in Alaska: A History of Wildlife and People* (New Haven, CT: Yale University Press, 1981), 82. Moose populations rise and fall in relation to browse available for them; they do not thrive in heavily forested areas. Regrowth after forest fires creates ideal habitat.

59. Quoted in Ken Ross, *Environmental Conflict in Alaska* (Boulder, CO: University Press of Colorado, 2000), 131.

60. Ernest Gruening, "The Plot to Strangle Alaska," *Atlantic*, July 1965, 55–59.

61. Ken Ross, *Pioneering Conservation in Alaska* (Boulder: University Press of Colorado, 2006), 391.

62. This is a common practice in oil leasing. The first lessee may not have the capability to develop the lease and instead sells its rights to the later lessee for a price and/or a percentage of whatever profits are generated by the second lessee's development, which is exactly what the Anchorage businessmen did.

63. Alaska Statehood Act, accessed March 12, 2015, http://avalon.law.yale.edu/20th_century/ak_statehood.asp.

64. *United States v. Santa Fe Pacific Railroad Company*, 314 U.S. 339; Felix Cohen, "Original Indian Title," *Minnesota Law Review* 32 (1947): 28; Lucy Kramer Cohen, ed., *The Legal Conscience: Selected Papers of Felix S. Cohen* (New Haven, CT: Yale University Press, 1960), 264–272, 273–304.

65. Stephen Haycox, *Law of the Land: A History of the Office of the Attorney General and the Department of Law in Alaska* (Juneau: Alaska Department of Law, 1998), 87–100.

66. Nell Jessup Newton, "Indian Claims in the Court of the Conqueror," *American Indian Law Review* 41 (1992): 753–80; Peter N. Jones, *Respect for the Ancestors: American Indian Cultural Affiliation in the American West* (Boulder, CO: Bauu Press, 2005).

67. Donald Craig Mitchell, *Take My Land, Take My Life: The Story of Congress's Historic Settlement of Alaska Native Land Claims, 1960–1971* (Fairbanks: University of Alaska Press, 2001), 55–95.

68. Dan O'Neill, *The Firecracker Boys* (New York: St. Martin's Press, 1994).

69. *Tundra Times*, October 28, 1966, quoted in Mitchell, *Take My Land, Take My Life*, 123.

70. U.S. Congress, Senate Executive Report No. 1, 89th Congress, 2nd Sess. (1966), 7, quoted in Mitchell, *Take My Land, Take My Life*, 95.

71. Remarkably, in 1964 Governor Egan, on the advice of officials in the state Department of Natural Resources, directed the selection of unreserved lands on Alaska's

North Slope between the Arctic National Wildlife Range and Petroleum Reserve No. 4, a selection Natives did not protest because they did not learn of it until the title conveyance had been made. The vast Prudhoe Bay oil field would be discovered on those lands in 1968.

72. *Alaska v. Udall*, U.S. Dist. Ct. Alaska, No. A-21-67 (1967).

73. Interview with Attorney General Edgar Paul Boyko in Haycox, *Law of the Land*, 75–80.

74. Alaska Department of Labor and Workforce Development, Research and Analysis Report, 2013, accessed September 14, 2014, http://almis.labor.state.ak.us/pop /popestpub.htm.

75. 30 U.S. Statutes 409, May 14, 1898.

76. James R. Shortridge, "The Alaska Agricultural Empire: An American Agrarian Vision, 1898–1929," *Pacific Northwest Quarterly* 69 (October 1978): 145–161.

77. Scott Goldsmith, *Structural Analysis of the Alaska Economy: What Are the Drivers?*, Institute of Social and Economic Research (Anchorage: University of Alaska, 2010), 3 (Table I:1), 14 (Table II:6).

78. Scott Goldsmith, revised. *Structural Analysis of the Alaska Economy: What Are the Drivers?* (Anchorage: University of Alaska, Institute of Social and Economic Research, 2010), 3, 17; Gunnar Knapp, *A Very Brief Introduction to the Alaska Economy* (Anchorage: University of Alaska, Institute of Social and Economic Research, 2013), 14.

79. Eric Sandberg, *A History of Alaska Population Settlement* (Juneau: Alaska Department of Labor and Workforce Development, 2013), 16.

80. John Strohmeyer, *Extreme Conditions: Big Oil and the Transformation of Alaska* (New York: Simon & Schuster, 1993), 124.

CHAPTER 2. THE ARCTIC NATIONAL WILDLIFE REFUGE

1. Morgan Sherwood, *Big Game in Alaska: A History of Wildlife and People* (New Haven, CT: Yale University Press, 1981), 48–49.

2. Charles Wohlforth, *From the Shores of Ship Creek: Stories of Anchorage's First 100 Years* (Anchorage, AK: Todd Communications, 2014), 20.

3. Sherwood, *Big Game in Alaska*, 22; Ken Ross, *Pioneering Conservation in Alaska* (Boulder: University Press of Colorado, 2006).

4. Sherwood, *Big Game in Alaska*, 237–250.

5. Richard A. Cooley, *Politics and Conservation: The Decline of the Alaska Salmon* (New York: Harper and Row, 1963), 27.

6. Now National Petroleum Reserve–Alaska.

7. Robert Marshall, "I Am an Ecologist," Articles, Speeches, and Studies, Robert Marshall Papers (RMP), Manuscripts Division, Bancroft Library, University of California.

8. Robert Marshall, *Arctic Village* (New York: H. Smith and Haas, 1933), 376.

9. National Resources Committee, *Alaska—Its Resources and Development, Part VII: Regional Planning* (Washington, DC: Government Printing Office, 1938), 140, 213.

10. Robert Marshall, "The Problem of Alaska Development," Articles, Speeches, and Studies, RMP.

11. Roger Kaye, *Last Great Wilderness: The Campaign to Establish the Arctic National Wildlife Refuge* (Fairbanks: University of Alaska Press, 2006), 15.

12. George Collins, "Consideration of the Arctic National Wildlife Range in the Proposal for a Trans Alaska-Canada Gas Transmission Line," 1973, "Notes on Alaska Recreation Survey, Special Reference ANWR Proposal," 1985, George L. Collins Papers (GCP), Alaska and Polar Regions Collections and Archives, University of Alaska.

13. George L. Collins, "The Art and Politics of Park Planning and Preservation, 1920–1979," oral interview, California Digital Library, Bancroft Library, University of California, Berkeley, 195.

14. Kaye, *Last Great Wilderness*, 20.

15. George L. Collins and Lowell Sumner, "A Proposed Arctic Wilderness International Park: A Preliminary Report Concerning Its Values," *Alaska Recreation Survey*, Preliminary Statement, November 1952, Arctic Wilderness International Park, US Department of the Interior, National Park Service, Region Four, GCP.

16. Ibid., 189.

17. Denver Public Library, Wilderness Society Records (WSR), Series 1, Governing Council, Box 1, Folder 22.

18. Bancroft Library, University of California, Sierra Club Records (SCR), Series 6, Council Records, 1952.

19. Kaye, *Last Great Wilderness*, 66–79.

20. Mark Harvey, *Wilderness Forever: Howard Zahniser and the Path to the Wilderness Act*, ed. William Cronon (Seattle: University of Washington Press, 2005), 113.

21. Samuel P. Hays, *Beauty, Health and Permanence: Environmental Politics in the United States, 1955–1985* (New York: Cambridge University Press, 1987); Mark W. T. Harvey, *A Symbol of Wilderness: Echo Park and the American Conservation Movement* (Albuquerque: University of New Mexico Press, 1994); Harvey, *Wilderness Forever*, 181.

22. Harvey, *Wilderness Forever,* 120–123, 178–221.

23. See Brian Allen Drake, *Loving Nature, Fearing the State: Environmentalism and Antigovernment Politics before Reagan* (Seattle: University of Washington Press, 2013), 12.

24. Roderick Nash, *Wilderness and the American Mind* (New Haven, CT: Yale University Press, 1967), 208–220.

25. Kaye, *Last Great Wilderness*, 72.

26. SCR, Series 6, Council Records, 1957.

27. William O. Douglas, *My Wilderness: The Pacific West* (Garden City, NJ: Doubleday & Co., 1960).

28. Lois Crisler, *Arctic Wild* (New York: Harper & Brothers, 1958), 77, 78.

29. Marshall, *Arctic Village*, 375–379.

30. "Would Set Aside Wilderness Area in Northeast Alaska," *Fairbanks Daily News-Miner*, January 27, 1954, 1.

31. Quoted in Kaye, *Last Great Wilderness*, 61.

32. "Arctic Wilderness Proposal Poses Threat to State," *Anchorage Daily Times*, November 3, 1958.

33. Kaye, *Last Great Wilderness*, 121–124.

34. *Fairbanks Daily News-Miner*, November 30, 1957; March 17, 1958.

35. Kaye, *Last Great Wilderness*, 118.

36. Ken Ross, *Pioneering Conservation*, 420–421.

37. It is arresting to reflect that this is the area where the great Prudhoe Bay oil deposit would be found in 1967–1968. That deposit was unknown in 1957, but the potential to explore the area greatly sweetened the federal announcement of the creation of the Arctic reserve.

38. Session Laws of Alaska, 1959, HJR 23. Although the legislation used the term "range," opponents often used the term "refuge" to call attention to the restrictive nature of the mandated management of the unit.

39. A mining patent is a form of title, defensible by the United States against claimant other than the patentee.

40. Gordon Harrison, *Alaska's Constitution: A Citizen's Guide* (Juneau: Alaska Legislative Affairs Agency, 1994), Article VII, Sections 11 and 12.

41. Public Law 85-508, 72 Stat. 339, July 7, 1958, Section 6e.

42. Claus-M. Naske, *Edward Lewis "Bob" Bartlett of Alaska: A Life in Politics* (Fairbanks: University of Alaska Press, 1979), 211–214.

43. Hearings Part 1, 1-30.

44. Kaye, *Last Great Wilderness*, 199.

45. US Congress, House, Committee on Merchant Marine and Fisheries, Subcommittee on Fisheries and Wildlife Conservation, Hearings, H.R. 7045, July 1, 1959, 86th Congress, 1st Sess.

46. William A. Egan Papers, Series 8, Memoranda 1952–74, File 4, Alaska Polar Regions Collections and Archives, University of Alaska, Fairbanks.

47. Harvey, *Wilderness Forever*, 178, 207–208.

48. US Department of the Interior, Public Land Order 2214, 1960.

49. Harvey, *Wilderness Forever*, 200, 224.

50. Report, March 3, 1958, Box 8, Folder 12, GCP.

51. Margaret E. Murie, *Two in the Far North* (New York: Alfred Knopf, 1962), 315.

52. Kaye, *Last Great Wilderness*, 172.

53. Ibid., 106.

CHAPTER 3. NATIVE CLAIMS AND ALASKA STATEHOOD

1. William C. Sturtevant, ed., *Handbook of North American Indians*, vol. 5, *Arctic*, vol. 6, *Subarctic*, vol. 7, *Northwest Coast* (Washington, DC: Smithsonian Institution, 1978); Ken Ross, *Pioneering Conservation*, 192–208; Alaska Native Heritage Center, Anchorage, Alaska, http://www.alaskanative.net.

2. Steve J. Langdon, *Native Peoples of Alaska: Traditional Living in a Northern Land*, 5th ed. (Anchorage, AK: Greatland Graphics, 2014).

3. David S. Case, *Alaska Natives and American Laws* (Fairbanks: University of Alaska Press, 1984).

4. *United States v. Santa Fe Pacific Railroad*, 314 U.S. 339 (1941).

5. Norma E. Forbes, "The State's Role in Suicide Prevention Programs for Alaska Native Youth," *American Indian and Alaska Native Mental Health* 4 (1994): 235–249; William Yardley, *New York Times*, May 14, 2007.

6. In 1966 the various regional Native associations formed a new organization, the Alaska Federation of Natives, the first statewide Native advocacy body. It is the principal voice of Alaska Native policy and political initiatives.

7. Donald Craig Mitchell, *Take My Land, Take My Life: The Story of Congress's Historic Settlement of Alaska Native Land Claims, 1960–1971* (Fairbanks: University of Alaska Press, 2001), 67–74.

8. The status of the reserve was unclear before the Interior Department secured a legal opinion supporting its definition as an Indian reservation, which entitled it to the oil lease revenue. Before that determination, however, state officials argued that it was not a reservation but unreserved federal land, and therefore the oil lease revenue should go to the US Treasury with 90 percent then rebated to the State of Alaska, per the terms of the statehood act.

9. Mitchell, *Take My Land, Take My Life*, 158–159.

10. George Sundborg, *Statehood for Alaska: The Issues Involved and Facts about the Issues* (Anchorage: Alaska Statehood Association, 1946).

11. Ernest Gruening to Secretary of the Interior Oscar Chapman, January 8, 1953, Series 4, Box 53, Ernest Gruening Papers (EGP), Alaska and Polar Regions Collections and Archives, University of Alaska.

12. Dan O'Neill, *The Firecracker Boys* (New York: St. Martin's Press, 1994), 206–214.

13. Patrick Daily and Beverly Ann James, *Cultural Politics and the Mass Media* (Champaign: University of Illinois Press, 2004), 93, 122, 289.

14. Peter A. Coates, *The Trans-Alaska Pipeline Controversy: Technology, Conservation and the Frontier* (Bethlehem, PA: Lehigh University Press, 1991), 130–131.

15. O'Neill, *The Firecracker Boys*, 210.

16. Two were Celia Hunter and Virginia Wood, former Army Air Service pilots who founded the first ecotourism operation in Alaska, Camp Denali, just west of the

original Mt. McKinley National Park boundary. Both would become formidable environmental activists. See Karen Brewster, ed., *Boots, Bikes and Bombers: Adventures of Alaska Conservationist Ginny Hill Wood* (Fairbanks: University of Alaska Press, 2012).

17. Alaska Conservation Society Papers (ACSP), Box 18, Folders 3–4, Archives, Alaska Polar Regions Collections and Archives, Rasmuson Library, University of Alaska, Fairbanks.

18. Paul Brooks and Joseph Foote, "The Disturbing Story of Project Chariot," *Harper's* 224 (April 1962), 62–67.

19. Robert Atwood, "Alaska Test Is Needed for the Progress of Man," *Anchorage Daily Times*, August 24, 1962.

20. Barry Commoner, *The Closing Circle: Nature, Man and Technology* (New York: Alfred A. Knopf, 1971).

21. Coates, *The Trans-Alaska Pipeline Controversy*, 131.

22. George W. Rogers, *The Future of Alaska: The Economic Consequences of Statehood* (Baltimore, MD: Johns Hopkins Press, 1962), 182.

23. Ibid., 94.

24. Marc Reisner, *Cadillac Desert: The American West and Its Disappearing Water* (New York: Viking Press, 1986).

25. ACSP, Box 1, Folder 16; Box 3, Folders 3, 10; Box 4, Folder 8; "No Rampart Say Villages," *Tundra Times*, November 18, 1963, 1.

26. Ernest Gruening, *Many Battles: The Autobiography of Ernest Gruening* (New York: Liveright Publishers, 1973), 496–501.

27. Coates, *The Trans-Alaska Pipeline Controversy*, 144.

28. "Rampart Dam Lacks Feasibility," *New York Times*, April 20, 1966.

29. Coates, *The Trans-Alaska Pipeline Controversy*, 157–158.

30. Stephen Haycox, "William Paul, Sr., and the Alaska Voters' Literacy Act of 1925," *Alaska History* 3 (Fall 1986).

31. *Tee-Hit-Ton Indians v. United States*, 120 F. Supp. 202, 128 Ct. Cl. 82; Stephen Haycox, "Tee-Hit Ton and Alaska Native Rights," in *Law for the Elephant, Law for the Beaver: Essays in the Legal History of the North American West*, ed. John McLaren, Hamar Foster, and Chet Orloff (Regina, Saskatchewan: Canadian Plains Research Center, University of Regina, and Pasadena, CA: Ninth Judicial Circuit Historical Society, 1992), 125–145.

32. 348 U.S. 272, 75 S. Ct. 313, 99 L. Ed. 314, reh. denied, 348 U.S. 965, 75 S. Ct. 521, 99 L. Ed. 753 (1955).

33. See Donald Craig Mitchell, *Sold American: The Story of Alaska Natives and Their Land, 1867–1959* (Fairbanks: University of Alaska Press, 2003), 405–408, 262–265; Peter M. Metcalfe, *A Dangerous Idea: The Alaska Native Brotherhood and the Struggle for Indigenous Rights* (Fairbanks: University of Alaska Press, 2014), 14–16.

34. Stephen Haycox, "Economic Development and Indian Land Rights in Modern Alaska: The 1947 Tongass Timber Act," *Western Historical Quarterly* 21, no. 1 (February 1990): 21–46.

35. James Mackovjak, *Tongass Timber: A History of Logging and Timber Utilization in Southeast Alaska* (Durham, NC: Forest History Society, 2010), 106–108, 123–124.

36. Quoted in Mitchell, *Take My Land, Take My Life*, 52.

37. Ernest Gruening, *The State of Alaska* (New York: Random House, 1954), 371.

38. *Miller v. United States*, 159 F. 2nd 997 (9th Cir. 1947).

39. Pub. L. 80-385, *Statutes at Large* 101, 920 (1947).

40. Mitchell, *Sold American*, 372.

41. "Sustained Yield from the Fisheries . . . from the Forests," *Pacific Fisherman* (July 1947): 24.

42. Quoted in Mackovjak, *Tongass Timber*, 345–346. Further explanation of the development of the Tongass National Forest appears in chapter 6.

43. Gruening to Chapman, EGP.

44. Author's interview with Robert Atwood, publisher, *Anchorage Daily Times*, January 21, 1992, Anchorage Pioneers Oral History Project, Series 2, University of Alaska Anchorage Archives and Special Collections.

45. Hugh Butler to Anthony W. Smith, June 2, 1950, Box 22, Hugh Butler Papers, Nebraska Historical Society, Lincoln.

46. *Statehood for Alaska: Hearings on H.R. 206 and H.R. 1808 before the Subcommittee on Territorial and Insular Possessions of the House Committee on Public Lands*, 80th Congress, 1st Session (1947), 14.

47. Alaska Statehood Act, accessed March 12, 2015, http://avalon.law.yale.edu /20th_century/ak_statehood.asp.

48. Metcalfe, *A Dangerous Idea*, 83–84.

49. Grand Camp resolution, 1950, Series 2, Box 1, Folder 10, Curry-Weissbrodt Papers, Sealaska Heritage Institute Archives, Juneau.

50. Metcalfe, *A Dangerous Idea*, 57.

51. Alaska Statehood Act.

52. Metcalfe, *A Dangerous Idea*, 45–55.

53. 100 *Congressional Record* 3167 (1954).

54. Alaska Statehood Act, Article VIII, Section 1.

55. Neil Risser Bassett Papers, Ted Stevens newsletter, March 1971, Box 14, Series 30, University of Alaska Anchorage Archives.

56. Mitchell, *Take My Land, Take My Life*, 94.

57. Kevin R. Marsh, "Wilderness Conference on Yellowstone Lake," *Living Wilderness* 77 (Summer/Fall 1961): 14–18.

58. Mitchell, *Take My Land, Take My Life*, 100.

59. *State of Alaska v. Stewart Udall*, US District Court for the District of Alaska, No. A-21-67 (1967); author's interview with John Havelock, attorney general, 1970–1973, April 22, 2014. The state would ultimately lose the suit.

60. Mitchell, *Take My Land, Take My Life*, 152.

61. Jack Roderick, *Crude Dreams: A Personal History of Oil and Politics in Alaska* (Fairbanks, AK: Epicenter Press, 1997), 167–169.

62. Mitchell, *Take My Land, Take My Life*, 186.

63. Ibid., 144.

CHAPTER 4. THE TRANS-ALASKA PIPELINE

1. Public Land Order 4582.

2. Jack Roderick, *Crude Dreams: A Personal History of Oil and Politics in Alaska* (Fairbanks, AK: Epicenter Press, 1997), 217–223.

3. "Richest Auction in History," *Time*, September 19, 1969, 54.

4. Mobil Oil, Phillips Petroleum, Union Oil, Amerada Hess, and Home Oil soon joined TAPS.

5. Ross Coen, *Breaking Ice: The Epic Voyage of the SS Manhattan through the Northwest Passage* (Fairbanks: University of Alaska Press, 2012).

6. Disagreement over the extent of opposition to nuclear power led the Sierra Club to accept David Brower's resignation in 1969. He then founded Friends of the Earth.

7. Edgar Wayburn, "Global Activist and Elder Statesman of the Sierra Club; Alaska, International Conservation, National Parks and Protected Areas, 1980–1992," an oral history conducted in 1992 by Ann Lage, Sierra Club Oral History Series, Regional Oral History Office, Bancroft Library, University of California–Berkeley, 1996, 366.

8. Quoted in Don Liston, "Pipeline Insures Alaska's Economic Future," *Anchorage Daily Times*, November 14, 1973, B1.

9. Elizabeth Tower, *Anchorage: From Its Humble Origins as a Railroad Construction Camp* (Fairbanks, AK: Epicenter Press, 1999), 149.

10. Sponsored by the American Association for the Advancement of Science.

11. E. L. "Bob" Bartlett died of a heart attack in December 1968. Before leaving the governor's office in Alaska, Hickel appointed Stevens to replace Bartlett. Stevens had served as US attorney in Alaska, had worked in the Interior Department during the Alaska statehood campaign, and had served two terms in the Alaska House of Representatives.

12. Quoted in Peter A. Coates, *The Trans-Alaska Pipeline Controversy: Technology, Conservation and the Frontier* (Bethlehem, PA: Lehigh University Press, 1991), 180; author's interview with Robert Weeden, president, Alaska Conservation Society, August 18, 1998.

13. Linda Luther, *The National Environmental Policy Act: Background and Implementation* (Washington, DC: Congressional Research Service, 2005).

14. Edgar Wayburn, *Your Land and Mine: Evolution of a Conservationist* (San Francisco: Sierra Club Books, 2004), 216.

15. Brock Evans, speech to award dinner, September 20, 1968, Box 78, Folder 7, Series IV, Brock Evans Papers, 03531, American Heritage Center, University of Wyoming, Laramie.

16. Mark Ganopole to Robert Weeden, June 2, 1969, Mark Hickok Papers, Box 1, Folder 4, University of Alaska Anchorage Archives.

17. Dave Hickok lecture, Anchorage Unitarian Universalist Fellowship, March 1, 1970, Dave M. Hickok Papers, Box 1, Folder 20, University of Alaska Anchorage Archives.

18. Robert Cahn, *The Fight to Save Wild Alaska* (New York: Audubon Society, 1982), 11.

19. Coates, *The Trans-Alaska Pipeline Controversy*, 190.

20. Federal Field Committee for Development Planning in Alaska, *Alaska Natives and the Land* (Washington, DC: Government Printing Office, 1968).

21. Donald Craig Mitchell, *Take My Land, Take My Life: The Story of Congress's Historic Settlement of Alaska Native Land Claims, 1960–1971* (Fairbanks: University of Alaska Press, 2001), 438–439.

22. Ibid., 391–399.

23. Wayburn, *Your Land and Mine*, 231.

24. Mitchell, *Take My Land, Take My Life*, 441.

25. Ibid., 454.

26. Ibid., 449.

27. Edgar Wayburn, "Sierra Club Statesman Leader of the Parks and Wilderness Movement: Gaining Protection for Alaska, the Redwoods, and Golden Gate Parklands," an oral history conducted in 1976–1981 by Ann Lage and Susan Schrepfer, Sierra Club Oral History Series, Regional Oral History Office, Bancroft Library, University of California, 1985, 407–412, accessed March 22, 2014, http://digitalassets.lib .berkeley.edu/roho/ucb/text/wayburn_edgar.pdf.

28. Michael McCloskey, "Sierra Club Executive Director: The Evolving Club and the Environmental Movement, 1961–1981," an oral history conducted in 1981 by Susan R. Schrepfer, Sierra Club Oral History Series, Regional Oral History Office, Bancroft Library, University of California, Berkeley, 1983, 194–196.

29. Mitchell, *Take My Land, Take My Life*, 491–493.

30. Sean Manget, "Senate Candidates Discuss Alaska Native, Rural Issues," *Alaska Journal of Commerce*, October 14, 2010, 1.

31. This is true, also, of the Alaska Permanent Fund.

32. See *McCrary v. Ivanof Bay Village*, as reported at http://www.narf.org/nill /bulletins/state/documents/mccrary_v_ivanof.html, Alaska Supreme Court S-13972, December 11, 2011; Indian Tribal List Act, 108 Stat. 4701.

33. By 1987 most of the 44 million acres of Native entitlement had been conveyed.

34. "Work on Pipeline Halted," *Anchorage Daily Times*, December 20, 1971.

35. Quoted in Coates, *The Trans-Alaska Pipeline Controversy*, 227–228.

36. Department of the Interior, *Final Environmental Impact Statement, Proposed Trans-Alaska Pipeline*, vol. 2 (Washington, DC: Government Printing Office, March 20, 1972), 217.

37. Coates, *The Trans-Alaska Pipeline Controversy*, 202.

38. The Wilderness Society, Friends of the Earth, and the Environmental Defense Fund, *Comments on the Environmental Impact Statement for the Trans-Alaska Pipeline*, 4 vol. (Washington, DC: Center for Law and Social Policy, May 4, 1972).

39. Department of the Interior, *Final Environmental Impact Statement*, vol. 7, M-5-3-5.

40. Coates, *The Trans-Alaska Pipeline Controversy*, 241.

41. "Vogler to Form New Party," *Anchorage Daily News*, February 24, 1973, B1; John McPhee, *Coming into the Country* (New York: Farrar, Straus and Giroux, 1977), 314–321.

42. Michael C. Castellon, "Standing to Challenge the Disposition of Land in Alaska," *Alaska Law Review* 2 (1985): 396.

43. Coates, *The Trans-Alaska Pipeline Controversy*, 239.

44. David Ross Brower, "Reflections on the Sierra Club, Friends of the Earth, and Earth Island Institute," an oral history conducted in 1999 by Ann Lage, Regional Oral History Office, Bancroft Library, University of California, Berkeley, 2012, 278.

45. McCloskey, Sierra Club Oral History Series, 194–196, 204–205; Coates, *The Trans-Alaska Pipeline Controversy*, 246.

46. The history of pulp mills on the Tongass National Forest and their relation to the Alaska lands act is discussed in chapter 6 of this book.

47. "Flawed Film Depicts Unknown Species," *Anchorage Daily News*, November 22, 1969, B5.

CHAPTER 5. THE ALASKA LANDS ACT

1. Lewis Lapham, "Alaska: Politicians and Natives, Money and Oil," *Harper's*, May 1970, 85–108.

2. "Economic Bonanza for Alaska," *Anchorage Daily Times*, December 19, 1971, 1.

3. Donald Craig Mitchell, *Take My Land, Take My Life: The Story of Congress's Historic Settlement of Alaska Native Land Claims, 1960–1971* (Fairbanks: University of Alaska Press, 2001), 476.

4. Daniel Nelson, *Northern Landscapes: The Struggle for Wilderness Alaska* (Washington, DC: Resources for the Future Press, 2004), 61.

5. Ibid., 78.

6. Interview with Virginia Wood and Robert Weeden, June 9, 2006, US Fish and

Wildlife Service National Digital Library, 1–2, http://digitalmedia.fws.gov/cdm/ref
/collection/document/id/1870.

7. Peter A. Coates, *The Trans-Alaska Pipeline Controversy: Technology, Conservation and the Frontier* (Bethlehem, PA: Lehigh University Press, 1991), 101.

8. Author's interview with Dave Hickok and Mark Ganopole, April 23, 1996; Nelson, *Northern Landscapes*, 119.

9. Author's interview with John Havelock, attorney general, 1970–1973, January 14, 1992.

10. Ibid.

11. ANCSA, 43 USC 1616. Members included Burt Silcock, then Jack Horton, as federal cochair; Joe Josephson as governor's cochair designate; Max Brewer; Harry Carter (the mandated Native member); Richard Cooley; Joseph Fitzgerald; Charles Herbert; Celia Hunter; James Hurley; and George Sullivan.

12. Nelson, *Northern Landscapes*, 122–124.

13. Ibid., 126–128.

14. Author's interview with John Havelock.

15. Ibid., 128.

16. Neil Risser Basset Papers, Box 23, Series 8, Reading File, University of Alaska Anchorage Archives.

17. Quoted in Nelson, *Northern Landscapes*, 129.

18. "Secretary Ignores Alaska Future," *Fairbanks Daily News-Miner*, January 15, 1974.

19. Judith Kleinfeld, *Frontier Romance: Environment, Culture and Alaska Identity* (Fairbanks: University of Alaska Press, 2012); Expert Panel Report, *Defining the Term "Frontier Area" for Programs Implemented through the Office for the Advancement of Telehealth* (Bismarck: Center for Rural Health, University of North Dakota, 2006). See the website for the Alaska Center for Rural Health, University of Alaska Anchorage, http://www.uaa.alaska.edu/hpd/acrh.cfm.

20. Edgar Wayburn, "Sierra Club Statesman Leader of the Parks and Wilderness Movement: Gaining Protection for Alaska, the Redwoods, and Golden Gate Parklands," an oral history conducted in 1976–1981 by Ann Lage and Susan Schrepfer, Sierra Club Oral History Series, Regional Oral History Office, Bancroft Library, University of California, 1985, 439.

21. Robert Cahn, *The Fight to Save Wild Alaska* (New York: Audubon Society, 1982), 15.

22. James Morton Turner, *The Promise of Wilderness: American Environmental Politics since 1964* (Seattle: University of Washington Press, 2012), 164–168.

23. Jay Hammond, *Diapering the Devil: A Lesson for Oil Rich Nations* (Homer, AK: Kachemak Resources Institute, 2011).

24. Jay Hammond, "What Will Happen to This Land?," testimony before Alaska

Lands Subcommittee, House Interior Committee, April 22, 1977, Jay S. Hammond Papers, University of Alaska Anchorage Archives.

25. Author's interview with William L. Hensley, March 22, 1993.

26. Nelson, *Northern Landscapes*, 171.

27. Ibid., 214–215.

28. Turner, *The Promise of Wilderness*, 166.

29. Timo Christopher Allan, "Locked Up!: A History of Resistance to the Creation of National Parks in Alaska" (PhD diss., Washington State University, 2010).

30. G. Frank Williss, *"Do Things Right the First Time": Administrative History, the National Park Service and the Alaska National Interest Lands Conservation Act of 1980* (Anchorage, AK: National Park Service, 1995), 140; Nelson, *Northern Landscapes*, 223.

31. Cahn, *The Fight to Save Wild Alaska*, 29.

32. On August 31, 2015, on the eve of an unprecedented three-day visit to Alaska to highlight concern about global climate change, President Obama, by executive order, renamed Mt. McKinley, restoring its Native name, Denali.

33. Turner, *The Promise of Wilderness*, 180.

34. Frank Norris, *Alaska Subsistence: A National Park Service Management History* (Anchorage, AK: National Park Service, 2002), 67–87. Although most rural subsistence harvesters are Native, the rural designation protects the right of non-Native nonurban residents to harvest traditional resources. Subsistence is addressed in chapter 6.

35. James Mackovjak, *Tongass Timber: A History of Logging and Timber Utilization in Southeast Alaska* (Durham, NC: Forest History Society, 2010), 262–263. Most of the subsidy was for road construction. The Tongass National Forest is addressed in chapter 6.

36. Scott Goldsmith, *Structural Analysis of the Alaska Economy: What Are the Drivers?*, Institute of Social and Economic Research (Anchorage: University of Alaska, 2010), 91. Alaska is the highest state in per capita federal spending (civilian and military). Conservation-unit management provides 15,000 jobs. Much summer tourism is directed at conservation units, the most popular being Denali National Park.

37. Rosemary Shinohara, "Senator Stevens Reflects," *Anchorage Daily News*, January 10, 2009.

38. Turner, *The Promise of Wilderness*, 180–181.

39. William Cronon, "The Trouble with Wilderness, or Getting Back to the Wrong Nature," in *Uncommon Ground: Rethinking the Human Place in Nature*, ed. William Cronon (New York: W. W. Norton, 1995), 69–90.

40. Joan Kluwe and Edwin Krumpe, "Interpersonal and Societal Aspects of Use Conflicts," *International Journal of Wilderness* 9 (December 2003): 28–33.

41. R. McGregor Cawley, *Federal Land, Western Anger: The Sagebrush Rebellion and Environmental Politics* (Lawrence: University Press of Kansas, 1993), 94–110.

CHAPTER 6. UNFINISHED BUSINESS:
SUBSISTENCE AND THE TONGASS

1. William Cronon, "The Trouble with Wilderness, or Getting Back to the Wrong Nature," in *Uncommon Ground: Rethinking the Human Place in Nature*, ed. William Cronon (New York: W. W. Norton, 1995).

2. Mark Harvey, *Wilderness Forever: Howard Zahniser and the Path to the Wilderness Act*, ed. William Cronon (Seattle: University of Washington Press, 2005).

3. 78 Stat. 890.

4. Ted Steinberg, *Down to Earth: Nature's Role in American History* (Oxford and New York: Oxford University Press, 2002), 3–7.

5. William Cronon, Samuel P. Hays, Michael P. Cohen, and Thomas R. Dunlap, "Forum: The Trouble with Wilderness," *Environmental History* 1 (1996): 7–55.

6. See James Morton Turner's discussion of the debate over the wilderness concept at *The Promise of Wilderness: American Environmental Politics since 1964* (Seattle: University of Washington Press, 2012), 88, 176, and especially 326. Turner is more sanguine that coalition leaders understood inhabited wilderness than are some other analysts.

7. In 2015 about 5.5 million acres remained to be conveyed.

8. In some early versions of H.R. 39 the preference was for Natives; it was changed to "rural" because "Native" was probably unconstitutional and because there are many non-Natives living in nonurban areas who depend on subsistence harvest of traditional resources.

9. Customary and Traditional Use Determination, Subsistence in Alaska, Department of Fish and Game, State of Alaska, accessed October 14, 2014,

http://www.adfg.alaska.gov/index.cfm?adfg=subsistence.customary.

10. Wallace Turner, "Alaska Hunters Seek to End Law Giving Natives Priority," *New York Times*, July 4, 1982.

11. "AFN Opposes Initiative," *Tundra Times*, September 14, 1982. Hensley's autobiography is William L. Iggiagruk Hensley, *Fifty Miles from Tomorrow: A Memoir of Alaska and the Real People* (New York: Farrar, Straus and Giroux, 2009).

12. R. McGregor Cawley, *Federal Land, Western Anger: The Sagebrush Rebellion and Environmental Politics* (Lawrence: University Press of Kansas, 1993), 2.

13. Malcolm B. Roberts, ed., *Going Up in Flames: The Promises and Pledges of Alaska Statehood under Attack* (Anchorage, AK: Commonwealth North, 1990).

14. The state attorney general ruled that the initiative violated the state constitution and ordered state officials to ignore it.

15. *McDowell v. State*, 85 Pac. 2nd 1 (1989).

16. Management of adjacent lands and waters was necessitated by the migration of wild species.

17. Dan Joling, "Native Group Urges Boycott of Sportsmen," *Juneau Daily Empire*, May 17, 2001.

18. Elizabeth Manning, "Prop. 1 Passes in Anchorage by a Landslide," *Anchorage Daily News*, April 3, 2002.

19. Alaska Constitution, Article XIII, Section 1.

20. *Sam McDowell et al. v. United States*, No. F90-034 CV (D-Alaska, 1990).

21. *Katie John v. State of Alaska*, No. A85-698 CV (D-Alaska 1989).

22. *Katie John v. United States*, 72 Fed. 3rd 698 (9th Cir. 1995); Ryan T. Peel, "Katie John v. United States: Balancing State Sovereignty with a Native Grandmother's Right to Fish," *BYU Journal of Public Law* 15 (2001): 263–279.

23. Bill McAllister, "Knowles: No Appeal of Lawsuit," *Juneau Daily Empire*, August 28, 2002.

24. The BIA is included because there are Native allotments and tribal councils in Alaska operating alongside the development corporations.

25. 16 U.S. Code Chapter 51 (1980).

26. Dan O'Neill, *A Land Gone Lonesome: An Inland Voyage along the Yukon River* (New York: Counterpoint, 2006).

27. Ken Ross, *Environmental Conflict in Alaska* (Boulder, CO: University Press of Colorado, 2000), 206–228.

28. Jack Hession, "'Good Neighbor' or 'Good Predator' Policy," *Sierra Club Alaska Newsletter*, July 1981.

29. Report on Borax Mine, May 1987, Box 44, Folder 10, Box 45, Folder 1, Alaska Conservation Society Papers, Archives, Alaska Polar Regions Collections and Archives, Rasmuson Library, University of Alaska Fairbanks.

30. Sierra Club Oral History Series, James W. Moorman interview, 1984, 73, 92, 148.

31. Tom Kizzia, *Pilgrim's Wilderness: A True Story of Faith and Madness on the Alaska Frontier* (New York: Crown Publishers, 2013).

32. Sally Gilbert, Report to the Citizens' Advisory Commission on Federal Areas, February 12, 2013, http://dnr.alaska.gov/commis/cacfa/documents/FOSDocuments/GibertPresentaiton.pdf.

33. Citizens' Advisory Commission on Federal Areas, http://dnr.alaska.gov/commis/cacfa/FOS.html.

34. Now the Yale School of Forestry and Environmental Studies.

35. Frank Heintzleman, "Forestry in Alaska," *Proceedings of the Alaskan Science Conference* (Washington, DC: National Academy of Sciences, 1951), 129–130.

36. Stephen Haycox, "Economic Development and Indian Land Rights in Modern Alaska: The 1947 Tongass Timber Act," *Western Historical Quarterly* (February 1990): 3–4.

37. A postwar wood shortage in Japan raised the possibility of purchases from the Soviet Union; the United States helped facilitate establishment of the Sitka mill to obviate that eventuality.

38. Both continued their support of forest development as US senators, 1958 to 1968.

39. 72 Stat. 339.

40. John R. Howe, *Bear Man of Admiralty Island: A Biography of Allen E. Hasselborg* (Fairbanks: University of Alaska Press, 1996).

41. Quoted in Ross, *Environmental Conflict in Alaska*, 248.

42. Ibid., 250; James Mackovjak, *Tongass Timber: A History of Logging and Timber Utilization in Southeast Alaska* (Durham, NC: Forest History Society, 2010), 260.

43. Kathie Durbin, *Tongass: Pulp Politics and the Fight for the Alaska Rain Forest* (Corvallis: Oregon State University Press, 1999), 121–122, 130–131.

44. Ross, *Environmental Conflict in Alaska*, 257–261; Durbin, *Tongass*, 197–202.

45. Timothy Egan, "Tongass Old Growth Tress at Risk," *New York Times*, August 22, 1989.

46. Stephen Haycox, "'Fetched Up': Unlearned Lessons from the *Exxon Valdez*," *Journal of American History* (June 2012): 219–228.

47. Marla Williams, "Sitka Saying Farewell to Japanese Mill," *Seattle Times*, August 26, 1993.

48. "Last Mill in Alaska Closes," *New York Times*, March 25, 1997.

49. Durbin, *Tongass*, 303–304.

50. Forest Service Employees for Environmental Ethics, http://www.fseee.org/index .php/stay-informed/projects/1003830.

51. Quoted in Ross, *Environmental Conflict in Alaska*, 257.

52. As noted, Senator Stevens had joined the Senate in 1968; Congressman Young was first elected in 1973.

53. "Timeline: The Roadless Rule," EarthJustice, accessed September 15, 2015, at http://earthjustice.org/features/timeline-of-the-roadless-rule.

54. McDowell Group, *Economic Impact of Alaska's Visitor Industry* (Juneau: Alaska Department of Commerce, Community and Economic Development, 2010), 18–21.

CHAPTER 7. ANTISTATISM PERSISTENT

1. James Morton Turner, "The Specter of Environmentalism: Wilderness, Environmental Politics, and the Evolution of the New Right," *Journal of American History* 96 (June 2009): 123–149; R. McGregor Cawley, *Federal Land, Western Anger: The Sagebrush Rebellion and Environmental Politics* (Lawrence: University Press of Kansas, 1993), 29.

2. Ken Ross reported that when Watt visited Juneau in 1981 he was met with a 21-chainsaw salute organized by the SEACC; he called it the most creative protest he

had encountered; Ken Ross, *Environmental Conflict in Alaska* (Boulder, CO: University Press of Colorado, 2000), 208.

3. Ibid., 207.

4. See chapter 6.

5. "Former Anchorage Lawyer Named to Bench in Idaho," *Peninsula Clarion*, August 18, 2000.

6. Malcolm B. Roberts, ed., *Going Up in Flames: The Promises and Pledges of Alaska Statehood under Attack* (Anchorage, AK: Commonwealth North, 1990).

7. Joseph Story, *Commentaries on the Constitution of the United States* (Boston: Hilliard Gray and Company, 1833), 318–319.

8. Garry Wills, *Lincoln at Gettysburg: The Words That Remade American History* (New York: Simon and Schuster, 1992).

9. Roberts, *Going Up in Flames*, 2.

10. 72 Stat. 339 (July 7, 1958), Section 4.

11. Claus-M. Naske, *Alaska: A History of the 49th State* (Norman: University of Oklahoma Press, 1994), 158.

12. Presidential Proclamation 3269, Alaska Statehood, Dwight D. Eisenhower Presidential Library, accessed November 3, 2014, http://www.eisenhower.archives .gov/research/online_documents/alaska_statehood.html; Roberts, *Going Up in Flames*, 20–21.

13. Not only was Texas permitted to retain title to most of its land, but in the 1848 Treaty of Guadalupe Hidalgo the United States assumed Texas's debt.

14. For these purposes and others, coal, oil, and natural gas are classified as minerals.

15. It is coincidental that the grant of land to the state, approximately 104 million acres, is the same amount as the new conservation lands reserved in ANILCA, approximately 104 million acres.

16. See, for example, *Horowitz v. United States*, 267 U.S. 458 (1925), *Great Northern Railway v. United States*, 155 Fed. 959 (1907), *Deming v. United States*, 1 Ct. Cl. 190 (1865).

17. Roberts, *Going Up in Flames*, 15–20.

18. Ibid., 11.

19. The BLM manages about 72 million acres of undesignated land in Alaska; Natives are titled to 44 million, the state to 104 million; about 155 million acres are in federal conservation units.

20. Roberts, *Going Up in Flames*, 69.

21. Dennis Kelso and Marshall Kendziorek, "Alaska's Response to the *Exxon Valdez* Oil Spill," *Environmental Science and Technology* 25 (1991): 16–23.

22. In 1957 Congress had amended the Mineral Leasing Act of 1920 to grant to Alaska 90 percent of mineral revenue collected on federal lands in Alaska: that was the original authorization; the statehood act merely confirmed the percentage.

23. The US Court of Federal Claims hears claims for monetary damages arising from the US Constitution, federal statutes, executive regulations, or express or implied contracts with the government. The case was filed in 1993, case number 93-454L; the decision was filed on May 31, 1996. See Stephen Haycox, "Owning It All in Alaska: The Political Power of a Rhetorical Paradigm," in *Land in the American West: Private Claims and the Common Good*, ed. William G. Robbins (Seattle: University of Washington Press, 2000), 164–189.

24. The mid-1980s collapse of oil prices and the 1989 *Exxon Valdez* catastrophe made opening the refuge at that time politically impossible.

25. *Alaska v. United States*, 35 Fed. Cl. 685 (1996).

26. In March 2015 the Alaska Permanent Fund was valued at $54 billion.

27. Charlie Cole, "Lawsuit Is Rooted in History of Alaska Statehood," *Anchorage Daily News*, September 30, 1993.

28. Ted Stevens, "Compact Lawsuit Critical to Alaska's Future," *Anchorage Daily News*, January 2, 1995.

29. 35 Fed. Cl. 687, 701.

30. Ibid., 685, 698.

31. *Alaska v. United States*, 119 Fed. 3rd 16; "Appeals Court Dismisses $29 Billion Hickel Lawsuit," *Juneau Empire*, July 15, 1997.

32. *Alaska v. United States*, 522 U.S. 1108 (1998).

33. Jeff Richardson, "Murkowski Mediates Panel Discussing Federal Role in Alaska Land Management," *Fairbanks Daily News-Miner*, August 15, 2011; John Coghill and Chad Hutchison, "Wrong on ANWR and Alaska's Rights as a State," *Alaska Dispatch News*, February 11, 2015.

34. David J. Hayes, "Rhetoric Doesn't Square with Reality in Alaska Drilling Debate," *Seattle Times*, March 16, 2015.

35. "Creating Alaska," University of Alaska, https://www.alaska.edu/creatingalaska /constitutional-convention/speeches-to-the-conventio/opening-session-speeches /bartlett.

36. Roberts, *Going Up in Flames*, 9.

37. Walter Hickel, "Decisions Made in 1959 Should Stand Forever," *Anchorage Daily News*, June 29, 1996. In his will Hickel said he wanted to be buried standing up, facing Washington, DC. He was.

38. Stephen Haycox, *Frigid Embrace: Politics, Economy and Environment in Alaska* (Corvallis: Oregon State University Press, 2002).

39. Frank Rue, "With Chuitna, Alaska Faces a Historic Decision for Wild Salmon Habitat Protection," *Alaska Dispatch News*, March 22, 2015.

40. Jack Roderick, *Crude Dreams: A Personal History of Oil and Politics in Alaska* (Fairbanks, AK: Epicenter Press, 1997), 167–169.

41. In June 2015 the Alaska Supreme Court ruled that Pebble Limited Partnership's suit against the EPA can move forward, though the court dismissed some portions of the suit. David Bendinger, "Pebble FACA Case to Go Forward," Alaska Public Media, June 5, 2015, accessed September 15, 2015, at http://www.alaskapublic.org/2015/06/05/pebble-faca-case-against-epa-to-go-forward.

42. The species are king, or Chinook; red, or sockeye; silver, or coho; pink, or humpback; and dog, or chum salmon. Red are the most valuable, pink the most prolific.

43. Ron Arnold, "Judge Orders EPA to Stop Anti-Mining Collusion," Daily Signal, February 19, 2015.

44. William Yardley, "Vote in Alaska Puts Question: Gold or Fish?" New York Times, August 23, 2008.

45. "The Midas Touch," Mother Jones, May 2006.

46. "About Pebble Mine," Trout Unlimited, accessed September 1, 2015, http://www.savebristolbay.org/about-the-bay/about-pebble-mine.

47. "Ground Truth Trekking Pebble Mine Seismic Studies," accessed September 1, 2015, http://www.groundtruthtrekking.org/pebble-mine-seismology-earthquake-science.

48. Svati Kirsten Narula, "Is Alaska's Pebble Mine the Next Keystone XL?" Atlantic, March 2024.

49. Clean Water Act Section 404, http://water.epa.gov/lawsregs/guidance/wetlands/sec404.cfm.

50. "EPA Bristol Bay Watershed Assessment, Second Review Draft (Do Not Quote)," accessed at http://www.epa.gov/ncea/pdfs/bristolbay/bristol_bay_assessment_erd2_2013_v011_exec_summary.pdf.

51. Sean Cockerham, "Anglo-American Pulls Out of Proposed Pebble Mine," Alaska Dispatch News, September 16, 2013.

52. Juliet Ellperin, "In Another Blow to Pebble Mine, Rio Tinto Pulls Out," Washington Post, April 7, 2014.

53. "Pebble Partnership Sues EPA over Records Request," Alaska Dispatch News, October 31, 2014.

54. Andrew Jensen, "Judge Puts Brakes on the EPA," Alaska Journal of Commerce, November 26, 2014.

55. Becky Bohrer, "Judge Sides with Interior Secretary in Refuge-Road Dispute," Associated Press, September 8, 2015, accessed September 15, 2015, at http://bigstory.ap.org/article/a2741bedca7a414ea854bb0065b88829/judge-sides-interior-secretary-refuge-road-dispute.

56. Dan Joling, "Alaska to Sue for Road through Izembek Wildlife Refuge," Huffington Post, April 8, 2014.

57. Alex DeMarban, "Myths Muddle Effort to Carve Road through Alaska's Izembek Refuge," *Alaska Dispatch News*, April 6, 2014.

58. US Interior Department, "Izembek National Wildlife Refuge," December 13, 2013, http://izembek.fws.gov.

59. "King Cove Residents Outraged that Interior Secretary Jewell Denies Land Exchange/Road Access to Cold Bay Airport," Aleutians East Borough, accessed September 15, 2015, at http://www.aleutianseast.org/index.asp?Type=B_PR&SEC=%7B 4625D388-43A1-4E17-A354-F5F12E4E7205%7D&DE=%7BA06D2017-C3A1-4D40 -8C5B-7044D69B4FE2%7D.

60. Bohrer, "Judge Sides with Interior Secretary in Refuge-Road Dispute."

61. Bruce Babbitt, "Alaska's 'Road to Nowhere' Is Still a Boondoggle," *Los Angeles Times*, March 11, 2014.

62. Defenders of Wildlife, "Costly, Unnecessary Road," March 4, 2014, http://www .defenders.org/press-release/costly-unnecessary-road-through-izembek-national -wildlife-refuge-wilderness-threatens.

63. Author's interview with Steve Cotton, chairman of the board, Trustees for Alaska, September 22, 2014.

CONCLUSION

1. US Geological Survey, Arctic National Wildlife Refuge, 1002 Area, Petroleum Assessment, accessed March 23, 2015, http://pubs.usgs.gov/fs/fs-0028-01/fs-0028-01 .htm. The original estimate for Prudhoe Bay was between 9 and 15 billion barrels; present estimates are 22 billion.

2. Joe E. LaRocca, *Alaska Agonistes: The Age of Petroleum, How Big Oil Bought Alaska* (Chapel Hill, NC: Professional Press, 2003), 135–155; Richard A. Fineberg, "The Arctic Refuge Coastal Plain: Pushing Development through a Litany of Lies," presentation to the Alaska Wilderness League and the Northern Alaska Environmental Center, November 27, 1995.

3. There is as yet no satisfactory summary and analysis of the Alaska corruption scandal in print, though there are myriad news stories retrievable online. Senator Stevens was convicted of failing to report prohibited gifts. The conviction was later set aside because of prosecutorial misconduct. Following a Justice Department investigation, no charges were brought against Justice Department prosecutors.

4. Zaz Hollander, "Lawsuit Targets Federal Approval of Mat-Su Coal Mine Permits," *Alaska Dispatch News*, March 19, 2015.

5. Office of Surface Mining, Reclamation and Enforcement, accessed September 1, 2015, http://www.osmre.gov/about/MissionVision.shtm.

6. "Red Dog Mine," Ground Truth Trekking, accessed September 1, 2015, http:// www.groundtruthtrekking.org/Issues/MetalsMining/RedDogMine.html.

7. "Climate Impacts in Alaska," Environmental Protection Agency, accessed September 1, 2015, http://www.epa.gov/climatechange/impacts-adaptation/alaska.html.

8. Jennifer A. Dlouhy, "U.S. Should Move to Tap Arctic Energy Reserves, Panel Concludes," *Alaska Dispatch News*, March 27, 2015.

9. McKenzie Funk, "The Wreck of the Kulluk," *New York Times*, December 30, 2014.

10. Dermot Cole, "Shell Stoppage Reflects More than Bureaucratic Opposition," *Alaska Dispatch News*, September 29, 2015.

11. Nathaniel Herz, "Alaska Gov. Walker Calls Special Legislative Session on Gas Line Megaproject," *Alaska Dispatch News*, September 24, 2015.

12. Nathaniel Herz, "Walker Administration Proposes Cutting Staff that Challenges the Feds," *Alaska Dispatch News*, February 11, 2015.

13. James Morton Turner, *The Promise of Wilderness: American Environmental Politics since 1964* (Seattle: University of Washington Press, 2012), 396–397.

14. Phillip Shabekoff, *A Fierce Green Fire: The American Environmental Movement* (Washington, DC: Island Press, 2003); Robert E. Dunlap and Angela G. Martig, "The Evolution of the U.S. Environmental Movement from the 1970s to the 1990s: An Overview," *Society and Natural Resources* 4 (1991): 209–218.

15. Turner, *The Promise of Wilderness*, 397.

16. Ibid., 407.

17. Timothy J. LeCain, *Mass Destruction: The Men and Giant Mines That Wired America and Scarred the Planet* (New Brunswick, NJ: Rutgers University Press, 2009), 230.

18. Charles Caldwell, *Hawley, a Kennecott Story: Three Mines, Four Men, and One Hundred Years, 1897–1997* (Salt Lake City: University of Utah Press, 2014), 322–325.

EPILOGUE

1. *Aquilar v. Kleppe*, 424 F. Supp. 433 (D. Alaska (1976) (48 U.S.C. Prec. Sec. I has been substantially incorporated into art. XII, sec. 12, Constitution of the State of Alaska).

2. 545 U.S. 75, 125 S. Ct. 2137, 162 L. Ed. 2nd 57 (2005).

3. 1982 Initiative Proposal No. 5.

4. 1983 Att'y Gen. Op. No. 2, 1983 Alas. AG LEXIS 365 (February 18, 1983).

5. Although the attorney general opined that the law enacted by the initiative is unconstitutional, AS 38.05.502 has been cited by some as a codification of the public trust doctrine, a common law principle that the state has the responsibility of a trustee to its citizens as beneficiaries of the state's resources. AS 38.05.502 reads as follows: "Sec. 38.05.502. Property of the People. Subject to valid existing rights of applicants for land, upon February 21, 1983, all land in the state and all minerals not previously appropriated are the exclusive property of the people of the state and the state holds title to the land and minerals in trust for the people of the state."

6. The Alaska State Legislature, "Bill History/Action for 29th Legislature," CSHB 115, accessed September 1, 2015, http://www.legis.state.ak.us/basis/get_bill.asp?bill =HB115&session=29.

7. Ecclesiastes 1:10. See Dermot Cole, "House Leaders Push Land Bill Despite Advice That It's Unconstitutional," *Alaska Dispatch News*, March 23, 2015.

BIBLIOGRAPHY

ARCHIVES AND COLLECTIONS

Alaska State Archives, Juneau
    Alaska State Legislature Records
    Department of Law Records
    Department of Natural Resource Records
Bancroft Library, San Francisco, CA
    Robert Marshall Papers
    Sierra Club Records, Michael McCloskey Papers
Denver Public Library, Denver, CO
    Harry Crandall Papers
    Theodore Swem Papers
    The Wilderness Society Records
National Archives and Records Administration, Alaska Region
    Record Group 220, Federal Field Committee for Development Planning
Nebraska State Historical Society, Lincoln
    Hugh Butler Papers
Rasmuson Library, University of Alaska Fairbanks
    Alaska Conservation Society Papers
    E. L. "Bob" Bartlett Papers
    Ernest Gruening Papers
    William A. Egan Papers
Sealaska Heritage Institute, Juneau
    Curry-Weissbrodt Papers
University of Alaska Anchorage
    Anchorage Pioneers Oral History Project
    Dave Hickok Papers
    Jay S. Hammond Papers
    Mark Ganopole Papers
    Neil Risser Bassett Papers
University of Wyoming, American Heritage Center, Laramie
    Brock Evans Papers

US Department of the Interior, National Park Service
George Collins Papers

GOVERNMENT DOCUMENTS

Alaska Citizens Advisory Commission on Federal Areas. "Report on Compliance," February 12, 2013, http://dnr.alaska.gov/commis/cacfa/documents /FOSDocuments/GibertPresentaiton.pdf.

Alaska Citizens Advisory Commission on Federal Areas. "Statement of Mission," accessed November 16, 2014, http://dnr.alaska.gov/commis/cacfa/FOS.html.

Alaska Department of Fish and Game. "Customary and Traditional Use Determination, Subsistence in Alaska," accessed October 14, 2014, http://www .adfg.alaska.gov/index.cfm?adfg=subsistence.customary.

Alaska Department of Labor and Workforce Development. "Research and Analysis Report." Juneau: State of Alaska, 2013.

Alaska Legislature, House of Representatives. Rep. Scott Ogan, "Statement on ANWR," January 2015, http://www.alaskool.org/projects/subsistence/timeline /akstatehood.htm.

Alaska Legislature. Session Laws, 1959.

Alaska Office of the Governor. Press release, "Obama, Jewell Attacking Alaska's Future," January 25, 2015, http://gov.alaska.gov/Walker/press-room/full-press -release.html?pr=7063.

US Congress. House, 80th Cong., 1st Sess., Subcommittee on Territorial and Insular Possessions of Public Lands. Report on H.R. 206, "A Bill to Provide for the Admission of Alaska" (1947); 85th Cong., 2nd Sess., Senate Report 1163 (1958); 104 Cong. Record 12 (1958).

US Congress. House, Committee on Interior and Insular Affairs. "Statehood for Alaska: Hearings on H.R. 206 and H.R. 1808 before the Subcommittee on Territorial and Insular Possessions of the House Committee on Public Lands." 80th Cong., 1st Sess. (1947).

US Congress. House, Committee on Merchant Marine and Fisheries, Subcommittee on Fisheries and Wildlife Conservation. "Hearings, H.R. 7045," July 1, 1959, 86th Cong., 1st Sess.

US Congress. Senate, Committee on Interstate and Foreign Commerce, Subcommittee on Merchant Marine and Fisheries. Hearings, S. 1899, "A Bill to Authorize the Establishment of the Arctic Wildlife Range and for Other Purposes." 86th Cong., 1st Sess.

US Congress. Senate, Hon. Lisa Murkowski, public appearance, January 25, 2015, https://www.youtube.com/watch?v=1dzCJExt_jM&feature=youtube.

US Department of the Interior. *Final Environmental Impact Statement, Proposed Trans-Alaska Pipeline*, vol. 2. Washington, DC, March 20, 1972.

US Department of the Interior. "Izembek Review," December 13, 2013, http://izembek.fws.gov.

US Department of the Interior, Office of Surface Mining, Reclamation and Enforcement. "Alaska Review," accessed November 10, 2014, http://www.usa.gov/directory/federal/surface-mining-reclamation-and-enforcement.shtml.

US Department of the Interior. Press release, "Obama Administration Moves to Protect Arctic National Wildlife Refuge," January 25, 2015.

US Department of the Interior. Public Land Order 2214, 1960 (Rescind Military Withdrawal, Alaska).

US Department of the Interior, Public Land Order 4582, January 19, 1969.

US Department of the Interior. *Trans-Alaska Pipeline Final Environmental Impact Statement*, vol. 6, A-63-8. Washington, DC, April 16, 1971.

US Environmental Protection Agency. "Bristol Bay Watershed Assessment," 2nd Review, accessed March 4, 2015, http://www.epa.gov/ncea/pdfs/bristolbay/bristol_bay_assessment_erd2_2013_v011_exec_summary.pdf.

US Environmental Protection Agency. "Clean Water Act Section 404," accessed January 4, 2015, http://water.epa.gov/lawsregs/guidance/wetlands/sec404.cfm.

US Environmental Protection Agency. "Climate Impacts in Alaska," accessed September 14, 2014, http://www.epa.gov/climatechange/impacts-adaptation/alaska.html.

US Geological Survey. "Arctic National Wildlife Refuge, 1002 Area, Petroleum Assessment," accessed March 23, 2015, http://pubs.usgs.gov/fs/fs-0028-01/fs-0028-01.htm.

US Public Law 85–508, 72 Stat. 339, July 7, 1958 (Alaska Statehood).

US Public Law 88–577 (Wilderness Act).

US Public Law 91–190 (National Environmental Policy Act).

US Public Law 94–579 (Federal Land Policy and Management Act 1976).

US Public Law 94–588 (National Forest Management Act 1976).

COURT CASES

Alaska v. Udall, US Dist. Ct. Alaska, No. A-21–67 (1967).

Alaska v. United States, 35 F. Cl. (1996).

Alaska v. United States, 119 Fed. 3rd 16 (1997).

Alaska v. United States, 522 US 1108 (1998).

Alaska v. United States, 545 US 75, 125 S. Ct. 2137, 162 L. Ed. 2nd 57 (2005) (re: statehood compact).

Aquilar v. Kleppe, 424 F. Supp. 433 (D. Alaska (1976) (re: statehood compact).

Deming v. United States, 1 Ct. Cl. 190 (1865) (statehood compact).

Great Northern Railway v. United States, 155 Fed. 959 (1907) (statehood compact).

Horowitz v. United States, 267 US 458 (1925) (statehood compact).

Katie John v. State of Alaska, No. A85–698 CV (D-Alaska 1989) (fishing rights).

Katie John v. United States, 72 Fed. 3rd 698 (9th Cir. 1995) (fishing rights).

McCrary v. Ivanof Bay Village, Alaska Supreme Court S-13972, December 11, 2011.

McDowell v. State, 85 Pac. 2nd 1 (1989) (rural subsistence preference).

McDowell et al. v. United States, No. F90–034 CV (D-Alaska, 1990) (rural subsistence preference).

Miller v. United States, 159 Fed. 2nd 997 (9th Cir. 1947) (aboriginal title).

Tee-Hit-Ton Indians v. United States, 120 F. Supp. 202, 128 Ct. Cl. 82 (aboriginal title).

United States v. Santa Fe Pacific Railroad Company, 314 US 339 (aboriginal title).

INTERVIEWS

Author with Steve Cotton, Chairman of the Board, Trustees for Alaska, September 22, 2014.

Author with John Havelock, attorney general 1970–1973, January 14, 1992.

Author with William L. Hensley, Native Leader, March 22, 1993.

Author with Dave Hickok and Mark Ganopole, Alaska Wilderness Council, April 23, 1996.

Author with Robert Weeden, Alaska Conservation Society, August 18, 1998.

California Digital Library, Bancroft Library, University of California, Berkeley, George Collins oral interview.

Sierra Club Oral History Series, David Brower.

Sierra Club Oral History Series, Michael McCloskey.

Sierra Club Oral History Series, James W. Moorman.

Sierra Club Oral History Series, Edgar Wayburn.

US Fish and Wildlife Service, National Digital Library, Robert Weeden, Virginia Wood.

NONGOVERNMENTAL ORGANIZATION WEBSITES

Alaska Center for Rural Health, University of Alaska Anchorage, http://www.uaa .alaska.edu/hpd/acrh.cfm.

Alaska Miners Association, http://alaskaminers.org.

Forest Service Employees for Environmental Ethics, http://www.fseee.org.

Ground Truth Trekking Pebble Mine Seismic Studies, http://www .groundtruthtrekking.org/pebble-mine-seismology-earthquake-science.

Resource Development Council, Alaska, http://www.akrdc.org.

Southeast Alaska Conservation Society, http://seacc.org.

Trout Unlimited, tu.org.

University of Alaska, Creating Alaska, http://www.alaska.edu/creatingalaska.

Wilderness Society, www.wilderness.org.

NEWS SERVICES AND PERIODICALS

Alaska Daily News

Alaska Daily Ties

Alaska Dispatch News

Alaska Journal of Commerce

Alaska Sportsman

Atlantic Magazine

Daily Signal

Fairbanks Daily News-Miner

Harper's

Living Wilderness

Los Angeles Times

Mother Jones

New York Times

Pacific Fisherman

Peninsula Clarion

Seattle Times

Time

Tundra Times

Washington Post

BOOKS AND ARTICLES

Allan, Timo Christopher. "Locked Up! A History of Resistance to the Creation of National Parks in Alaska." PhD diss., 2010, Washington State University.

Arendt, Hannah. *On Revolution.* New York: Viking Press, 1963.

Arnold, David F. *Fishermen's Frontier: People and Salmon in Southeast Alaska.* Seattle: University of Washington Press, 2011.

Arnold, Ron. "Judge Orders EPA to Stop Anti-Mining Collusion." *Daily Signal,* February 19, 2015.

Ascott, Ivan L. "Comments: The Alaska Statehood Act Does Not Guarantee Alaska Ninety Percent of the Revenue from Mineral Leases on Federal Land in Alaska." *Seattle University Law Review* 27 (2004): 999–1034.

Babbitt, Bruce. "Alaska's 'Road to Nowhere' Is Still a Boondoggle." *Los Angeles Times,* March 11, 2014.

Berry, Mary Clay. *The Alaska Pipeline: The Politics of Oil and Native Land Claims.* Bloomington: Indiana University Press, 1975.

Borneman, Walter R. *Alaska: Saga of a Bold Land.* New York: Perennial, 2003.

Bowkett, Gerald E. *Reaching for a Star: The Final Campaign for Alaska Statehood.* Kirkland, WA: Epicenter Press, 2009.

Brewster, Karen, ed. *Boots, Bikes and Bombers: Adventures of Alaska Conservationist Ginny Hill Wood.* Fairbanks: University of Alaska Press, 2012.

Brooks, Paul, and Joseph Foote. "The Disturbing Story of Project Chariot." *Harper's* 224 (April 1962): 62–67.

Cahn, Robert. *The Fight to Save Wild Alaska.* New York: Audubon Society, 1982.

Callicott, J. Baird, and Michael P. Nelson, ed. *The Wilderness Debate Rages On: Continuing the Great New Wilderness Debate.* Athens: University of Georgia Press, 2008.

Campbell, Ballard C. "Federalism, State Action, and 'Critical Episodes' in the Growth of American Government." *Social Science History* 16 (1992): 561–577.

Carson, Rachel. *Silent Spring.* Boston: Houghton Mifflin, 1962.

Case, David S. *Alaska Natives and American Laws.* Fairbanks: University of Alaska Press, 1984.

Castellon, Michael C. "Standing to Challenge the Disposition of Land in Alaska." *Alaska Law Review* 2 (1985): 396.

Catton, Theodore. *Inhabited Wilderness: Indians, Eskimos and National Parks in Alaska.* Albuquerque: University Press of New Mexico, 1997.

Cawley, R. MacGregor. *Federal Land, Western Anger: The Sagebrush Rebellion and Environmental Politics.* Lawrence: University Press of Kansas, 1993.

Clark, John H., Andrew McGregor, Robert D. Mecum, Paul Krasnowski, and Amy M. Carroll. *The Commercial Salmon Fishery in Alaska.* Alaska Fishery Research Bulletin 12. Juneau: Alaska Department of Fish and Game, 2006.

Coates, Kenneth. Review, Webb, *The Last Frontier. BC Studies* 74 (Summer 1987): 42–44.

Coates, Peter A. *The Trans-Alaska Pipeline Controversy: Technology, Conservation and the Frontier.* Bethlehem, PA: Lehigh University Press, 1991.

Coen, Ross. *Breaking Ice: The Epic Voyage of the SS Manhattan through the Northwest Passage.* Fairbanks: University of Alaska Press, 2012.

Cohen, Felix. "Original Indian Title." *Minnesota Law Review* 32 (1947).

Cohen, Lucy Kramer, ed. *The Legal Conscience: Selected Papers of Felix S. Cohen.* New Haven, CT: Yale University Press, 1960.

Cole, Charlie. "Lawsuit Is Rooted in History of Alaska Statehood." *Anchorage Daily News,* September 30, 1993.

Cole, Terrence. *Blinded by Riches: The Permanent Funding Problem and the Prudhoe Bay*

Effect. Anchorage: Institute of Social and Economic Research, University of Alaska Anchorage, 2004.

Colt, Steve. *Salmon Fish Traps in Alaska: An Economic History Perspective.* ISER Working Paper. Anchorage: University of Alaska Institute for Economic and Social Research, 2000.

Commoner, Barry. *The Closing Circle: Nature, Man and Technology.* New York: Alfred A. Knopf, 1971.

Cooley, Richard A. *Politics and Conservation: The Decline of the Alaska Salmon.* New York: Harper and Row, 1963.

Cotton, Steve, ed. *Earth Day: The Beginning.* New York: Bantam Books, 1970.

Crandall, Harry B., Celia M. Hunter, and Urban C. Nelson. "Discussion: Alaska's Wilderness Wildlife." In *Wilderness: the Edge of Knowledge,* edited by Maxine E. McCloskey, 183–192. San Francisco: Sierra Club, 1969.

Crisler, Lois. *Arctic Wild: The Remarkable True Story of One Couple's Adventures Living among Wolves.* New York: Harper and Brothers, 1958.

Cronon, William. "The Trouble with Wilderness, or Getting Back to the Wrong Nature." In *Uncommon Ground: Rethinking the Human Place in Nature,* edited by William Cronon, 69–90. New York: W. W. Norton, 1995.

———, Samuel P. Hays, Michael P. Cohen, and Thomas R. Dunlap. "Forum: The Trouble with Wilderness." *Environmental History* 1 (1996): 7–55.

Crutchfield, J. A., and G. Pontecorvo. *Pacific Salmon Fishery: A Study of Irrational Conservation.* Baltimore, MD: Johns Hopkins University Press, 1963.

Daily, Patrick, and Beverly Ann James. *Cultural Politics and the Mass Media.* Champaign: University of Illinois Press, 2004.

Douglas, William O. *My Wilderness: The Pacific West.* Garden City, NJ: Doubleday, 1960.

Drake, Brian Allen. *Loving Nature, Fearing the State: Environmentalism and Antigovernment Politics before Reagan.* Seattle: University of Washington Press, 2013.

Dunlap, Robert E., and Angela G. Martig. "The Evolution of the U.S. Environmental Movement from the 1970s to the 1990s: An Overview." *Society and Natural Resources* 4 (1991): 209–218.

Durbin, Kathie. *Tongass: Pulp Politics and the Fight for the Alaska Rain Forest.* Corvallis: Oregon State University Press, 1999.

Edling, Max M. *A Revolution in Favor of Government: Origins of the U.S. Constitution and the Making of the American State.* New York: Oxford University Press, 2003.

Egan, Timothy. "Tongass Timber Fiasco." *New York Times,* August 22, 1989.

Eilperin, Juliet. "Obama Administration to Propose New Wilderness Protections in Arctic Refuge—Alaska Republicans Declare War." *Washington Post,* January 26, 2015.

Expert Panel Report. *Defining the Term "Frontier Area" for Programs Implemented through the Office for the Advancement of Telehealth*. Bismarck: Center for Rural Health, University of North Dakota, 2006.

Farber, David A. "Completing the Work of the Framers: Lincoln's Constitutional Legacy." *Journal of the Abraham Lincoln Association* 27 (Winter 2006): 1–12.

Federal Field Committee for Development Planning in Alaska. *Alaska Natives and the Land*. Washington, DC: Government Printing Office, 1968.

Finley, Carmel. *All the Fish in the Sea: Maximum Sustained Yield and the Failure of Fisheries Management*. Chicago: University of Chicago Press, 2011.

Forbes, Norma E. "The State's Role in Suicide Prevention Programs for Alaska Native Youth." *American Indian and Alaska Native Mental Health* 4 (1994): 235–249.

Gates, Paul Wallace. *History of Public Land Law Policy Development*. Washington, DC: Wm. W. Gaunt & Sons, 1967.

Goldsmith, Scott. *Structural Analysis of the Alaska Economy: What Are the Drivers?* Anchorage: University of Alaska Anchorage, Institute of Social and Economic Research, 2010.

———. *Structural Analysis of the Alaska Economy: What Are the Drivers?*, rev. ed. Anchorage: University of Alaska Anchorage, Institute of Social and Economic Research, 2010.

Gruening, Ernest. "Let Us End American Colonialism." Keynote speech at Alaska Constitutional Convention, November 9, 1955.

———. *Many Battles: The Autobiography of Ernest Gruening*. New York: Liveright Publishers, 1973.

———. *The State of Alaska*. New York: Random House, 1954.

Hammond, Jay. *Diapering the Devil: A Lesson for Oil Rich Nations*. Homer, AK: Kachemak Resources Institute, 2011.

Harrison, Gordon. *Alaska's Constitution: A Citizen's Guide*, 5th ed. Juneau: Alaska Legislative Affairs Agency, 2013.

Hartz, Louis. *The Liberal Tradition in America: An Interpretation of American Political Thought since the Revolution*. New York: Harcourt Brace, 1955.

Hartzog, George, Jr. "The Impact of Recent Litigation on Administrative Agencies." In *Wilderness in a Changing World*, edited by Bruce M. Kilgore, 172–180. San Francisco: Sierra Club Books, 1966.

Harvey, Mark. *A Symbol of Wilderness: Echo Park and the American Conservation Movement*. Albuquerque: University of New Mexico Press, 1994.

———. *Wilderness Forever: Howard Zahniser and the Path to the Wilderness Act*. Seattle: University of Washington Press, 2005.

Hawley, Charles Caldwell. *A Kennecott Story: Three Mines, Four Men, and One Hundred Years, 1897–1997*. Salt Lake City: University of Utah Press, 2014.

Haycox, Stephen. *Alaska: An American Colony*. Seattle: University of Washington Press, 2002.

———. "Economic Development and Indian Land Rights in Modern Alaska: The 1947 Tongass Timber Act." *Western Historical Quarterly* (February 1990): 21–46.

———. "Felix Cohen and the Legacy of the Indian New Deal." *Yale University Library Gazette* (April 1994): 135–156.

———. "'Fetched Up': Unlearned Lessons from the *Exxon Valdez*." *Journal of American History* (June 2012): 219–228.

———. *Frigid Embrace: Politics, Economy and Environment in Alaska*. Corvallis: Oregon State University Press, 2002.

———. *Law of the Land: A History of the Office of the Attorney General and the Department of Law in Alaska*. Juneau: Alaska Department of Law, 1998.

———. "Mining the Federal Government: The War and the All-American City." In *Alaska at War, 1941–45: The Forgotten War Remembered*, edited by Fern Chandonnet, 203–210. Fairbanks: University of Alaska Press, 2007.

———. "Owning It All in Alaska: The Political Power of a Rhetorical Paradigm." In *Land in the American West: Private Claims and the Common Good*, edited by William G. Robbins, 164–189. Seattle: University of Washington Press, 2000.

———. "Tee-Hit Ton and Alaska Native Rights." In *Law for the Elephant, Law for the Beaver: Essays in the Legal History of the North American West*, edited by John McLaren, Hamar Foster, and Chet Orloff, 125–145. Regina, SK: Canadian Plains Research Center University of Regina; and Pasadena, CA: Ninth Judicial Circuit Historical Society, 1992.

———. "William Paul, Sr., and the Alaska Voters' Literacy Act of 1925." *Alaska History* 3 (Fall 1986).

Hayes, David J. "Rhetoric Doesn't Square with Reality in Alaska Drilling Debate." *Seattle Times*, March 16, 2015.

Hays, Samuel P. *Beauty, Health and Permanence: Environmental Politics in the United States, 1955–1985*. Studies in Environment and History. New York: Cambridge University Press, 1987.

———. *Conservation and the Gospel of Efficiency*. Forge Village, MA: Murray Printing, 1959.

———. *Wars in the Woods: The Rise of Ecological Forestry in America*. Pittsburgh, PA: University of Pittsburgh Press, 2006.

Heintzleman, B. Frank. "Forestry in Alaska." *Proceedings of the Alaskan Science Conference*, 129–130. Washington, DC: National Academy of Sciences, 1951.

Hellenthal, John Albertus. *The Alaskan Melodrama*. New York: Liveright Press, 1936.

Hensley, William L. Iggiagruk. *Fifty Miles from Tomorrow: A Memoir of Alaska and the Real People*. New York: Farrar, Straus and Giroux, 2009.

Hession, Jack. "'Good Neighbor' or 'Good Predator' Policy." *Sierra Club Alaska Newsletter*, July 1981.

Hickel, Walter J. "Decisions Made in 1959 Should Stand Forever." *Anchorage Daily News*, June 29, 1996, B6.

Hinckley, Ted C. *The Americanization of Alaska, 1867–1896*. Palo Alto, CA: Pacific Books, 1972.

Howe, John R. *Bear Man of Admiralty Island: A Biography of Allen E. Hasselborg*. Fairbanks: University of Alaska Press, 1996.

Hunt, William R. *Alaska: A Bicentennial History*. New York: W. W. Norton, 1976.

Jaffa, Harry V. *A New Birth of Freedom*. Lanham, MD: Rowman and Littlefield Publishers, 2000.

Jensen, Andrew. "Judge Puts Brakes on the EPA." *Alaska Journal of Commerce*, November 26, 2014.

Joling, Dan. "Native Group Urges Boycott of Sportsmen." *Juneau Daily Empire*, May 17, 2001.

Jones, Peter N. *Respect for the Ancestors: American Indian Cultural Affiliation in the American West*. Boulder, CO: Bauu Press, 2005.

Kammen, Michael. "The Problem of American Exceptionalism: A Reconsideration." *American Quarterly* 45, no. 1 (March 1993): 1–43.

Kaye, Roger. *Last Great Wilderness: The Campaign to Establish the Arctic National Wildlife Refuge*. Fairbanks: University of Alaska Press, 2006.

Keilor, Francine. "Alaska's Senator Murkowski Says War Declared against Alaska." *Christian Science Monitor*, January 27, 2015.

Kelso, Dennis, and Marshall Kendziorek. "Alaska's Response to the *Exxon Valdez* Oil Spill." *Environmental Science and Technology* 25 (1991): 16–23.

Ketcham, Christopher. "The Great Republican Land Heist: Cliven Bundy and the Politicians Who Are Plundering the West." *Harpers's*, February 2015, 23–31.

Kizzia, Tom. *Pilgrim's Wilderness: A True Story of Faith and Madness on the Alaska Frontier*. New York: Crown Publishers, 2013.

Kleinfeld, Judith. *Frontier Romance: Environment, Culture and Alaska Identity*. Fairbanks: University of Alaska Press, 2012.

Kluwe, Joan, and Edwin Krumpe. "Interpersonal and Societal Aspects of Use Conflicts." *International Journal of Wilderness* 9 (December 2003).

Knapp, Gunnar. *A Very Brief Introduction to the Alaska Economy*. Anchorage: University of Alaska Anchorage, Institute of Social and Economic Research, 2013.

Kollin, Susan. *Nature's State: Imagining Alaska as the Last Frontier*. Chapel Hill: University of North Carolina Press, 2001.

Langdon, Steve J. *Native Peoples of Alaska: Traditional Living in a Northern Land*, 5th ed. Anchorage, AK: Greatland Graphics, 2014.

Lapham, Lewis. "Alaska: Politicians and Natives, Money and Oil." *Harper's*, May 1970.

LaRocca, Joe E. *Alaska Agonistes: The Age of Petroleum, How Big Oil Bought Alaska.* Chapel Hill, NC: Professional Press, 2003.

LeCain, Timothy J. *Mass Destruction: The Men and Giant Mines That Wired America and Scarred the Planet.* New Brunswick, NJ: Rutgers University Press, 2009.

Lind, Michael. "The American Creed: Does It Matter? Should It Change?" *Foreign Affairs* (March/April 1996): 665–694.

Lipset, Seymour Martin. *American Exceptionalism: A Double-Edged Sword.* New York: W. W. Norton, 1997.

Lowery, David, and William D Berry. "The Growth of Government in the United States: An Empirical Assessment of Competing Explanations." *American Journal of Political Science* 27 (November 1983): 665–694.

Luther, Linda. *The National Environmental Policy Act: Background and Implementation.* Washington, DC: Congressional Research Service, 2005.

Mackovjak, James. *Alaska Salmon Traps.* Gustavus, AK: Cross Sound Publications, 2013.

———. *Tongass Timber: A History of Logging and Timber Utilization in Southeast Alaska.* Durham, NC: Forest History Society, 2010.

Manget, Sean. "Top Alaska Businesses." *Alaska Journal of Commerce*, October 14, 2010.

Manning, Elizabeth. "Prop. 1 Passes in Anchorage by a Landslide." *Anchorage Daily News*, April 3, 2002.

Marsh, Linnie. *John of the Mountains: The Unpublished Journals of John Muir.* Madison: University of Wisconsin Press, 1938.

Marshall, Robert. *Arctic Village.* New York: H. Smith and Haas, 1933.

———. "I Am an Ecologist." Articles, Speeches, and Studies. Robert Marshall Papers. Manuscripts Division, Bancroft Library, University of California, Berkeley.

———. "The Problem of Alaska Development." Articles, Speeches, and Studies. Robert Marshall Papers. Manusctripts Division, Bancroft Library, University of California, Berkeley.

———. "The Problem of Wilderness." *Scientific American* 2 (1930).

Mauer, Richard, Alex DeMarban, and Nathaniel Herz. "Obama Plans to Block Development in Arctic Refuge; Alaska Leaders Irate." *Alaska Dispatch News*, January 25, 2015.

McAllister, Bill. "Knowles: No Appeal of Lawsuit." *Juneau Daily Empire*, August 28, 2002.

McBeath, Gerald. *The Alaska State Constitution.* New York: Oxford University Press, 2011.

————, Matthew Berman, Jonathan Rosenberg, and Mary F. Ehrlander. *The Political Economy of Oil in Alaska: Multinationals vs. the State*. Boulder, CO: Lynne Rienner Publishers, 2008.

McCloskey, Michael M. "Wilderness Movement at the Crossroads." *Pacific Historical Review* 41 (1972): 346–362.

McDowell Group. *Economic Impact of Alaska's Visitor Industry*. Juneau: Alaska Department of Commerce, Community, and Economic Development, 2010.

McPhee, John. *Coming Into the Country*. New York: Farrar, Straus and Giroux, 1977.

Merrill, Karen R. "In Search of the 'Federal Presence' in the American West." *Western Historical Quarterly* 30 (Winter 1999): 449–473.

Metcalfe, Peter M. *A Dangerous Idea: The Alaska Native Brotherhood and the Struggle for Indigenous Rights*. Fairbanks: University of Alaska Press, 2014.

Milkis, Sidney M. *The President and the Parties: The Transformation of the American Party System since the New Deal*. New York: Oxford University Press, 1993.

Mitchell, Donald Craig. *Sold American: The Story of Alaska Natives and Their Land, 1867–1959*. Dartmouth, NH: University Press of New England, 1997.

————. *Take My Land, Take My Life: The Story of Congress's Historic Settlement of Alaska Native Land Claims, 1960–1971*. Fairbanks: University of Alaska Press, 2001.

Mitchell, Jerry, and Richard Feiock. "A Comparative Analysis of Government Growth in the 50 American States." *State and Local Government Review* 20 (Spring 1988): 51–58.

Morse, Kathryn. *The Nature of Gold: An Environmental History of the Klondike Gold Rush*. Seattle: University of Washington Press, 2010.

Murie, Margaret E. *Two in the Far North*. New York: Alfred Knopf, 1962.

————. "Wilderness Concept." *Living Wilderness* 34, no. 110 (1970): 63.

Narula, Svati Kirsten. "Is Alaska's Pebble Mine the Next Keystone XL?" *Atlantic*, March 2014.

Nash, Roderick. *Wilderness and the American Mind*. New Haven, CT: Yale University Press, 1967.

Naske, Claus-M. *Alaska: A History of the 49th State*. Norman: University of Oklahoma Press, 1994.

————. *Edward Lewis "Bob" Bartlett of Alaska: A Life in Politics*. Fairbanks: University of Alaska Press, 1979.

————. *Ernest Gruening: Alaska's Greatest Governor*. Fairbanks: University of Alaska Press, 2004.

————. *49 at Last: The Fight for Alaska Statehood*. Kirkland, WA: Epicenter Press, 2009.

————. *History of Alaska Statehood*. Lanham, MD: University Press of America, 1985.

National Resources Committee. *Alaska—Its Resources and Development: Part VII, Regional Planning*. Washington, DC: Government Printing Office, 1938.

Nelson, Daniel. *Northern Landscapes: The Struggle for Wilderness Alaska.* Washington, DC: Resources for the Future Press, 2004.

———. *A Passion for the Land: John F. Seiberling and the Environmental Movement.* Kent, OH: Kent State University Press, 2009.

Newton, Neil Jessup. "Indian Claims in the Court of the Conqueror." *American Indian Law Review* 41 (1992): 753–780.

Nichols, Jeannette Paddock. *Alaska: A History of Its Administration, Exploitation and Industrial Development during Its First Half Century of Rule by the United States.* Cleveland, OH: Arthur H. Clark Publishing, 1924.

———. "Alaska's Search for a Usable Past." *Pacific Northwest Quarterly* 59 (April 1968): 57–67.

Nie, Martin. *The Governance of Western Lands: Mapping Its Present and Future.* Lawrence: University Press of Kansas, 2008.

Norris, Frank. *Alaska Subsistence: A National Park Service Management History.* Anchorage, AK: National Park Service, 2002.

Novak, William J. "The Myth of the 'Weak' American State." *American Historical Review* 113 (June 2008): 752–772.

O'Neill, Dan. *The Firecracker Boys.* New York: St. Martin's Press, 1994.

———. *A Land Gone Lonesome: An Inland Voyage along the Yukon River.* New York: Counterpoint, 2006.

Peel, Ryan T. "*Katie John v. United States:* Balancing State Sovereignty with a Native Grandmother's Right to Fish." *BYU Journal of Public Law* 15 (2001): 263–279.

Reisner, Marc. *Cadillac Desert: The American West and Its Disappearing Water.* New York: Viking Press, 1986.

Richardson, Jeff. "Murkowski Mediates Panel Discussing Federal Role in Alaska Land Management." *Fairbanks Daily News-Miner,* August 15, 2011.

Robbins, Roy M. *Our Landed Heritage: The Public Domain, 1776–1936.* Princeton, NJ: Princeton University Press, 1942.

Roberts, Malcolm, ed. *Going Up in Flames: The Promises and Pledges of Alaska Statehood Under Attack.* Anchorage, AK: Commonwealth North, 1990.

Roderick, Jack. *Crude Dreams: A Personal History of Oil and Politics in Alaska.* Fairbanks, AK: Epicenter Press, 1997.

Rogers, George. *The Future of Alaska: Economic Consequences of Statehood.* Baltimore, MD: Johns Hopkins University Press, 1962.

Rohrbough, Malcom J. *The Land Office Business: The Settlement and Administration of American Public Lands, 1789–1837.* New York: Oxford University Press, 1968.

Ross, Ken. *Environmental Conflict in Alaska.* Boulder: University Press of Colorado, 2000.

———. *Pioneering Conservation in Alaska.* Boulder: University Press of Colorado, 2006.

Sandberg, Eric. *A History of Alaska Population Settlement.* Juneau: Alaska Department of Labor and Workforce Development, 2013.

Scheiber, Harry N. "Federalism and Legal Process: Historical and Contemporary Analysis of the American System." *Law and Society Review* 14 (Spring 1980): 663–722.

Scott, Doug. *The Enduring Wilderness: Protecting Our National Heritage through the Wilderness Act.* Golden, CO: Fulcrum Publishing, 2004.

Shabekoff, Phillip. *A Fierce Green Fire: The American Environmental Movement.* Washington, DC: Island Press, 2003.

Sherwood, Morgan. *Big Game in Alaska: A History of Wildlife and People.* New Haven, CT: Yale University Press, 1981.

Shortridge, James R. "The Alaska Agricultural Empire: An American Agrarian Vision, 1898–1929." *Pacific Northwest Quarterly* 69 (October 1978): 145–161.

Spence, Mark. *Dispossessing the Wilderness: Indian Removal and the Making of the National Parks.* New York: Oxford University Press, 1999.

Standlea, David M. *Oil, Globalization, and the War for the Arctic Refuge.* Albany: State University of New York Press, 2006.

Stegner, Wallace. "Wilderness Letter." In *Marking the Sparrow's Fall: The Making of the American West,* edited by Page Stegner, 111–117. New York: Henry Holt, 1998.

Stein, Mark. *How the States Got Their Shapes.* New York: Smithsonian Books/Collins, 2008.

Steinberg, Ted. *Down to Earth: Nature's Role in American History.* Oxford and New York: Oxford University Press, 2002.

Stevens, Ted. "Compact Lawsuit Critical to Alaska's Future." *Anchorage Daily News,* January 2, 1995.

Story, Joseph. *Commentaries on the Constitution of the United States.* Boston: Hilliard Gray and Company, 1833.

Strohmeyer, John. *Extreme Conditions: Big Oil and the Transformation of Alaska.* New York: Simon & Schuster, 1993.

Sturtevant, William C., ed. *Handbook of North American Indians,* vol. 5, Arctic, vol. 6, Subarctic, vol. 7, Northwest Coast. Washington, DC: Smithsonian Institution, 1978.

Sundborg, George. *Statehood for Alaska: The Issues Involved and Facts about the Issues.* Anchorage: Alaska Statehood Association, 1946.

Tower, Elizabeth. *Anchorage: From Its Humble Origins as a Railroad Construction Camp.* Fairbanks, AK: Epicenter Press, 1999.

Turner, James Morton. *The Promise of Wilderness: American Environmental Politics since 1964.* Seattle: University of Washington Press, 2012.

———. "The Specter of Environmentalism: Wilderness, Environmental Politics, and the Evolution of the New Right." *Journal of American History* 96 (June 2009): 123–149.

Turner, Wallace. "Alaska Hunters Seek to End Law Giving Natives Priority." *New York Times*, July 4, 1982.

Udall, Stewart. *The Quiet Crisis*. New York: Holt, Rinehart and Winston, 1963.

Walker, Bill. "Walker to Obama: ANWR Wilderness Call Violates Statehood Compact and ANILCA." *Alaska Dispatch News*, January 31, 2015.

Walker, Bruce. "Running against Washington." *American Thinker*, August 9, 2014.

Webb, Melody. *The Last Frontier: A History of the Yukon Basin of Canada and Alaska*. Albuquerque: University of New Mexico Press, 1985.

Weeden, Robert B. "Arctic Oil: Its Impact on Wilderness and Wildlife." In *Wilderness: The Edge of Knowledge*, edited by Maxine E. McCloskey, 174–179. San Francisco: Sierra Club Books, 1969.

Weyburn, Edgar. *Your Land and Mine: Evolution of a Conservationist*. San Francisco: Sierra Club Books, 2004.

White, Richard. *"It's Your Misfortune and None of My Own": A New History of the American West*. Norman: University of Oklahoma Press, 1991.

The Wilderness Society, Friends of the Earth, and the Environmental Defense Fund. *Comments on the Environmental Impact Statement for the Trans-Alaska Pipeline*. 4 vols. Washington, DC: Center for Law and Social Policy, May 4, 1972.

Wilentz, Sean. "Against Exceptionalism: Class Consciousness and the American Labor Movement, 1790–1920." *International Labor and Working Class History* 26 (Fall 1984): 1–24.

———. *The Rise of American Democracy: Jefferson to Lincoln*. New York: W. W. Norton, 2005.

Williams, Marla. "Sitka Saying Farewell to Japanese Mill." *Seattle Times*, August 26, 1993.

Williss, G. Frank. *"Do Things Right the First Time": Administrative History, the National Park Service and the Alaska National Interest Lands Conservation Act of 1980*. Anchorage, AK: National Park Service, 1995.

Williss, Roxanne. *Alaska's Place in the West: From the Last Frontier to the Last Great Wilderness*. Lawrence: University Press of Kansas, 2010.

Wills, Gary. *Lincoln at Gettysburg: The Words That Remade American History*. New York: Simon and Schuster, 1992.

Yardley, William. "The Challenge of Village Alaska." *New York Times*, May 14, 2007.

———. "Vote in Alaska Puts Question: Gold or Fish?" *New York Times*, August 23, 2008.